# DIGITAL ENCOUNTERS

*Digital Encounters* is a cross-media study of digital moving images in animation, cinema, games and installation art.

In a world increasingly marked by proliferating technologies, how we encounter and understand these story-worlds, game spaces and art works reveals aspects of the ways in which we organize and decode the vast amount of visual material we are bombarded with each day.

Working with examples from *The Incredibles*, *The Matrix*, *Tomb Raider: Legend* and Bill Viola's *The Five Angels For the Millennium*, Aylish Wood considers how viewers engage with the diverse interfaces of digital effects cinema, digital games and time-based installations and argues that technologies alter human engagement, distributing our attention across a network of images and objects.

A groundbreaking study of digital technology, *Digital Encounters* will revitalize this area of research.

**Aylish Wood** is a Senior Lecturer in Film Studies at the University of Kent. Her current research interests are the impact of digital technologies on the expressive possibilities of different moving image media, including animation, digital cinema, digital games and the time-based gallery installations.

# DIGITAL ENCOUNTERS

*Aylish Wood*

R Routledge
Taylor & Francis Group

LONDON AND NEW YORK

First published 2007
by Routledge
2 Park Square, Milton Park, Abingdon, Oxon OX14 4RN

Simultaneously published in the USA and Canada
by Routledge
270 Madison Ave, New York, NY 10016

*Routledge is an imprint of the Taylor & Francis Group, an informa business*

© 2007 Aylish Wood

Typeset in Perpetua by
Taylor & Francis Books
Printed and bound in Great Britain by
Antony Rowe Ltd, Chippenham, Wiltshire

*British Library Cataloguing in Publication Data*
A catalogue record for this book is available from the British Library

*Library of Congress Cataloging in Publication Data*
Wood, Aylish.
Digital encounters / Aylish Wood.
p. cm.
Includes bibliographical references.
(pbk. : alk. paper) 1. Technology and the arts. 2. Digital art. 3. Digital
Cinematography. I. Title.
NX180.T4W66 2007
776–dc22        2006036839


ISBN10: 0–415–41065–7 (hbk)
ISBN10: 0–415–41066–5 (pbk)


ISBN13: 978-0-415-41065-6 (hbk)
ISBN13: 978-0-415-41066-3 (pbk)

# CONTENTS

# FIGURES

# ACKNOWLEDGEMENTS

I would like to acknowledge the support of the Leverhulme Trust for a Research Fellowship which allowed me to undertake the early stages of research for this project. I would also like to thank the Carnegie Trust and the British Academy for travel awards.

For their time and support I particularly thank Ling-Yen Chua, Su Holmes, Nina Wakeford and, most importantly, Jean Daintith.

Sections of this work have been published in different versions in the following:

- 'Re-Animating Space', *Animation: An Interdisciplanary Journal*, November 2006, Sage.
- 'Encounters at the Interface: Distributed Attention and Digital Embodiments', *Quarterly Review of Film and Video*, forthcoming.
- 'The Metaphysical Fabric that Binds Us: Proprioceptive Coherence and Performative Space in *Minority Report*', *New Review of Film and Television Studies* 2(1), May 2004: 1–18.
- 'The Timespaces of Spectacular Cinema: Crossing the Great Divide of Spectacle versus Narrative', *Screen* 43(4), winter 2002: 370–86.
- 'The Expansion of Narrative Space: *Titanic* and CGI Technology', in Sarah Street and Tim Bergfelder (eds) *Titanic as Myth and Memory: Representations in Visual and Literary Culture*, I.B. Tauris, 2004, pp. 225–34.

# INTRODUCTION

People adapt to perturbation in their own way.
(McCarthy and Wright 2004: 31)

iPods are the latest digital device to enable audio-visual imagery to go mobile, allowing viewers to watch and listen in almost any context, providing they have first downloaded their tunes and podcasts. I participated in this mobile network by downloading *Aan Rika* (2005), a short cartoon, onto my iPod; created as part of a series of poetry-based animations, it tells the story of a man distracted by the poster image of a woman.[1] So entranced is he by the details of her image, the man misses his train and also fails to notice a live appearance by the woman herself. It would be easy to use *Aan Rika* as a metaphor for viewing moving image technologies, with viewers as individuals who get hung up on the image, paying attention only to their iPod, distracted as the world and its possibilities pass them by. Below, as I take a closer look at the details of the animation, I find an alternative view of digital technologies, one that thinks through processes of engagement rather than distraction. In *Digital Encounters* I take this alternative view and use it to reconceptualize our thinking about technology and the moving image. Rather than simply seeing images as a means of entering into a story-world, I argue that they are a place where viewers also interact with technological interfaces. I situate such encounters within a broader context of technologies interceding in human engagement, distributing our attention across a network of images and technological objects, which in turn frame how we see the world. Although networks of images are often typified by webpages, I argue that moving image media more generally, including animations, digital effects films, digital games and time-based gallery installations, are also sites where the impact of technology is becoming evident. Understanding how these media tell their stories, or offer opportunities for play and contemplation, requires an account of the ways traces of technology intercede in a viewer's engagement with the imagery, and how these in turn generate new kinds of encounters.

A central claim of *Digital Encounters* is that moving image media are becoming increasingly marked, or inscribed, by visible evidence of the technological interventions used in their creation, and that these inscriptions frame or intercede in a

1

viewer's engagement with such imagery. This kind of technological inscription is seen in the opening section of *Aan Rika*. In the story-world of the animation, a woman's face on a poster distracts the man, causing him to almost miss his train (see Figure 0.1). The action is shown in ways that exploit the possibilities of animation: familiar shot structures unusually arranged vertically or horizontally, with the frame shape varying between squares and oblongs. This story arc is joined by a second, that of the woman's imminent arrival at the same station as the man. As her story appears, the screen splits so that both arcs appear together, running alongside each other, again in both vertical and horizontal orientations, each playing a role in taking the narration of the animation further. In Figure 0.2 we see the screen split in a horizontal orientation, with the two trains moving in opposite directions. This arrangement not only breaks with a singular focus typical of much filmmaking, revealing the technologies of image construction as they appear through the inscription of a split screen, but also echoes a broader shift in our media landscape, where proliferating interfaces offer numerous screens for our engagement.[2]

The example of watching *Aan Rika* on a portable digital device reveals two features that inform both the context and content of *Digital Encounters*: the proliferation of media platforms and the emergence of digital inscriptions on the interface. The proliferation of media platforms is familiar. At this point in the early twenty-first century, a domestic space can include imagery accessible through a multiplicity of interfaces, including televisions connected to networks of digital channels, DVD players/recorders, game platforms, numerous hand-held devices, as well as computer systems linked to the internet, itself a vast reservoir of connectivity. Such a dispersal of media interfaces does not stop with domestic spaces, as, having travelled

*Figure 0.1* The focus of this image from *Aan Rika* is centred on the man and his action of looking at the poster of the woman. Still from *Aan Rika* (2005, directed by Juan de Graaf © il Luster Productions). Courtesy of www.illuster.nl.

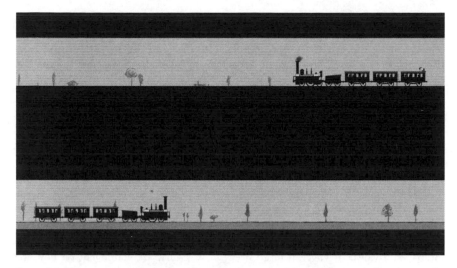

*Figure 0.2* The screen is split horizontally, with the two trains, which are travelling in opposite directions, separated by the blackness of the screen. Still from *Aan Rika* (2005, directed by Juan de Graaf © il Luster Productions). Courtesy of www.illuster.nl.

into the home, moving image technologies are in the process of becoming mobile and are going outside once again, gaining visibility in public spaces. Throughout the twentieth century and into the beginning of the twenty-first, inhabiting a media landscape has undergone a number of shifts. The experiencing of the world through moving image technology has relocated from public spaces to domestic settings, only to re-emerge into public spaces again via burgeoning arrays of hardware. Making sense of a world framed by moving image technology has become complex, no longer the domain of a single public screen, but of a multiplicity of domestic and public spaces. Tiziana Terranova approaches this proliferating media landscape through the concept of information, arguing that we live with a chaos of information. The proliferating screens described above are an example of such chaos, as each interface aims to communicate by 'clear[ing] out a space and establish[ing] a contact' (Terranova 2004: 17). The establishment of contact, however, has an uncertainty associated with it, since information is conveyed to someone when they select a probable message from a range of possible messages with which they are presented. In this dispersed landscape where does the agency of a viewer emerge?

Although the proliferation of media interfaces is the context for this book, its subject matter is the nature of the interfaces themselves and the ways they too reveal the changing technological landscape which we inhabit. When I started this project I was more narrowly concerned with digital effects cinema and whether digital technologies had the capacity to alter the narrational strategies of such films. As I describe more fully in Chapter 2, I took the view that digital effects were establishing different organizations of narrative space in which the viewer's focus was split between character and effects-based elements, and that these two elements distributed a viewer's attention. At around this same moment, I happened to be in a gallery in which there was a major exhibition of mixed-media installations, and when walking through it I began to recognise the same tendency for competing elements. In time-based installations in particular, the competing elements again had the effect of distributing a viewer's attention. *Digital Encounters* is the product of this coincidence of experiences, in which I recognised something equivalent in my viewing of *The Matrix* and *The Five Angels For the Millennium*. This seemingly peculiar conjunction motivated a series of questions which led to the distinctive approach I have developed. This builds through a discussion of what I call the interface, moving towards an understanding of how our encounters with these interfaces offer viewers agency. As I follow through these two sets of ideas, I will argue that digital technologies have led to an increasing appearance of competing elements in digital effects cinema, games and gallery installation art, and that the degree to which viewers have to distribute their attention varies within the organization of the interface. From this I develop my position that rather than being disengaged by such interfaces, a viewer is engaged in a variety of ways that are contingent on how the technologies operate within the organizations of the interface.

Before more fully describing the approach I take in this book I briefly state what I mean by digital encounters and interfaces, as, like moving image hardware, the term 'digital' has proliferated within the literature of cinema studies, often without a clear definition. I use 'encounter' straightforwardly, meaning to come up against something, in the sense of coming face to face with it. But what is the face of a digital encounter and what in turn is the nature of the agency such an encounter offers? At its most fundamental, digital means a form of numeric information, the flow of which generates meaningful data for a computer to read. Taken in terms of recording colour or sound, the quality of light or sound is registered by a light or sound sensor on the digital recording device and converted into a numeric entity, a binary code that is then executed by an interface as it recreates those colours and sounds. A digital projector, or computer monitor, reads the binary code input and outputs a colour by activating the appropriate region of its colour array. Digital information is inaccessible to direct experience by humans, as we are not hard wired, unless perhaps we have some kind of implant directly stimulating our muscles. Instead, we encounter the means through which digital information is displayed or relayed as text, sound or visual elements; in other words, we encounter it through a range of interfaces. As moving image hardware proliferates, so the physical structure of these interfaces varies from static screens of many dimensions to computer and television monitors and various hand-held devices. In this context, one way that digital encounters might be understood is as an account of how we engage with the multiplicity of media in our world.[3] In *Digital Encounters*, however, I approach this multiplicity of media by looking instead at how these different interfaces are themselves marked by multiplicities, offering complexity within the domain of an individual interface.

Debates within film and television studies tend to understand the screen as the place where images appear to the viewer, with the majority of intellectual effort

4

expended on the form and content of the images. One of the central ideas of *Digital Encounters* is that the screen is not simply a way into a story-world, document, game or artwork, but an interface which, to lesser or greater degrees, intercedes with the ways in which a viewer gains access to the story-world, document and so forth. The interface can be seen as being created by elements that work to organize a viewer's attention. The distinction I make between screen and interface becomes clearer by comparing continuity and non-continuity editing patterns. The idea of elements working together to organize a viewer's attention is already familiar from *mise-en-scène* analysis in cinema and television studies, but mostly this is attributed to pro-filmic aspects of set and costume design and camera placements. Editing patterns come closer to establishing an interface that intercedes in the ways that a viewer gains access to the audio-visual material. Continuity editing, for instance, typically creates a seamless interface that effectively acts as a transparent window into the story-world. By contrast, avant-garde practices often involve editing patterns that aim to disturb a viewer's easy engagement with a story-world or image content, jump cuts or a montage of fragmented parts, as is often seen in Stan Brahkage's films, for instance. A visible editing pattern breaks down the unified focus typical of continuity editing, establishing an interface where a viewer is far more aware of the inventions of the filmmaker. Increasingly, digital technologies are used to create elements that also visibly break with the unified focus of continuity editing, producing an interface in which the technological intervention is evident. As such, these elements form an interface that intercedes in a viewer's engagement with the story-world. To enter the story-world viewers have first to negotiate their way through the competing elements on the interface of the screen, adding a new dimension to how we view:

> If we only look *through* the interface, we cannot appreciate the ways in which the interface itself shapes our experience. We should be able to enjoy the illusion of the interface as it presents us with a digital world. But if we cannot also step back and see the interface as a technical creation, then we are missing half of the experience that new media can offer.
>
> (Bolter and Gromala 2003: 27)

I suggest that this new dimension of experience is offered on two levels. The first level is a material one, in which technology leaves traces on the interface of the screen through the emergence of competing elements either on a single screen or more radically dispersed as in installations. The second level of this new experience follows from the first. If competing elements are able to distribute a viewer's attention, they create the opportunity for choices in viewing, which in turn engenders agency. Agency emerges as viewers, in addition to their acts of interpretation, orient their perceptual apparatus in order to decide which competing element they attend to and which they choose to set aside. The second level of experience is not only a textual one, as it is also a technological one. Inscribed interfaces reveal the presence of technology and so not only intercede in access to a story-world but also present a view of a technological system. This idea of an interface constructed around competing elements is familiar to users of Windows environments, as Jay David Bolter and Richard Grusin have stated:

> The multiplicity of windows and the heterogeneity of their concerns mean that the user is repeatedly brought into contact with the interface, which she learns to read just as she would any hypertext. She oscillates between manipulating the windows and examining their contents, just as she oscillates between looking at a hypertext as a texture of links and looking through the links to the textual units as language.
>
> (Bolter and Grusin 1999: 33)

Although Bolter and Grusin's comments are suggestive of a user's capacity for agency as she oscillates between windows, their interest in the processes of remediation ultimately tends towards whether images expose or obscure their aesthetic influences through the double logic of immediacy and hypermediacy. In *Digital Encounters* I begin by taking a different approach, using the idea of seamless and non-seamless, or what I call inscribed, interfaces to reveal the influences of technologies on the construction of images, and from there develop a model for thinking about the impact of these influences on viewers' experiences of interfaces.

The approach I take in this book is to use each of the media I discuss to develop and explore different aspects of my framework. Chapters 1 and 2 describe the ways in which images are inscribed by technologies through a detailed analysis of animations and digital effects cinema. Both of these chapters offer distinctive views of these two kinds of cinema, as well as articulating key terms of my framework: inscribed interfaces and competing elements. Once they have been introduced, these key terms are in turn built into a model of embodied viewers who have agency in their encounters with interfaces. As a consequence, Chapter 3 is the most theoretically explicit, and for this reason might more conventionally be placed at the beginning of my account. But since the terms of my framework rely on the interventions I make in the first two chapters, this material is placed at the centre of my argument. The ideas about agency, embodiment and textual architectures are then developed further in the final chapters on digital games (Chapter 4) and gallery installations (Chapter 5). The evolution of ideas in *Digital Encounters* begins with the emergence of digital inscriptions in texts and ends with embodied viewers encountering interfaces.

Animation is the starting point for my analysis, and I use it to re-articulate our familiar understanding of the technologies of sound and moving images, reconfiguring them into an interface whose textual elements claim the attention of viewers. Just like live-action cinema, animation has a history of technological innovation, and my approach is to pay close attention to the diverse ways in which technologies are involved as an organizing principle, as they both extend and limit the possibilities of expression. Frequently, everything in an animation has to be drawn or modelled and then given movement, making it a rich resource for thinking about how technologies play a role in the organization of textual elements. As I move from a discussion of seamless interfaces, in which the presence of technologies is displaced, towards inscribed ones, where the technologies of animation are more in evidence, I argue that inscribed interfaces reveal the ways in which technologies can manipulate not only what is seen but also *how* it is seen. Using examples from early animations by Winsor McCay, the *Felix* and *Out of the Inkwell* series, as well as the developments instigated through the Disney Studio's experimentation in the *Silly Symphonies*, the shift away from visible inscriptions of technology to ones hidden by the operations of narrative and naturalistic drawing styles is highlighted. Through examples of cel-animation technologies, including the multi-plane camera, I describe the several influences – technologies, narrative, drawing styles – that coexist to seamlessly embed elements of the animated image on the screen. Although computer-generated animation such as *Monsters, Inc.* and *The Incredibles* also has a predominantly seamless interface, I argue that the presence of technology begins to surface through a display of unusual camera movements and framing devices. Chapter 1 ends with a section on more experimental works whose play with animation conventions (such as *Flatworld*, *Feeling My Way* and *Waking Life*) exposes the extensive manipulations of moving image technologies, and how this has an impact on a viewer's experience and engagement with imagery. When spatio-temporal organizations no longer only serve the purpose of giving support to character action, they generate meanings of their own. I argue that such moments hold the potential to articulate a more direct experience of the impact of technologies, transferring narration within a story-world to an experience directed on the viewer. This final point demonstrates a particular facet of this book. My aim is not to talk about representations of technology, but articulations of technology, where the viewer is engaged in a more direct encounter with the spatio-temporal transformations that technologies enable.

My analysis of animation presents a means of excavating the presence of technology as an organizing principle in seamless interfaces, as well as considering the impact of increasingly visible inscriptions on a viewer's experience of an interface. In Chapter 2 I build on this idea via discussions of digital effects cinema. Such films are sites where innovative technologies are often on display, and I use them to introduce a second key term of this book: competing elements. Although digital technologies are now used in many different aspects of filmmaking, from the Dogme films to independent genre features such as *28 Days Later*, in contemporary film-going culture digital effects cinema is probably the most widely seen example of the new technology, although this will undoubtedly change within the next few years as digital technologies become more prevalent in different areas of filmmaking.[4]

Special effects films of all kinds have always involved composite images constructed around live-action elements and synthetic ones, and I will argue that digital effects cinema extends the potential already present in earlier special effects technologies to generate competing elements within an image. Although effects remain embedded within the conventions of storytelling in many films (including *Gladiator*, *King Kong* and the *Lord of the Rings* trilogy), in others a different kind of spatio-temporal organization is becoming visible. Advancing the debate about spectacle and narrative, I show that effects technologies expand narrative space in *The Matrix*, *Twister*, *Titanic* and *Minority Report*. In doing so, I demonstrate how digital effects both create an alternative means for narration and also generate elements that compete for a viewer's attention. In a discussion of *Batman Returns*, the *Spider-Man* films, *Pleasantville* and *Sin City* I also claim that these films provide an alternative perspective on digital technologies, one which goes beyond the surface play of effects.

As I begin to suggest through my discussion of digital effects cinema, the presence of competing elements in an image puts viewers in the position of having to distribute their attention between characters and effects on the interface of the screen. This idea is fully articulated in Chapter 3, as I argue that the capacity of competing elements to distribute attention creates the ground on which a viewer can generate varying degrees of agency. This argument makes an intervention in debates that would see competing elements as further evidence of a distracted viewer. In the context of proliferating hardware, Jonathan Crary has stated:

> [T]elevision and the personal computer ... are antinomadic procedures that fix and striate. They are methods for the management of attention that use partitioning and sedentarization, rendering bodies controllable and useful simultaneously, even as they simulate the illusion of choices and 'interactivity.'
>
> (Crary 2001: 75)

Although Crary is not here discussing textual organizations, the implied other, the unpartitioned and uncontrolled body revelling in 'real' choice, which haunts his remarks is relevant to my argument, albeit as a false idol. In a world marked by proliferating media there is no such thing as an uncontrolled body, and arguably such a thing never has existed nor could exist, since bodies as persons are always apprehended within the social organizations in which they are embedded. But as Pierre Bourdieu has observed, in being placed within a nexus that aims to exert control, people are rarely subjugated, fully interpellated into a system, as they seek instead to find routes where their choices may generate degrees of agency (Bourdieu 1990).

I aim to find these routes in inscriptions on the interfaces of moving image technologies that are themselves emerging within the context of proliferating hardware. Since the 1990s audio-visual technologies have gradually begun to display the kinds of fragmented imagery previously associated with avant-garde practices. Just as it common to find ourselves making sense of the world by engaging with a range of different media, either as individuals or as groups, it is equally common to find fragmentary, mixed media audio-visual materials on the otherwise singular interface, or screen, through which films, digital games, television and webpages are encountered. Although there remains a tendency to see these engagements through spatializing metaphors – fixed, striated, partitioned, fragmented – what this emphasis misses is our ability to make sense of those fragments by traversing the striating impulses of technologies, an ability that relies on time and movement, things which are inherent in time-based media that create moving images. Making sense of the world involves temporally negotiating the structures put in place through the proliferating array of media, oscillating between their competing poles of determinism and choice, creating degrees of freedom. We inhabit the world, not through single points of contact, but through multiple ones, and we also interact with a range of media, not single ones. Making sense of texts constructed from fragmented imagery suggests a model for understanding how we inhabit such a world.

In the narrative of *Digital Encounters* established by my analysis of animation and digital effects cinema, the visibility of inscribed interfaces leads to the emergence of competing elements, which act in turn to distribute a viewer's attention. These terms are taken further in Chapter 3 as I use them to develop a distinctive model of a viewer's agency by bringing together theorists from cinema studies and the social sciences. Katherine Hayles has argued that the cognitive capacities of users of technological networks are distributed, but at the same time these users remain embodied rather than dispersed (Hayles 1999). I draw on this idea by suggesting that the competing elements of the split-screen organization of *Timecode* establish an interface at which viewers are put in the position of having to distribute their attention. Working with the ideas of Vivian Sobchack, Maurice Merleau-Ponty, Pierre Bourdieu and Lois McNay, I mobilize concepts of embodiment, freedom and agency, and use them to explore how the imagery and soundscape of *Timecode* consequently offer both freedoms and restrictions through which the viewer can be understood to have agency.

To more fully describe the processes through which embodiment and agency emerge, I also offer an innovative approach to thinking about the structures and organizations of texts. In order to more fully comprehend the spatio-temporal nature of a viewer's embodied encounter with interfaces I utilize the term 'architecture'. This allows me to break with the convention of seeing narrative films only in terms of their linearity. Instead, I suggest that competing elements introduce an array of spatio-temporal connections, and it is these that enable more complex interfaces for a viewer. This argument is explained by looking at several split-screen films, sections of *Hulk* and the two-, four- and eight-way split-screen films *The Boy Who Saw the Iceberg*, *Timecode* and *The End of the World in Four Seasons*, the first and last of which are animated films. Through this model, I argue that while competing elements are increasingly common, their differing organizations within a narrative structure offer different degrees of freedom and modes of embodiment to a viewer.

To articulate how different degrees of freedom are offered to a viewer I introduce the term 'attractor'. If an architecture is understood to exist as a spatio-temporal organization, then competing elements tend to describe only an architecture's spatial organization. Each competing element, however, has its own temporality, one established in its individual spatio-temporal organization of images. The concept of an attractor emphasizes the different temporalities of competing elements. A simple example is Alighiero e Boetti's installation *Ping Pong* (1966).[5] *Ping Pong* is a two-way split-screen installation where the illuminated words 'PING' and 'PONG' sequentially switch on and off, so that 'PING' appears on the left, 'PONG' on the right and so on. The installation can be described spatially as consisting of two competing elements, but their ability to attract attention varies over time through the on/off mechanism of the installation. Each time one of the words is illuminated it directs viewers' attention away from the non-illuminated one, causing them to 'ping–pong' their attention between the two screens of the installation. Where competing elements are created from more complex moving imagery, their ability to act as attractors also becomes complex, an aspect I consider in relation to digital effects and various split-screen films as they reveal both the limits and opportunities in our encounters with technological interfaces.

In the final chapters of *Digital Encounters* I take the idea of textual architectures and use it to understand the technological interfaces offered by the distinctive organizations of digital games (Chapter 4) and time-based gallery installations (Chapter 5). Playing a digital game, whatever the kind of platform, involves a more complex interface than those already discussed, as a gamer has to watch a series of images and use a console to manipulate characters within the game. The concept of immersion has often been used to think about how a gamer engages with the spatiality of digital game environments. I use the idea of competing elements, distributed attention and architecture to challenge oversimplified understandings of the spatio-temporal architecture of a game. Referring to *Myst*, *Half-Life 2* and *Tomb Raider: Legend*, I argue that the gameworld, the 'playspace' of a game's environment, is structured around several spatio-temporal organizations. For instance, a gamer's engagement with a digital game is very different depending on whether they are puzzle-solving without temporal pressures or whether they are having to contend with the attractor of an AI (artificial intelligence) agent, an element within the game which demands action from the gamer, often an enemy who will otherwise cause an avatar to die. Playing a game does not involve a simple immersion within a virtual environment, but requires gamers to distribute their attention across different spatio-temporal structures, in which attractors operate to both limit and expand the possibilities of agency for the gamer. One of the key differences between playing a digital game and watching animations or digital effects films is that gamers are embedded in the technological interface, in the sense they are required to make their presence felt within the game's structure, through a keystroke say. A consequence of my analysis is to argue that as a gamer's agency is constituted, they too become embedded as an element within the architecture of the game. They are not simply viewers in an ongoing world, but active elements in the construction of that world.

In the final chapter of *Digital Encounters* I focus on time-based gallery installations, including both video and digital work. Unlike the technological interfaces already discussed, which have been confined to the single place of a screen, in installations the competing elements often extend beyond single interfaces into multiple ones, resulting in an interaction that requires attention to be distributed between an array of monitors (Fred Wilson, Nam Jun Paik and Bruce Nauman's multi-monitor installations) or between separate screens (Bill Viola's *The Five Angels for the Millennium* and *Going Forth By Day*). By discussing works by Sam Taylor Wood, Olafur

Eliasson and Tony Oursler, I consider installations as interfaces consisting of competing elements that cue and distribute attention, creating architectures within which viewers gain agency as they make an interpretation of the whole of the artwork. Although they are active in the sense of being interpretive agents, something equally true of viewers of films and players of games, installations also activate the viewer in a different sense. To make this point, I consider how time-based media have 'taken hold' of space, and in doing so situate viewers as the site at which the meaning of space is organized, making them central to the process of the installation, incorporating them within the processes of the artwork. I argue that this incorporation varies from an embodiment based only on frontally distributed attention to one in which viewers are surrounded by the competing elements and so are made more aware of the partiality of their perception. The ability of installations to surround a viewer makes explicit the ways in which installations work on bodies, causing them to take on orientation in space and time. Some installations take the process of bodily incorporation further by including the body as a competing element in the installation. In this way, time-based installations not only create interfaces where viewers can be embodied agents, but embody viewers as an element of the technological interface itself.

Early in this introduction I stated that there is an equivalence in the experience of viewing of *The Matrix* and *The Five Angels For the Millennium*. The equivalence lies in their status as spatio-temporal interfaces at which a viewer can be embodied and gain agency. Maurice Merleau-Ponty (2002) describes freedom as somewhere between determinism and absolute choice, and the idea of freedom, or agency, is central to the explorations of *Digital Encounters*. Moving from animation and digital effects cinema, through digital games and installations, I describe the temporal and spatial complexities of textual elements as competing elements make an appearance on their interfaces. Rather than dispersing viewers, these elements engage them in a variety of ways. The agency of a viewer in making sense of these images is contingent on the kind of interactivity created by the spatio-temporal organization of any given technological interface, with the different textual organizations neither fully determining nor open to absolute choice. *Digital Encounters* is innovative in claiming that moving image technologies offer a range of embodied experiences through distributed viewing, a position that resonates with broader human experiences of technologies and the actual world.

# 1

# RE-ANIMATING THE INTERFACE

> The mutability of the body, and indeed, the whole material
> environment, is a fundamental aspect of the way animation
> revises and questions aesthetic norms and social orthodoxies.
>
> (Wells 2002: 39)

Throughout its history cinema has taken viewers to all kinds of places, from romantic sunsets or the farthest-flung reaches of a galaxy, to abstract patches of colour spiralling to music. We are used to thinking about how technologies are implicated in generating the many imaginative and intellectual possibilities of cinema as they organize time and space, as flickering patterns of light and dark, while changing colours and shapes establish the place inhabited by characters. While these ideas are important, they take us directly into the story-world of the film, displacing the location of our first encounter – the interface of the screen. The work of *Digital Encounters* is to step back from story-worlds and the alternative spaces of cinema, and instead pay attention to the screen as an interface where viewers come into contact with technologies of image construction. It seems important to look more fully at this interface, as by thinking about how technologies are used to manipulate the different elements making up an image's placement and transformation we can begin to see how the organization of these elements is central to processes of viewing, playing a part in enabling and orchestrating engagements and identifications. While much writing has pointed to different aesthetic practices in cinema, paying attention to how its technologies are used in the expressivities of the medium, I place an alternative emphasis here, one that reveals the ways in which technologies shape what and how we see, not only in creative practices, but also in the world more generally.

My purpose is to investigate how technology co-operates with other influences to shape what we see, and not to argue for technology as a determining factor orchestrating engagements and identifications. Technology is only one influence brought to bear on the production of images and sounds; others include narrative organizations, set design, lighting and costume. To excavate these co-operative influences I start with animation, as it is a mode of cinema especially dependent on technology to give viewers access into the worlds it creates. Technologies of animation help create worlds, but the visible evidence of the place of technology in this process varies, revealing more or less about how it shapes what is seen. The *Silly Symphonies* collection, for instance, contains a series of cartoons through which it is possible to trace the innovations explored by the Disney Studio from the late 1920s and into the 1930s, from the introduction of colour and sound to the use of a multi-plane camera. Yet the visibility of these technologies is displaced in favour of characterization and storytelling. A similar argument can be made in relation to more recent computer-generated animations such as *Antz* (1998), *A Bug's Life* (1998), *Shrek* (2001) and *Finding Nemo* (2003). Again, characterization and the credibility of the story-worlds obscure the ways in which technologies influence what is seen on the screen. To expose these influences, instead of looking at the screen as a window into a story-world I take it as an interface where traces of technologies are inscribed to greater or lesser degrees. Through this perspective, the ways in which technologies co-operate with other influences to shape the world seen begin to become more apparent. A number of the cartoons discussed below, including *The Old Mill* (1937), *Daffy Duck in Hollywood* (1938) and *Monsters, Inc.* (2001), are narrative based, with strong characterization, and in them the presence of technology is mostly displaced in favour of the plot. The interface is seamless, one that holds our attention to the story with an intensity that bears little in the way of distraction.

Like other kinds of cinema, seamless or otherwise, animations act as interfaces through which viewers enter into fictional worlds, but, more than other kinds of cinema, animation is extremely dependent on technologies. Where cinema has always relied on technology to record and project live-action scenarios or events occurring in front of the camera, in either actual or constructed worlds, animation's reliance on technologies is more emphatic. It needs technologies to give its objects motion; from abstract shapes processing across a screen to the gestural movements of figures, animated objects would literally not *be* without technology. The phrase 'illusion of life' is often used to describe animation and in many ways captures its essence – a technological system giving movement to inanimate objects.[1] While 'illusion of life' conveys the notion that animations are uncanny reminders of life and death, it also implies a positioning of viewers in a place of contemplation, objectively reacting to images flowing before them. If, however, the screen is understood as an interface, the technology of animation need not be perceived as only allowing images to flow and move, but also as playing a role in positioning a viewer's relationship to the contents of audio-visual imagery.

Technology has an impact on the organization of any audio-visual text. The structures by which a text is organized are as much an aspect of the technologies of animation as they are of the expressive possibilities available through different narrational strategies, and it follows that these organizations also position a viewer. *The Secret Adventures of Tom Thumb* (1993) is open to a range of analyses, and accounts can be given of the ways the animation expresses a perspective on the discourse on technoscience, or its post-apocalyptic dystopian vision of a social organization, or its retelling of the traditional tale of Tom Thumb. Activating these discourses, while opening out a series of potentially interesting questions, overlooks other aspects of the animation such as the techniques used, as well as the kind of interface established for a viewer. This point emerges more fully through looking at the different cinematic versions of Tom Thumb, as their technological display demonstrates two distinct interfaces in the cinema. The earlier *Tom Thumb* (1958), a musical made at MGM, directed by George Pal and featuring the apparently diminutive singing and dancing Russ Tamblin decades before the hobbits of *The Lord of the Rings* trilogy trundled into cinema history along with Gandalf in a cart. Images of Tamblin as Tom Thumb were fully integrated with those of the seemingly larger humans. The cinematic technology used in *Tom Thumb* involved careful camera angles, set design and optical compositing to generate images in which the different-sized figures were made to appear as though they existed within the same space. The technologies effectively maintained the continuity structures typical of Hollywood films in this era, so creating a seamless interface.

In *The Secret Adventures of Tom Thumb* technologies were also employed to integrate the live-action figures with the animated ones, but, by contrast to *Tom Thumb*, the aim of *The Adventures of Tom Thumb* was to create a far from comfortable interface. The process of making the animation, pixilation, involved shooting both the live-action and model sequences using frame-by-frame stop motion. The animators, while generating the movement of a puppet through stop–motion techniques, were at the same time controlling live-action actors as though they too were puppets. This technique not only allows the integration of live action and puppets, but also creates an estranged interface where the movement of live action is rendered curious as the normal and often overlooked motion of even the simplest of gestures is reconfigured and stylized through the process of pixilation. Where the integration of live action and animation in *Tom Thumb* created an interface in keeping with the more easygoing entertainment offered by the musical, in *The Secret Adventures of Tom Thumb* the estrangement of the interface can provoke a degree of anxiety suited to the more acerbic world-view operating in the story-world of the animation. In both instances, cinematic technologies integrate live-action and animated images, but the interfaces generated by the technologies are very different. The expressive possibilities of storytelling reside not only in the content of the story, but also in how the technologies are mobilized to organize the different elements constituting both the sound and also the imagery.

The ability to achieve expression in animation is contingent on technology, making it is a rich source for exploring how emergent technologies enable and place the viewer in different kinds of relationships to the interfaces of the screen. As Norman Klein has discussed, from the late 1920s and throughout the 1930s the Disney Studio developed an animation style which proved so popular with audiences that the more graphic style of the earlier 1920s was overtaken (Klein 1993). These changes included a more naturalistic drawing style, use of music, as well as the development of a multi-plane camera set-up. Such shifts also reveal the place of technology in organizing the interfaces of the different animations, a point made more evident by looking closely at two particular aspects of animations – the embeddedness of characters in the drawn space of an animation and the dimensionality and stability of that space. In the following, I use both of these aspects to think through questions of how technologies organize elements of the screen, tracing the emergence of interfaces that are both seamless and inscribed, which circumvent or extend the freedoms of a viewing experience.

In order to make this argument I especially focus on the interplay between characters, space and action, as the relationship between these elements in many ways determines the extent to which the traces of technology are inscribed on the screen. In continuity systems, where seamless interfaces are most consistently in operation, character actions establish the meanings of any given space. In particular, character actions unify spatial organizations and often draw the eye to a single point of focus. For instance, in the evil toy sequence in *Toy Story* (1995) the damaged toys may look odd, but the relationship between the actions of the toys and the space they inhabit remains a unified one — their movements are dislocated and awkward, but they move within space in a conventional sense. That is, their actions draw a viewer's eye, while all the other space of the screen is used simply as the location in which the movements can occur. By contrast, in *Snack and Drink* (2000), a work created using live-action documentary footage animated by Rotoshop, elements of the image change in such a way that the unifying presence of character action is displaced.[2] Such a displacement releases the space, allowing it to become active on its own terms. In a sequence at a local store, the central figure, Ryan, is mixing himself a drink from the drinks counter, and the flip taps are animated in rhythms and patterns that have no relationship to his actions. As such, they are no longer simply taps for Ryan's use, their meaning fully determined by his actions of drink mixing; instead, they gather meanings of their own. In breaking the unified relationship between character, space and action, two points of focus are opened up in the images – Ryan's actions and the changing look of the flip taps. The presence of these two points of focus, elements that compete for a viewer's attention, inscribe the traces of technology on the screen interface. Such an extensive manipulation of live-action footage has only become possible through the emergence of digital technologies and the development of the Rotoshop program. The inscribed traces of these developments on the screen act as a reminder that technologies of animation not only tell stories, but also manipulate what we see and how we see it.

As this point suggests, I also aim more generally towards technology and its manipulation of the ways in which the world is perceived. Just as animations either invisibly deploy conventions or actively reflect upon or even break conventions, technologies can be used invisibly or visibly to create images of the world. Although such a position might imply a rather simplistic 'use or abuse' view of technology, it does not, as technologies in themselves are far from innocent objects integrated in different ways into the world. Commenting more specifically on computers, Bolter and Gromala suggest:

> The computer is not a neutral space for conveying information any more
> than the printed book, film or television are neutral. The computer shapes

the information it conveys and is shaped in turn by the physical and cultural worlds in which it functions.

(Bolter and Gromala 2003: 86)

Technologies are usually created with a specific purpose in mind, and that sets the criteria through which they are developed. The internet, for instance, emerged out of the need for a sustainable command and control network for the military, and though its usage has exceeded this rationale, its structure remains indebted to those original demands (Wilson 1996). Similarly, technologies used in the creation of moving images and sound are created and refined with particular requirements in mind, and these confine the possibilities of expression – even when someone is working against the conventions established by a particular kind of animation package such as Maya or Animo, they can only break the conventions of that package. Technologies, then, offer different kinds of freedom, but it is always a limited freedom contingent on the structures established by the possibilities of that technology. This is not to begin from a position where technologies necessarily limit human existence. Just like everything else in the world, technologies impose limitations even as they establish new freedoms.

## The beginnings: animation as an emergent cinematic technology

Different kinds of animated technologies create strange yet often oddly familiar worlds, and do so through interfaces that both reveal or displace their status as moving image technologies. Historians of animation have begun the task of piecing together exact histories of the technological, economic and artistic practices from which these worlds have emerged.[3] However, I discuss interfaces in the light of contemporary debates that specifically address the interplay between humans and technologies. Given this perspective, I explore the different ways animation technologies play a role in the organization of the elements that make up their storyworlds, rather than paying attention to the particular chronologies of the development of those technologies. Initially, I work with some early examples of animation, such as those of Winsor McCay, before going on to discuss animations that create a seamless interface for a viewer, where the presence of technologies is unmarked, including the *Silly Symphonies* and more recent digital animations such as *Monster's Inc.* and *The Incredibles* (2004). This is followed by a discussion of examples of animations where the technology of animation is more fully visible, inscribed on interfaces of animations such as *Flatworld* (1997) and *Waking Life* (2002).

As historians of early cinema have described, some of the initial pleasures of looking in the cinema lay in its ability to give motion to things previously only photographically represented in stillness. These included the fascination of moving leaves, of trains pulling into stations, the flow of a crowd of people leaving a factory or familiar spaces reconfigured through the images taken by a cameraman in the audience's town earlier in the day.[4] At this very early point in cinema's history its abilities as a technology to give movement to images were as much a part of the spectacle of entertainment as was the content. As cinematic technology became familiar to audiences and filmmakers began to experiment with the storytelling possibilities of the new media, the emergence of narrative displaced this element of cinema as a particular point of interest. Instead, movement and the technologies generating it were taken for granted, only gaining attention again when significant innovations such as sound, colour or widescreen were introduced as a distinctive and transformative presence in the cinema-going experience.

In its early stages, the place of technology in the process of animation was similarly a part of the spectacle, though again it was quickly displaced. This transition is visible in early cartoons by James Stuart Blackton, working at the Edison Laboratories, and Winsor McCay, who both combined live action with lightning drawing in their demonstrations of animated filmmaking. In 1900 when James Stuart Blackton, then working at the Edison Studio, made an early cartoon, *The Enchanted Drawing*, live-action cinema was already becoming a commonplace, and so the technological surprise focused on the possibilities of cartooning via frame-by-frame photography. The innovation lay in an ability to animate the inanimate, and the potential pleasures of the novel technological experience existed again in seeing something familiar anew. *The Enchanted Drawing* shows a man sketching a face on a large, vertically hung sheet of paper, and two effects are visible. First, drawn objects, such as a hat, bottle and cigar, become actual objects through substitution, and parts of the face move – mouth and eyes – effects achieved through stop–action photography. Second, the animator's activities are visible on-screen, so that his actions appear to be directly responsible for generating the motion of the figure. These two elements, the live-action and drawn elements, coexist as two points of attention for a viewer, but the potential for this to split a viewer's attention is negated by the co-ordination of the live action with the animated action. In a way which prefigures later compositing conventions, the two elements are made to appear as though they exist in the same spatio-temporal organization – as the man reaches towards the hat, a well-timed substitution of drawn for actual object makes the action of reaching appear seamless. As the technology of frame-by-frame photography allows co-ordinated action and movement, the organization of the structural elements (live action *and* drawn) draws a viewer's attention to the same place on the screen, so creating a unifocal viewing interface. The use of camera technology to film frame by frame enables a structure seamlessly integrating live-action and animated elements.

Released eleven years later, *Little Nemo* (1911) also explicitly plays with the possibilities of animation, but instead of simply emphasizing facial movements gives movement to a trio of figures, Nemo and his playmates. For those familiar with the cartoon strip, the pleasure in seeing *Little Nemo* lay not simply in bringing any drawn figure to life, but in the bringing to life of this particular figure.[5] As well as animating his already famous character, in showing shapes deforming in the tradition of distorting mirrors McCay showed off one of the distinctive features of animation – the manipulability of shape. Just as *The Enchanted Drawing* combines explanatory live-action sequences with the drawn segments, the animated sequences of *Little Nemo* are framed by a device telling the story of McCay's bet with his friends, but, more importantly for this analysis, also demonstrate the technology of animation. Initially, the same tactic seen in *The Enchanted Drawing* is repeated – McCay standing in front of a vertically hung sheet of paper drawing the figure of Little Nemo. Later the work of animating is shown more explicitly – the labour and materials needed to draw the 4,000 individual cards said to make up the animated sequences, giving them motion via a hand cranked device, and finally a projector suggesting that there has been a transfer between cards and film. While the doubled role of the animator and the technology in generating an animation is made clear in *Little Nemo*, with *How a Mosquito Operates* (1912) the hand of the animator that ended *Little Nemo* has become opaque, out of sight behind the telling of the story. On this, Giannalberto Bendazzi comments:

> *Little Nemo* is truly a 'first movie'; without plot or background, it is little more than a sequence of images, materializing and then vanishing as if to prove their ability to exist on screen. The experimentalism is overcome in *The Story of a Mosquito*, the funny, ironic tale of a huge mosquito, wearing a top hat, which is insatiably hungry for the blood of a drunkard. The gluttonous bug ends up exploding.
>
> (Bendazzi 1994: 16–17)

The displacement of animation technology in *How a Mosquito Operates* (referred to as *The Story of a Mosquito* in the quotation above) allows a full view of the animation itself. It is a moment where the story of being able to animate gives way to storytelling. While Bendazzi sees this as an overcoming of experimentalism, it is equally when technology and visible play go into hiding. With some notable exceptions, such as the Fleischer Studio's *Koko the Clown* series, begun in the later 1910s and running through much of the 1920s, and Disney's *Alice Comedies* series, which ran in the 1920s, use of live action and explicit allusions to the processes of filmmaking cease until the 1940s and 1950s.[6] This, of course, only means that as narrative-based animation becomes predominant the place of technology in organizing the elements of the cartoon on the screen is less obvious. It nevertheless is present, embedded within a system of conventions.

## Traces of technology

Although the visibility of animation technology does not disappear completely, its presence is displaced, making it necessary to excavate its traces. Some of these traces are more strongly present than others, their evidence demonstrable at a macro level of studio production practices. For instance, the emergence of cel-animation as the dominant technique within the animation studios by the late 1910s determined the look of animation within the mainstream of American studio productions (Furniss 1998: 16). Donald Crafton argues that the various developments of pegs holding the sheets in place for drawing or shooting enabled sharper alignments, and the subsequent use of celluloid sheets for drawing 'disclosed a new visual world . . . [where] figures could obscure the background, move in and out of pictorial space, and repeat motions with relative ease' (Crafton 1984: 150–51). The comfortable fit between the need for rapid production of cartoons and the systemized process of cel-animation facilitated its implementation in animation studios, a co-operative influence that demonstrates the pervasive impact of technology on what would become possible in studio-produced animations.

The influence of technology can be further revealed by looking more closely at details at the interface of a cartoon animation. As I described in relation to the Tom Thumb films, the organization of the interface can work to draw in its viewers, seamlessly locating them within its story-world, or it can equally dislocate its viewers. One way to give an account of the immersive qualities of an interface is to look at how character actions operate in the drawn space of an animation, seeing how they are embedded within the spaces of the story. As characters are often the main point of focus in viewing a character-based animation, they are a key element around which other elements are organized. The embeddedness of a character is central both in effacing the traces of technology and also in positioning the viewer in relation to the interface. If the character is not effectively embedded, no matter how minimal or detailed the animation style, the credibility of the story-world is reduced.

This aspect of a character's location in space is something almost taken for granted in live action. In continuity systems, for instance, the editing allows them frequently to move without disruption across and through spaces. But many other elements of the set-up also embed the figure. Unless manipulated to be otherwise, shadows move with characters, figures move with the 'weightedness' expected of a body inhabiting the gravitational and spatial dimensionality of the planet earth. Whereas such things are taken for granted in live action, in animation all these cues of embeddedness have to be added. The developments of animation in the transition from the 1920s through into the 1930s reveal the techniques used increasingly to embed characters in animated spaces, both through drawing styles and also through the use of technologies. By the 1920s, the initial wonderment offered by the technologies of animation had long been exceeded by the establishment of cel animation as the main mode of production, along with the solidification of conventions for narrative structures – plotting, characterization, detailed drawing of background. Within these kinds of structures, the organization of the elements making up an animation increasingly generated a seamless interface. This reorganization can be traced through the changes evident between the *Felix* cartoons of the 1920s and the *Silly Symphonies* of the 1930s. Where the *Felix* cartoons are something of a forerunner to the more anarchic Warner Bros cartoons, with Felix involved in numerous escapades with other more peripheral characters, the *Silly Symphonies* are renowned as a series in which the Disney Studios experimented with the possibilities of characterization and depth of space, developing the style of the subsequent feature-length cartoons that began with *Snow White and the Seven Dwarfs*, released in 1937.

A major series of the 1920s, *Felix the Cat* was produced at the Pat Sullivan Studio, and drawn by Otto Mesmer. In a drawing style still typical of the 1920s, the animations were line drawn with block (black and more latterly grey) and tonal filling and a simple but effective illusion of perspective. The spaces the characters operated within were credible ones, rural or urban spaces, farmyards or street scenes, drawn always with enough detail to locate the character in terms of narrative place. Nevertheless, the figure of Felix itself was slightly disconnected from the space, always hovering on the edge of settling into the gravity of any situation. This edge of uncertainty in a character's embeddedness finds greater expression in Felix's and other figures' abilities to metamorphose. Felix's mutable tail frequently facilitated otherwise unexpected transitions in space, becoming, for instance, a ladder or an aircraft. In *Felix Takes a Hand* (1922) there is a quite extraordinary transition when sausages process from a butcher's store into a phone line. Felix, involved in a battle between rats and cats, has called up his friend the butcher for reinforcements. The butcher gestures towards the sausages, which promptly march across the screen into the phone, and so quickly cross the miles to the battlefield from where Felix is calling. Such transformations could occur at any moment in Felix cartoons and, in the absence of cues through which to anticipate these moments, create characters that resist being completely secured in the space of the cartoon. A similar argument can be made for the *Out of the Inkwell* cartoon series, in which Koko and more latterly Fitz both jump between animated and live-action spaces.[7] In both instances, though action and gag narrative systems are in play, one of the great pleasures allowed by the still insecure interface is the strange transformations of space and time.

In the late 1920s as the Disney Studio began experimenting with the emergent sound technologies, creating the syncopated Mickey Mouse vehicle *Steamboat Willie*, they also developed a drawing style with artfully drawn backgrounds of increasingly full perspective, as well as further extending character animation. In this drive towards equivalence with both the spatiality and deeper characterizations of live action, the spatio-temporal playfulness of the Felix series was displaced.[8] In conjunction with changes in drawing techniques, the use of multi-plane camera technology added another organizational possibility to the imagery.[9] Frequently discussed as a key element in the Disney Studio's success throughout the 1930s, multi-plane camera inaugurated a period in which spatial parameters increasingly approached a look-alike of live-action cinema through depth perspective and shaded spaces, not to mention the use of cinematic framing and camera movement.[10] Although its influence on the realism of depth perspective is the most often discussed aspect of this technology, it was also used for fantastical sequences, the drunken-dream sequence in *Dumbo*, for instance, was created using the camera. However, whether discussing live-action depth perspective or that of fantasy sequences, in both instances the characters began to be secured within dimensional space, made to inhabit it more fully.[11] A more detailed comparison of *The Skeleton Dance* and *The Old Mill* makes this apparent.

The first of Disney's *Silly Symphonies*, *The Skeleton Dance*, released in 1929, already reveals a dense style of drawn space, but one against which less-defined figures look flattened and unintegrated. The graveyard of the cartoon is a crafted image, with tonal spaces and detailing in the grass and trees. Within this space the skeleton dance is set carefully to music and sound effects. Looking at the cartoon, it is clear that the studio had not yet perfected the interaction of relatively low definition characters within a high definition space. The tonal detail of the background is at odds with the details of the figures, making the figures seem exactly what they are – two-dimensional figures overlaid onto a background. This observation is not meant as a criticism of the cartoon, only as a comment on the nature of the cartoons in that period, and also as an index against which the Disney Studio subsequently worked. As a series, the *Silly Symphonies* is credited as the site of Disney Studio experimentation, and many of the cartoons show not only the development of personality animation in the characters, but also a drawing style achieving greater integration of character and space, leading to a more secure and seamless viewing interface. This style, which included adjusting to the three-colour Technicolor process in 1932, became increasingly complex, often with naturalistic backgrounds into which a less delineated moving character was integrated. Two key means of achieving integration were use of depth and markers for a figure's presence within a space.

The use of multi-plane camera allowed shot set-ups where a 'zoom' through the multi-plane layers created an impression of greater dimensional depth. This effect is furthered by the ability of characters to move between objects placed at different depths, such as the clouds passing by in the *Water Babies* (1935). Within such an organization, movement across the layers of depth is always certain, as the point is to show the movement through depth, rather than distract from it by introducing the spatio-temporal leaps of a Felix or a Koko. The technological innovation of multi-plane camera operated within a more general convention of a 'spatio-temporal realism' that fully secured the interface.[12] As well as integrating figures into depth through use of the multi-plane camera, other devices used more frequently to solidify the dimensions of the interface included shadows and reflections as 'markers of presence'. Markers of presence are those aspects of the animation added to create equivalences with actuality. Shadows and reflections are particularly good markers of presence, and they became increasingly sophisticated from the relatively shapeless and blob-like shadows of *Just Dogs* (1932) to the almost full and responsively mobile reflections on the floors, walls and pools of the colour cartoon *Music Land* (1935), enabling a more effective embedding of figures into the locations of the imagery.

The release of *The Old Mill* (1937) combined these effects and demonstrated the range of the Disney Studio's skills in integrating characters more fully within the drawn spaces. The images of the opening establishing shot are detailed, carefully coloured and naturalistic. In the later action-filled storm sequence, the use of responsive shadows around the birds and mice makes them look as though they inhabit the space, particularly during the lighting flashes. The frog sequence showcases another kind of presence marker: ripples in the water accompany their movements on the lily leaves. *The Old Mill* also showed off the possibilities of the multi-plane camera, allowing for movement through animated layers – the cartoon opens with a zoom through cel-layers from the foreground of rushes up to the mill, and includes an upward movement through the different levels inside the mill. As well as showcasing the various innovations of the Disney Studio, *The Old Mill* also demonstrates one of the central organizational structures within which studio-based animation technologies operated in the 1930s. Technology does not enable anything strange; instead it co-operates with other influences, mediated through changes in drawing styles, to call to mind live-action cinema and, through that, evokes a representational version of actuality. The security of a seamless interface is central to this organizational structure.

The innovations of the *Silly Symphonies* throughout the early 1930s show how characters were integrated into spaces through detailed depth perspective and presence markers. Other animations, however, demonstrate that the seamless quality of the interface is not absolutely dependent on the detailing of full animation, but on the placement of a character within space in a sequence of shots, whose detail can vary from the fully drawn aesthetics of Disney to more minimalist ones. This becomes clearer through the idea of anticipation. Discussing Disney animation, Norman Klein suggests that character movements can be anticipated, and these secure the integration of a character within a shot sequence. That is, a figure makes micro adjustments prefiguring larger movements to come: a look or a turn of the head toward the next point of motion ensures an appearance of seamless action. The notion of anticipation is not only relevant to characterization, but also to the organization of the elements making up the images. In the Sorcerer's Apprentice section of *Fantasia*, Mickey's backward glances towards the Sorcerer's hat as he watches the Sorcerer go upstairs to bed anticipate the character's subsequent action of borrowing the hat *and* locate the hat in the same space as Mickey.

The ability of a glance or movement of a character to unify the spaces in which actions occur holds true for many kinds of animation, not only those of the Disney Studio, and as such is another means through which a seamless interface is established. As I will discuss further, this is especially true in relation to animations combining different kinds of cinematic technique, such as live action and animation, or cel- and digital animation. However, it is also a facet of drawing styles that avoid conventional depth perspective, using instead a more flattened perspective and graphic spaces. The United Productions of America (UPA) Studio, established in the 1940s and coming to critical notice in the 1950s following the Oscar-winning *Gerald McBoing Boing* (1951), took a different direction to the more established animation of its era, that of Warner Bros and the Disney Studio, in turning to a more graphic style of drawing.[13] In this cartoon, and also in *The Tell-Tale Heart* (1953), the spaces where actions occur are angular, and figures drawn with heavy lines lessen the depth perspective. Non-action spaces are frequently unfilled by any detail, often simply coloured space existing off the centre established by the actions of the character. Despite the distinctive look of UPA animations, characters still hold the animation together, in that their actions give coherence to the spaces. The ability of character actions to hold together space is more obvious in cartoons using a minimalist drawing style. For instance, in a more recent animation, *Second Class Mail* (1984), an older woman buys a blow-up doll version of a male companion. By comparison with other cel-animations the spaces look very pared down, and the character unintegrated through presence markers. However, the insubstantiality of much of the space is inconsequential as the flow of the character's actions gives it sense.

One of the outcomes of these character-led organizations is that traces of the technology vanish behind the coherence of the interface. The inscriptions of technologies become shallow since they tend to be dissipated by the other influences having an impact on the animation's structure and organization, especially character embeddedness. This effect is most clear in films combining live action and animation. Even the early animations such as *The Enchanted Drawing* and *Little Nemo*, whose narratives were more about the ability to animate than creating fictional stories, demonstrate the tendency to displace the potentially disruptive combination of live action and animation in a single sequence of images, as the spectacle of the illusion covers over the join between the two technologies of live-action and animated cinema. Subsequently, it has become conventional to find the gap between live action and animation joined by gestures that secure the connectivity of the space, markers of presence that cross the junction. Although the *Out of the Inkwell* series was popular and Koko and Fitz could jump space without any particular motivating event, combinations of live action and animation went into abeyance, and throughout the later 1920s and the 1930s the combination only occurred through framing devices such as the song and dance routines opening a number of cartoons in the *Betty Boop* series, with little actual crossover between such spaces.

When they re-emerged in the 1940s, studio-produced combinations of live action and animation ensured not only that such transitions were always cued rather than abrupt, but also that live-action figures were fully integrated within the animated space and animated characters embedded within the live-action spaces. For instance, in the Worry Song sequence of *Anchors Aweigh* (1945) Gene Kelly's character, Joseph Brady, dances with King Jerry (from *Tom and Jerry*). This sequence begins with Brady entering into the animated kingdom, where he talks to the animals, and ends with him dancing in a live-action space with the animated Jerry. The integration of Jerry into the live-action space is ensured not only by the matched choreography of the two dancing figures, but also by the matching movements of Jerry's animated shadow. The latter operates to embed the animated figure into the live-action space. Subsequent combinations of live action and animation such as *Song of the South* (1946), *Bedknobs and Broomsticks* (1971), *Tron* (1982), *Who Framed Roger Rabbit?* (1988) and the more recent *Looney Tunes: Back in Action* (2003) all ensure integration in the different elements of the film. *Tron*, for instance, combines not only conventional animation and live action, but also early digital animation. The similar stylization of all the elements coexisting within the story-world adds cohesion to the different elements, and so displaces the traces of the technologies used in the creation of the audio-visual imagery, even though much of the action of *Tron* is spent inside a digital environment.

## Moving into the digital era

The rhetoric surrounding the emergence of computer-generated animation suggests that it too continues to generate a seamless technological interface, in spite of the fact that in its early stages it represented a distinct mode of animation, one exploited by experimental filmmakers. The success of *Toy Story* (1995) led the way in opening up the marketplace to computer-generated character animation. And although there are 60 years between *Toy Story* and the *Silly Symphonies*, there is clearly an equivalent displacement of technological traces in the later animation, even as the developments in computer technology were essential to its completion. But this is not the whole story. John Lasseter, the director of *Toy Story* and a key figure in the development of computer animation within mainstream filmmaking, has spoken of his vision of animating objects on the computer, with early examples such as *Luxo Jnr* (1987) and *Knick Knack* (1989) demonstrating Pixar's animation aesthetic of not only making familiar objects inhabit three-dimensional space, but also giving those objects characterization.[14] Julia Moszkowicz writes about the tendency for commentators of computer animation to fixate on computer animation's ability to go ever closer to depictions of reality, and aims to counter this view by arguing for the idea of a 'pictorial reality':

> Too many people seem persuaded that digital animation should be understood as yet another 'extension of man', enhancing his capacity to reproduce the world in all its Technicolored, shaded and rendered glory. Whilst it cannot be contested that the computer has, indeed, provided us with some useful tools with which to visualize the world and make its image incredibly realistic, the outcome is not informed solely by the machine nor by its capacity to mimic the physical aspects of human perception. The realism on offer is more crucially informed by prior engagements, on the part of animators and audiences alike, with existing media.
>
> (Moszkowicz 2002: 314)

The merging of conventions implied by the idea of pictorial reality is evident in a range of different computer-generated animations, and it is possible to note differing degrees of attachment to live-action and/or animation traditions.[15] In seeking out evidence for such attachments, it becomes clear, especially in cartoons aiming to showcase how digital technologies push the boundaries of possibility in animation aesthetics, that there is also a leakage of technological inscription onto the screen interface. For instance, animations such as *Final Fantasy: The Spirits Within* (2001) or the short *The Final Flight of the Osiris* (2003) both aim for the look of live-action science fiction films generally, and in particular *The Matrix* (1999) in the case of *The Final Flight of the Osiris*. The latter shows the relative complexity of this merging of conventions, though the innovatory techniques serve the aim of achieving a resemblance to the short's live-action antecedents. The animation is based around a fight between two characters within a simulator, where the existence of such a simulator is first established within *The Matrix*. *The Final Flight of the Osiris* uses the same kinds of movements as the action sequences of the live-action film, which were themselves built around the influences of wire-fu and the possibilities of digital manipulation of live-action footage.[16] In addition, the animators on *The Final Flight of the Osiris*, as in *Final Fantasy*, were striving towards a look that simulated human figures. As such, embedding the characters, even within the more unconventional spatiality of the *Matrix* world order, is paramount. All the technological possibilities of digital animation are focused on this simulation, which again displaces its potential as anything other than a technology operating to reproduce a series of pre-existing conventions.

Not all computer animations strive as emphatically towards the kind of simulation seen in *The Final Flight of the Osiris* and *Final Fantasy*. In examples such as *Monsters, Inc.* and *The Incredibles* there is the potential for the technology to be visible, to inscribe the possibilities of a different kind of interface. The quality of seamlessness still secures the interface through narrative and depth, but coexisting with these two influences is a digital one. Thus, both features draw on the traditions of animating in depth running from the *Silly Symphonies* to *Toy Story*, and they also include imagery that simulates objects in the actual world, such as Sulli's fur in *Monsters, Inc.* and the foliage in *The Incredibles*. But these influences are combined with elements that could only be effectively achieved through digital animation. The extraordinary door store is an instance of this in *Monsters, Inc.* Although it might be possible to imagine the door store being drawn without a computer, its scale, in conjunction with the movement of the 'camera', make this a space that draws attention to the technology of computer animation.[17] The sweeping movement of the camera as it follows Sulli, Boo and Mike along the rails of the door store captures the point of view of the characters as they speed along twists and turns, and swoop across wide chasms, while also allowing the viewer to see these characters rapidly moving within a vast space in which the doors recede into the depth at all angles of the viewpoint. *Monsters, Inc.* is full of expertise, with the filmmakers drawing on the Pixar tradition of strong story-telling and characterization, brought into being with cutting-edge digital animation technologies used in conjunction with a developed experience of longer-standing techniques.[18] The door store sequence stands out in a film about encounters between the two worlds of monsters and humans. It is one of the few moments where *viewers* are given a distinctive interface through which they more directly encounter technological manipulation. Instead of only telling the story of a character's encounter with a different space, the impact of such an encounter is transferred to viewers by giving them access to a space that is somehow unexpected. Such a moment suggests the possibility for other kinds of interfaces, an idea explored later in this chapter.

There is a tendency to see computer-generated animations within a tradition of an aesthetic of encroaching realism, whether pictorial or actual, all aspects of which are served by technological advancements. A closer look at some of these animations suggests, however, another aesthetic in play, one that is about 'showing off' the latest possibilities of technologies in any given moment. Although all the structures of a secure interface are still in play, as the door store example from *Monsters, Inc.* suggests, the innovations of the technology are beginning to surface. While not creating images fundamentally distinct from the ones preceding it, *The Incredibles* combines a number of different influences, but its movement towards simulation of live-action figures and objects in the actual world is tempered by the particularities of digital animation. The way the animators speak about the construction of the

25

characters demonstrates several of the competing influences at play in the animation of the characters. Listening to the DVD interviews, it is clear that the animators modelled the figures as a caricature of gender conventions. Mr Incredible's narrow hips and impossibly wide shoulders are given an angular aspect that is most pronounced when he is in shape. By contrast, Elasti-Girl's proportions invert this: her wide hips curve out below a cinched waistline, while her slender shoulders accentuate her narrow upper body. At the same time, the animators speak of their desire to evoke an ordinary human body through modelling the movements of muscle and fat under skin during gestures and more substantial motion, something which owes a debt to a tradition within special effects cinema creature modelling rather than cel-animation.[19] Yet these, too, are subject to exaggeration: for instance the excessive, squeezed-in movement of Mr Incredible's paunch when he is being forced into the launch device to enable him to land on the island. The mutability of Elasti-Girl's extraordinary body pushes all this further. The modelling of these bodies reveals a gesture towards anatomical realism, but this is packaged within another series of conventions from animation – exaggeration of expression and body movements.

The competing influences of pictorial realism also make more explicit the surfacing of digital inscriptions on the interface of the screen. In the sequence where Mr Incredible first journeys to the island, he lands on a lush green area. As Mr Incredible runs down a path following the slope of a hill, a camera shot plunges from mid-air down into the undergrowth. Although similar in kind to a live-action crane shot, the extent of its movement as it falls from mid-air, dropping down to the ground, gives it an untethered quality demonstrating its status as a virtual camera.[20] This digitally constructed shot, however, reveals the detail of the foliage, which moves in reaction to the passing superhero, apparently reflecting the light of the sun. The realism of these images creates a counterpoint to the untethered digital shot, and it is this kind of counterpoint that establishes the distinctive interface of *The Incredibles*. Other instances of this distinctive counterpoint include the speed of the camera movements used in Dash's run. Again, the imagery relies on a pictorially realistic construction of the space of the forest, but such speeding movement by the camera would be impossible to achieve using cel-animation technologies. The tumbling sphere of Violet's force field, when Mr Incredible and Elasti-Girl become attached, is another example. As Violent and Dash remain inside the field's bubble, Mr Incredible and Elasti-Girl, caught on its outside, rapidly rotate around them. In a view apparently from within its dimensions, they remain fully visible through the transparent sphere as they react to being squashed.

Evident in *Monsters, Inc.* and *The Incredibles* is the surfacing of technology on an otherwise seamless interface. Unlike earlier animations where the technology was effaced, here the double positioning reveals its inscription. However, this is not necessarily one that provokes questions about the limits of representation; rather, it is a display of the possibilities of animation technologies in a way that is not so dissimilar to *Little Nemo*. While these animations are different in terms of narrative devices, length and the combinations of live-action and animation technologies, both show off technologies in the eras of their creation. The early cartoon literally shows the technologies of its creation, while the later cartoon showcases its technologies through the distinctive combination of aesthetic influences, those of pictorial reality and digital imaging.

Animation technologies create interfaces of moving sounds and images, with different kinds of technological developments opening up a vast array of expressive possibilities. As I have argued, the technologies in themselves are not determining of those possibilities, but coexist with other kinds of influences, such as drawing styles and narrative organizations. As an example of seamless interfaces, 1930s mainstream animation, heavily influenced by the successes of the Disney Studio, tended towards a very secure interface in which characters were fully embedded within spatial depth. This kind of seamless interface locates its viewers by immersing them within its content, primarily encouraging a purchase on the story-world, whether structured by fabular, action or gag devices. Broadening this point out, emphasis is placed on the information being given and not on the process by which that information came into being. A viewer at this interface is, therefore, engaged at a screen where the sense of mediation is minimal. To borrow Bolter and Grusin's language of remediation, a seamless interface is 'a transparent interface ... that erases itself, so the user is no longer aware of confronting a medium, but instead stands in an immediate relationship to the contents of that medium' (Bolter and Grusin 1999: 5). Furthermore, it is not simply the medium that is erased, but also the technological implications of that medium. In most of the examples discussed so far, if attention is drawn to the technology this is in order to display its possibilities and not to question its operations and manipulations.

The contemporary rush of computer-generated animation, then, is at most a display of the possibilities of digital technologies, as *Monsters, Inc.* or *The Incredibles* remains seamless overall. Even though the unusual combination of convention with novel uses of animating tools generates moments of having seen something anew, these moments are embedded within a secure interface, working inside the overarching organization of a narrative system, and so although questions about the technological interface may surface they quickly dissipate as the action moves on. However, when such moments begin to slip away from the arch-controller of narrative coherence – characters and their actions – a different kind of interface starts to emerge. As the expressive possibilities of technological systems become more explicit, technology is more obviously placed within the discursive operations of the text.

## Making inscriptions visible

Traces of technology begin to deepen in animations in which character actions are no longer able to give full meaning to their spaces, allowing space to escape the organization frame of character action. By escaping such a frame, I mean those moments where the mutability of objects and figures exceeds the support they give to characters and instead draws attention and meaning to the objects and figures themselves. The idea of self-reflexivity is relevant here, but whereas this is normally used to think about the conventions of narrative or editing, it can be extended to think about technology. An animation such as *Monsters, Inc.* tweaks a seamless interface by displaying the possibilities of animating using a virtual camera, but its conventions of time and space still remain stable. It does not, in the end, pose questions about organizations of time and space and how a technological system may be implicated in positioning viewers. By contrast, in an animation such as *Flatworld* the organizations of space come into focus through manipulations of the dimensionality of its various figures. In combination with a plot device in which a technology (a television remote) gives access to other worlds, the role of technology in locating a viewer is explicit in the both the form and content of the animation.

To begin exploring how technological inscriptions appear on interfaces, I look at animations in which space escapes the meaning given to it by character action; that is, when characters cease to be fully embedded in a coherent spatial organization and their presence does not fully unify the relationship between character, actions and space. Before looking at how conventions are warped or stretched, a distinction needs to be made between mutability in animations generally and in those which draw particular attention to spatio-temporal organization. For instance, in *Daffy Duck in Hollywood* (1938) Daffy's actions subvert the normal functions of objects, including phones, camera and lighting equipment, but the locations for these actions are drawn in the more straightforward dimensional style of Warner Bros. cartoons. In some other Warner Bros cartoons, such as *Dough For the Do-Do* (1949) and *Duck Amuck* (1953), the mutability crosses over from the characters and objects to the spatiality of the animations. *Dough For the Do-Do* combines an already surrealist landscape – Dali-esque clocks and oddly shaped formations – with a chase sequence in which the do-do leaps downward off-screen into other spaces, creating doors and windows in air. In the do-do's world the organizing logic allows space itself to be mutable. Similarly, in *Duck Amuck* conventions of studio-based animation are broken as Daffy's background and costume alter without any motivation or warning as the cartoon works through its story of a battle between Daffy and the animator.[21] These three examples reveal a distinction between the more usual mutability of figures and objects and the less usual mutability of space.

Characters are embedded in space by various strategies, including depth, markers of presence and anticipatory gestural cues, as well as narrative organizations, especially gag and fable-based structures.[22] In many cartoons, the space in which the figures and objects are embedded is contained by the actions of characters: characters act in space and the meaning of space is to give sense to those actions. *Dough For the Do-Do* and *Duck Amuck* break with these conventions when the unity between character, space and action dissolves. In discussing live-action cinema Stephen Heath observes how space is conventionally 'used up' in the construction of place or narrative setting:

> The vision of the image is its narrative clarity and that clarity hangs on the negation of space for place, the constant realization of centre in function of narrative purpose, narrative movement: 'Negatively, the space is presented so as not to distract attention from the dominant actions: positively, the

space is "used up" by the presentation of narratively important settings, character traits ... or other causal agents.' Specific spatial cues – importantly, amongst others, those depending on camera movement and editing – will be established and used accordingly, centring the flow of the images taking place.

(Heath 1981: 39)

The opposite of the idea of space as 'used up' is useful here; that is, to think about space when it is *not* used up, when it emerges in an abundance escaping the setting of place or the control of character. This is not to say space is redundant, or in excess, but rather it introduces a dimension allowing space to emerge as a distinct element in the organization of an interface.

In a seamless interface character actions always control the meaning of space, even where the drawn space is minimal or where two kinds of images are composited together. By contrast, an inscribed interface may be one where actions do not use up the meaning of space. One way of approaching the presence of 'un-used' space is to move beyond its revelations about the conventions of spatial organizations and consider instead how it opens up a discussion about the ways in which the organization of the interface creates different experiences of technologies. In what I have been calling a seamless interface the experience is contained as a viewer is immersed in the story-world. In more inscribed interfaces organizations of the elements making up the imagery are not always directed towards the story-world in ways that support only character action. Instead, the organization of the interface includes elements evoking direct experiences for a viewer, ones that are motivated by the story-world. As the examples of *Dough For a Do-Do* and *Duck Amuck* suggested, one of these direct experiences can be that of unexpected spatial transitions; however, if we understand animation as a technological system that plays a part in organizing elements on the interface of the screen, it follows that this spatial experience is also a technological one, drawing on its capacity to alter spatio-temporal experiences.

Images of spatial transformation not only create a direct experience of space for a viewer, but also remark on the relationship between technologies and space. In a general way, technologies have the ability to create different kinds of spaces and to establish different kinds of relationships with older and newer spatial organizations. Transport systems are very familiar to people in the early twenty-first century, and, in addition to getting people from A to B, also alter the ways in which the spatiality of the world can be experienced. Fast transport, for instance, alters perceptions of distance and the dimensions of geography. Webcams are another technology altering our experience of the world. Even if we cannot visit places physically, webcams allow people to look, giving them a limited perspective on another space. However, the limits of this perspective become apparent in the time-lapse of image capture or the stasis of the camera. The viewing experience offered by webcams is clearly delimited by the possibilities and settings of the technologies.

This concept of possibilities opening out through technology yet also being constrained by it emerges in a number of animations. Daniel Greaves' animation *Flatworld*

evokes a sense of spatial experience that is both expanded and limited by technological systems through the interplay of its content and form. The story of *Flatworld*
is centred on Matt, a character who lives on the planet of Flatworld. Following an
accident, Matt is led into a series of encounters with spaces made accessible to him
by technology. Instead of simply watching television through the interface of a
screen, Matt and various other characters are able to cross into the different worlds
existing within the television. Technology makes this possible, as each of these
characters has been zapped by the multicoloured aura escaping from a cut cable
wire, giving them the ability to gain entry to the different televisual worlds. This is
an instance of fully embodied remote access, as the technological intervention
allows characters to fall through puddles from one space into another and then
control access to a myriad of other spaces through the use of a remote control. The
introduction of these spaces technologically expands the spatiality of the planet of
Flatworld and allows the zapped inhabitants to distribute their existence across
multiple dimensions.

The emergence of such an expanded interface within Flatworld is treated with
some ambivalence within the story-world and style of the animation. At first these
alternative spaces seem like a literal escape from the chase between a series of
characters – Matt; Geoff, his cat; Chips, his fish; a policeman and his dog – who are
all chasing or are chased by a thief (see Figure 1.1). As all these figures cross into the
technological world their colours become brighter and more vivid, except that of

*Figure 1.1* Matt Phlatt is chased by a policeman wielding a staple gun. The dimensional play of the
animation is visible in Matt's ability to slide through the lift door. Still from *Flatworld*
(1998, directed by Daniel Greaves © Tandem Films). Courtesy of Tandem Films.

the thief, who remains in his original greyscale. But it also becomes clear that each world has its own set of rules, and so offers an often confusing and limited experience. As Matt *et al.* channel hop, the different spaces present new domains, but they are each structured by generic TV conventions. For instance, the events in the western channel culminate in a spaghetti western shoot-out; Geoff gets bounced on the basketball channel; trapped in a microwave on the cookery show; threatened by a rattlesnake in a romantic desert saga; and so forth. The chaotic yet always structured chase breaks down completely when Chips eats the remote and the channels and spaces begin to leak into each other, or rather they begin to leak into Flatworld itself. The rules of each world cease to operate as everything begins to emerge within a single space, with objects and figures of warfare, nature programmes and a sports channel all running around in the same space. Even as the technological interventions incite a breakdown of order, the pandemonium is transcended by a reassertion of the laws of Flatworld – the channel-hopping thief is brought to justice by a member of Flatworld police, while Geoff and Matt contain the multi-channel escapees. The gleeful multiplicity of possibilities initially encountered in crossing over, of going beyond the interface and inhabiting the technological world, is revoked in the face of mayhem. As these technological interventions are accidental ones, the ambivalence exists not so much towards technology itself but in its impact of breaking down too many boundaries, provoking a wild disorder. In pulling back from these possibilities, Matt throws his television set out at the end of the story, and *Flatworld* seems to advocate resisting the promise of new interfaces, but the return of the figures to their more drab colour palette hints perhaps that something is lost with this gesture.

Where *Flatworld's* story of multiple dimensions, told through the actions of the characters, seems in the end to resist the possibilities of experiencing the different spaces offered by technological interfaces, it nevertheless offers its viewers a more direct experience of such unusual parameters through its formal playfulness. *Flatworld* and an earlier work by Greaves, *Manipulation* (1991), constantly pick at assumptions about space by playing with the dimensionality of the figures who move within the image. Noting the effect of projecting in two dimensions, in which filmed objects retain a sense of their three-dimensional perspective, Rudolph Arnheim has addressed the precarious dimensionality of projected images, and how a viewer 'sees' the projected image as between two dimensions and three dimensions (Arnheim 1958). Although films are images of three-dimensional spaces viewed via their projection onto a flat screen, as viewers we also understand the image to retain depth, even in those works where the illusion of depth is not a particular facet of the work. It is as though we attribute '3-D-ness' to the images even as we know them to be on a two-dimensional screen, and in doing so create a sense of in-between.

Arnheim was talking about live-action cinema, but his comments are also relevant to animation. Cel-animations, for instance, are two-dimensional images projected on a two-dimensional surface, but depth is introduced through perspective drawing. And because of this a viewer of animation is able to attribute a sense of depth to two-dimensional animation. Whilst three-dimensional space has been evident in animation through stop–motion models, puppets, claymation and depth-based sets for many years, three-dimensional computer animation is currently creating an emergent space in the animation market. Daniel Greaves' animations are an interesting counterpoint to those aiming for a dimensional equivalence with live-action film, as they constantly call attention to the dimensional organizations of the figures who move in the image. In doing so they reveal a different kind of interface, one inscribing a technologically enhanced experience of different spatial organizations, rather than presenting those possibilities more transparently as an interface unmarked by the presence of technologies.

The opening sequence of *Flatworld* introduces the key characters: Matt Phlatt, Geoff the Cat and Chips the Fish, who pop up as flat figures. This is followed by an introduction to the planet of Flatworld, which looks far from flat, as the dimensions of the space are established through the perspective of the set, the use of light and shadow and the rain effects, giving perspective even to the surface of the street. Initially, it appears that the objects of Flatworld are flat, as flat vehicles pass along the streets and a flat figure sweeps the rubbish. However, as soon as one might have come to this understanding, it is undermined as a flat figure appears pulling an object with three dimensions. Such shifts continue throughout the animation, and are not cued so that a viewer could anticipate the transition: Chips the fish appears both flat and puffed; Matt can iron part of his leg flat; and a chasing police dog's face is unexpectedly flattened at right angles to his body. The play on the dimensionality of the objects and characters is a result of the different techniques of drawing, modelling and use of set (with some computer assistance used in the final images).[23] The animation combines conventional cel-animation with flat cut-outs on a three-dimensional set. Throughout the police car chase, for instance, the flat cars move along streets whose lighting and detailing is three-dimensional (see Figure 1.2). The cut-outs have shadows, move into depth and behind objects and buildings, and when turning reveal another aspect to their profiles, all of which builds the illusion of substance and material dimensions. At other times they are made to slip through impossibly narrow gaps, remain flat when turning, are given heavily drawn outlines which flatten them out, and crumple up like paper. All these things reduce the illusion of substance and materiality, especially when the figures and objects are both flat and round depending on the moment at which they are seen. Through such constant shifts in the dimensions of the characters, *Flatworld* continually explodes assumptions about the spatial dimensions of its characters and objects – as viewers, it turns out that we can never be certain as to what we will see next. The immersive potential of the story of *Flatworld* is counterbalanced by the shifting dimensionalities of characters and objects. As these reverberations allow a character to exist beyond the usual constraints of spatial conventions, the interplay between characters, space and action is transformed by the temporality of unexpected transitions. Combined with *Flatworld*'s more overt story about alternative technological spaces, the instability of the characters more directly evokes the possibility for technology to take a viewer into unexpected places.

*Figure 1.2* The low-angle shot of the car chase shows the three-dimensional cityscape of Flatworld, in which are embedded two-dimensional cars. Still from *Flatworld* (1998, directed by Daniel Greaves © Tandem Films). Courtesy of Tandem Films.

Although Caroline Leaf's work does not make any explicit references to technologies, the unusual spatio-temporal organizations she achieves through her use of animation technologies allow them to also stand as examples of technologies taking viewers into unexpected places. The main difference between Leaf's animations and Greaves' work in *Manipulation* and *Flatworld* is that, rather than placing an emphasis on the dimensionality of characters, Leaf's animations instead allow space itself to emerge. Her most well-known works exploit the frame-by-frame capacities of animated filmmaking. Where cel-animation demonstrates this process by filming a series of drawings, Leaf uses materials through which she can produce a gradually changing series of images. Making little use of conventional framing and establishing set-ups, her images are variously picked out on celluloid, sand on glass or paint on glass, creating a series of transitions referred to as 'sustained metamorphoses'.[24] Through this technique an image is altered, then filmed, and, given the materials used by Leaf, the final sequence of images has a remarkable quality of fluidity. *The Street* (1976), perhaps Leaf's most celebrated animation, features images created using under-lit ink on glass, with individual frames generated by small changes to the previous one; in *Entre Deux Soeurs* (1990) images are created by scratching on the surface of 70mm i-Max film stock. Leaf's fluid animations establish interfaces that again reveal elements of space not contained by character action, but which in the narrative contexts of Leaf's story-worlds offer a different perspective on technology than that seen in *Flatworld*. Since *Entre Deux Soeurs* and *The Street* both explore feelings of entrapment, the relationship set-up with a technological interface is one in which the transformational effect is of a release from something, one that captures a sense of the uncertainty of the outcome of that release.

The interfaces created by *Entre Deux Soeurs* and *The Street* contain two kinds of elements, both of which work together within the organization of the narrative. As in the previous animations, a number of influences, including drawing style, technology, characterization and narrative organization, all co-operate in the creation of the interface, but this interface is of a different order. The interfaces of either *The Old Mill* or *Toy Story* are carefully structured to allow all the elements of the image to work together, co-operating at any given moment in the telling of the story, with the actions of the figures using up the space. In *Entre Deux Soeurs* and *The Street* the influences co-operate, but the relationship between character and actions is sometimes separable from the operations of the spatial elements, as at times the elements of the image depicting space function on their own terms. The presence of the two kinds of elements on the screen creates two different but interactive modes of viewing on the same interface: places where characters act and through which the narrative unfolds, and other places where viewers are themselves caught by the transitional qualities of the images. Even in an interface that appears so simply drawn there are layers – layers of characters and layers of space – and together they tell stories. One of these is explicit and grounded in the content of the emotional lives of the characters. The second is the story I want to tell about how moving images can give us insights into technological experiences more generally. Where a seamless interface aims to be transparent, locating the viewer in the story-world of the fiction with ease, this one locates viewers in a position in which they have an experience of encountering the space for themselves. The interface in this sense reveals the technology of the system by exposing its ability to take hold of spatiality.

*Entre Deux Soeurs* is the story of two sisters, Viola and Marie, living together in a secluded house, whose mutually dependent relationship is reconfigured through a brief and unexpected visit by a stranger. At the level of the narrative, the change in the sisters' relationship is apparent in their interaction with both each other and the space within which they live. The initial visual impressions of this space, their house, are indirect; the materiality of the place only created through the sequential appearance of objects used as lives are being lived – hair being brushed, a coffee pot and flowers on a table. These ongoing activities gain substance as they are cued by components of the soundtrack, but the objects themselves are rendered with minimal visible detail, only recognizable because of their highlighted edges, while the body of the object is as undefined as the rest of the space in the image. Any sense of dimension has to be assumed since it is not present in the images; in a sense they are full of unused space. When actual dimensions do appear, emerging as the writer Viola paces, struggling with her words, they seem strangely mutable – Viola apparently defies gravity by walking across a wall. But since it is difficult to make sense of the space, the anti-gravity walk may not be what it seems. Indeed, a brief cut back to Viola at her keyboard during this walk suggests it may be occurring in her head rather than in the real space of her home. The overall effect of these images is to create a space that simultaneously has substance and yet is oddly insubstantial. This combination of presence and absence turns an apparently ordinary space into one tinged with a degree of strangeness. The activities of brushing hair, drinking coffee and working at the keyboard do not seem able to contain the possibilities immanent at the interface. Again, technology as an element that organizes interfaces, placing viewers in different ways, is rendered visible. In the context of Leaf's animations, its capacity for generating a different spatial experience is made present through the juxtapositioning of coexisting spatial organizations. One is grounded, defined and knowable; the other is hinted at, its structure accessible only as an in-between state engendered by the technology used to inscribe the interface.

Leaf's animations emphasize another aspect of relationships between space and technology: the extent to which spatial organizations can be transformed through technological interventions. There are many ways technologies alter the ways we inhabit the spaces of the world. The most obvious examples are travelling technologies, which alter perceptions of distance. However, as we get used to each new innovation there is a tendency to forget the initial experience of the transformation. Leaf's animations have the potential to reinvoke such transformative moments as her fluid technique in *The Street* generates spaces and times in which transformation and change take precedence. Given often blank or cursory backgrounds and figures which are sometimes only rudimentary lines, rather than being used up in providing locations for action, the changing dimensions themselves take the narrative forward. Despite this quality, the animation is essentially realist rather than abstract. The human figures, whilst broadly drawn, always evoke the moment of the story – the emotions of weariness, anger, grief and accommodation. It is this aspect that gives substance to the images of time and space in *The Street*. Yet this substance is always tempered by the continual transformations of figures and spaces into different figures and spaces. The insubstantial quality is derived from the different devices Leaf uses to establish transitions between events, spaces and temporal moments. Up to a point, these transitions recall those of live-action films – straightforward cuts, dissolves and fades – and there even seem to be moving camera-like effects, the most noticeable of which is a 360° panorama of the street. The dissolves, however, are different from those found in live action. Usually a dissolve occurs as one image fades in and another fades out, where both can be discerned briefly competing with each other for a viewer's attention. By contrast, in *The Street* the image literally dissolves and then resolves into another. For instance, the first figurative images of the film emerge as the screen, blank and almost black, resolves into a clasped pair of hands, which in turn dissolves and then resolves into an old woman lying in her bed. More so than with a conventional live-action dissolve, the in-between is briefly present on the screen as one object, seen and comprehended, gives way to another as yet uncomprehended.

It is from these resolves that the tendency for Leaf's transitions to disassemble the relationship between time, space and action is revealed, allowing traces of technology to enter more fully into the organization of the images. In such resolves everything is reconfigured as the dissolution of the image results in a complete jump in time and space. Characters resolve from one to another, or objects turn into other objects: space in use as opposed to used up. There are several examples of this:

the transitions from the grandmother to the family at table which establish her separation from the family she lives with; the boy's hair translating into the children's bedroom; the dissolve from the mother to the nurse; and the transformation of the family group into the ambulance. These sequences have a dynamic quality, disrupting the rhythm of an easy transition by introducing a fluid but nonetheless abrupt change in terms of the time and space. In some of these, the abruptness is bridged by the linked actions of characters. The mother resolves into the nurse or the family meeting to decide the fate of the grandmother resolves into the ambulance that will take her to a home. The presence of linked action re-establishes a coherence in the images, whilst also making a point about the transformation of care-giving. In others, however, there is no bridging connection or action, and there is a strong sense of uncertainty in the moments before the image revolves into a distinct time and space within the narrative. Writing about *The Street*, Thelma Schenkel describes these resolves as 'moments of metamorphosis when the laws of physics are called into question' (Schenkel 1988: 45). Schenkel continues with the suggestion that the transitions evoke a shift from a grounded reality to a more fantastical magical space of storytelling. Another way of thinking about these transitions, however, is to remain grounded. Rather than seeing these as moments when the laws of physics are called into question, take them instead as evocations of encounters in which technologies reconfigure our more habitual experiences of spaces. Like the dissolve in live-action cinema, the transitions introduce a momentary uncertainty: as the dimensions change, space and time emerge before place and recognition have taken hold.

My analysis of *Flatworld*, *Entre Deux Soeurs* and *The Street*, as well as the cartoons discussed in the previous section, reveals the impact of technologies on how we see the world. Although in *Flatworld* the narrative about technology is explicit in the story of the animation, the dimensional shifting reveals the impact of technologies by transferring some of the surprise to the viewers as they adjust to the cartoon's dimensional play. In *Entre Deux Soeurs* and *The Street*, technology is not an explicit aspect of the story, yet the formal work of the animations also yields technologically transformed spaces. As an analysis, the above relies on a willingness to seek out the traces of technology, to look beyond the self-reflexivity of breaking conventions as only a comment about textual organizations. Instead, it requires that we think about the organizations of interfaces in terms of technologies of image production, and then that we comprehend these interfaces as examples of technological experiences in themselves. In the remainder of this discussion about animation, I take examples in which the inscription of technology on the screen is fully visible, where the impact of technology on how the world is made visible is literally seen.

## Active inscriptions

Looking beyond textual reflexivity or unconventional spatio-temporal organizations and seeing them as examples of technological experiences does, perhaps, require something of leap of faith, especially if the content of the animation does not make any explicit reference to technologies. The animations I have considered so far do reveal traces of technologies on their interfaces, but claiming their unusual spatio-temporal transformations as direct evocations of technological interfaces relies on an act of interpretation constructed by the viewer. In the final set of animations discussed here, the technological inscription is explicit, as the capacity of technology to manipulate what is seen is visibly rendered on the interface of the screen. The inscription literally appears before the viewer, especially in those works that exploit rather than seamlessly join up the junction between live action and animation.

Jane Aaron's animation *Remains to Be Seen* (1986) combines live-action footage of landscapes, cityscapes, gardens, hearth and home with animated inserts moving across the image. As these move they outline partial sections of the whole image. The animation technology visibly reconfigures the view, suggesting past or future temporalities. For example, an oblong insert crosses the centre of the screen, animating a live-action image of an unlit fire in a sitting room; in the insert the fire is lit and there is a cat dozing on the floor. Every time an insert appears, each has the same contours and colour scheme of the live-action space, and its motion activates the space in some way. Other examples of elements added by the animated inserts include a ball and running figure in a beach scene, a reclining female nude in the grass and on a sofa, a woman framed in a window. Since each segment is a scrolling animated version of the live-action image, this activation shifts the temporality of the space. However, just like the title *Remains to Be Seen*, this temporality is ambiguous and viewers are left wondering whether these animations are the remains of things that have already happened or a set if possibilities that remain to be seen. In one segment the live-action images progress from garden chairs and a table, to a fireplace and then to a bed. Overlaid on each of these, the animated inserts place two women relaxing in the chairs, show four people sitting down to eat, with only the two women visible, a cat sleeping in front of the burning fire and the two women lying asleep in the bed. But what do such sequences actually mean: have these events happened or will they happen? And what connections exist, if any, to the woman posing for holiday snaps on a city balcony and to the reclining nude? Whatever answer a viewer decides on, it is at least certain that the inserts show technology animating space, reconfiguring it and forcing a reconsideration of their histories and/or possibilities. The ability of technology to alter one's sense of time and place is fully inscribed on the interface of the animation.

*Feeling My Way* (1997) and *Dad's Dead* (2003) are other animations in which the filmmaker visibly manipulates the image, but rather than alter its temporality activates a series of emotional resonances that changes the meaning of the imagery. In both films live-action footage is edited and manipulated using various techniques. In *Feeling My Way* the internal monologue of someone walking across London on his way to work is made visible as live-action footage is edited into a sequence depicting the man's point of view. Throughout, the footage is annotated by animation and collage, with colour tints altering the look of images. Outline drawings take the place of detailed background while a figure is still visible in the foreground, and word tag labels directly comment on people seen or objects on the ground. These latter include wondering whether a man lying prone on the pavement is dead or sleeping, while scurrying people in King's Cross station are labelled as dead inside (see Figure 1.3). In *Dad's Dead* a very different kind of story is being told through memories of a childhood friendship. The narrator is a man who has been sent to prison because he was blamed for the actions of his friend. It begins with the man speaking of his affection for Johnno, but then catalogues the latter's escalating acts of violence and ends on an image of Johnno's smirking face as we learn that the imprisoned man's mother is now one of Johnno's targets. The initially jaunty monologue of the narrator that accompanies the live-action footage moving through an estate in Everton takes a more unsettling turn as digital manipulations visually add to the verbal reminiscences. These include dead pigeons and cats and a burning ice-cream van, as the violence of the pranks worsens. The most arresting digital effect is used on Johnno, the childhood friend, whose face and body are distorted. As these moments are accompanied by changes on the soundtrack, a deep rushing, grinding sound conveying the impression of a visceral twist, the visual memories are given both a haunted quality and one that more directly speaks to Johnno's malignant presence in the social network both men inhabit.

*Feeling My Way* and *Dad's Dead* both have mixed interfaces, but, unlike organizations where all the elements are seamlessly embedded, in these two films the animation

*Figure 1.3* A live-action figure in King's Cross, filmed on Hi-8, is annotated using paint on the surface of the image, a process that inscribes the technology of animation on the interface of the screen. Still from *Feeling My Way* (directed by Jonathan Hodgson, © 1997). An *animate!* commission funded by Arts Council England and Channel Four. Courtesy of Jonathan Hodgson.

technologies are visible on the screen. While remaining part of the overall narration of each film, these elements exist in a different relation to the visible figures and characters. In *Feeling My Way* the additional animation alters how viewers might respond to what they see on the screen, and in *Dad's Dead* the visual and aural digital manipulations heighten the anxiety pervading the piece. In their different ways, these two animations demonstrate the impact of technological manipulations on our emotional engagement with the world. The visible combination of different elements on the interface filters each set of images through the operations of the other: the live action re-animated by the animation, and the latter given a purchase on actuality. Because this purchase on reality operates within a clear narrational system, these technological interventions are encountered as expressive possibilities that add to an understanding of the story. *Waking Life* (2002) uses technology in a different way, as an expressive device adding to the deliberate obscurity of meaning. The feature-length animation was created through a version of digital rotoscoping – live-action sounds and images taken on DV (digital video) camera were downloaded to a computer and the images manipulated by an animation program called Roto-shop.[25] *Waking Life* progresses via a central character who encounters a series of figures, many of whom talk about agency through the tropes of individual responsibility, evolution, free will, lucid dreaming and language. Through these encounters he becomes aware of himself as someone caught in an extended dream from which he can never awaken or of which he can never gain control. The final images ambiguously show him floating away into the sky, a scene echoing the opening sequence of a young boy, possibly a younger self, also floating but with one hand anchoring him to the ground.

Different animators worked on different segments of the live-action footage used in *Waking Life*, so the detail and the stylization of the Rotoshopped figures and objects and the use of colour change from segment to segment. What is particularly distinctive about the look of the animation is the instability of the images, something especially obvious in the background. To an extent this instability is a feature of the animation process. Individual frames were digitally rotoscoped, and then a smoothing program used to keep the discrepancies in line placement between frames to a minimum. In different segments, according to the look required by the animators, the potential for discrepancy is exaggerated so that some elements of the image appear to be shifting and unstable. The segment featuring two women talking about curiosity as an essential aspect of humanness already has a high degree of motion originating from the movement of the hand-held camera through the space of the room. Throughout their conversation the focus remains on the women, and their framing in medium close-up distracts from the background. Since the talking heads mostly fill the screen, the shifting elements in the background, the edge of the chair and pictures on the wall, tend to be less distracting. By contrast, in a later sequence the central character meets a man on a bridge who speaks about life understood and lived. Throughout, the background formed from the detail of bridge spans and cables and the skyline of city buildings constantly shifts as though these elements are unanchored from the ground. Silhouettes of skylines against which figures in the foreground are set is a familiar device in both moving and still photography. What is especially peculiar about this image sequence is the framing established by the lines of the bridges and the skyline, which are ungrouped so that each seems to float on an individual locus of motion. Visible on the screen in *Waking Life* is the ability of technology to intervene in a view of the world in ways that literally disassemble its organizations.

## Encounters at the interface: to disassemble or reassemble?

The possibilities of a digital technology such as Rotoshop intervening in *Waking Life* to disassemble views of the world opens out a series of questions that inform the remainder of *Digital Encounters*. One way of responding to the notion that technology disassembles how we see the world is to think of this as a negative effect, one in which technology irretrievably alters our place in the world, lessens our engagement with it, because we no longer encounter it in the same way. Another way to respond to this problem is to accept that technologies do intervene in human relationships with the world, and each other, but rather than seeing this as a lessening of our engagements, take it instead as a reconfiguration that brings both losses and gains.

The animation *The End of the World in Four Seasons* (1995) disassembles a cartoon interface by breaking it up into eight oblong segments, each of which has different dimensions. In a way that prefigures *Timecode*, each of the oblongs is animated to tell a part of the narrative about water consumption and global warming. Making sense of this cartoon requires several watchings through, so the first time around it may indeed seem like a disengagement with the interface as a viewer is having to try and pay attention to all the boxes, not really able to properly attend to any of them. However, if viewers are interested they will want to try and make sense of it, to see if their initial impressions of the cartoon can be followed through. Does the bottom-left corner ever show anything other than elephant-like humanoids guzzling water? Is the figure diving off a sandbank in one panel the same figure seen entering the water in another? And why does the bather in one panel cross over and steal a tree from another? As a device for telling a story from a set of multiple perspectives this split interface works very well, but it requires a different kind of processing from its viewer. Instead of viewing a seamless interface where all the elements already operate together within a coherent story-world, fully supporting a central narrative, in this kind of interface viewers have to put the elements together for themselves. As I explain more fully in Chapter 2, viewers have to distribute their attention across the different elements of the screen in order to synthesize a meaning. In moving between the seamless interfaces of many of the later *Silly Symphonies* towards the more inscribed interface of *Waking Life*, I have described how animation technologies in different eras have been used to displace or exploit this potential. Continuing with this movement, I argue in *Digital Encounters* that digital technologies have led to an increasing appearance of competing elements in digital effects cinema, games and gallery installation art. The degree to which viewers have to distribute their attention varies within the organization of the interface. From this follows my position that rather than being disengaged by such interfaces a viewer is engaged in a variety of ways that are contingent on how the technologies operate within the organizations of the interface. In Chapter 2 I continue to develop this position through digital effects films, arguing that digital technologies are expanding the constructions of narrative space and that these expanded spaces offer viewers a different kind of interface with which to engage.

# 2

# DIGITAL EFFECTS AND EXPANDED NARRATIVE SPACE

My desire [was] to do something we hadn't seen before, a superhero story told in a realistic fashion. And doesn't step outside itself and acknowledge the form and the medium it's coming from, but one in which the audience is just immersed in the reality that's going on.

(Christopher Nolan in 2005[1])

When computer-generated images first began to make their appearance in the cinematic world of the 1960s and 1970s, they were confined to abstract and experimental animations.[2] John Whitney's *Matrix No. III* (1972) is an animation in which seemingly simple geometric patterns of lines, squares and rectangles spiral into and out of the screen, coloured lines building into shapes as they move to the rhythm of the score.[3] In this abstract work based on an algorithm for harmonic progression, it is possible to discern what would become the achievable future: figure-based computer animation. As the chain of cubes twisted from the foreground into the background, depth perspective seemed to be present and to exist in combination with the suggestion of linked sections of a whole able to move independently of its other elements. These were the rudimentary precursors to animated bodies that animation packages would eventually allow to be segmented into linked parts that could be separately controlled into walk cycles, actions, gestures and so forth. As a viewer seeing these images for the first time in the first years of the new millennium, I cannot say if I would have been struck by the prescience of these images in quite the same way if I had not acquired 'a knowledge' from watching the numerous computer-generated figures created since the mid-1980s, but that question is a distraction. What is important, however, was my experience of a technological system – computer-generated images transferred to celluloid and then projected – with the ability to completely define both how I saw and what I saw.

My encounter with the image, as well as the sound envelope in which it took place, occurred within a complex network. Even with what retrospectively seems like a simple construction, the intermediate ground between the possibilities and limits of a technology defined my response, as well as the knowledge I brought to it. Making sense of *Matrix No. III* relies on a relatively straightforward awareness of lines and shapes, and the pleasure comes in seeing how they tumble on the screen. Since *Matrix No. III* was made, computer technologies have developed and new programming techniques have emerged, allowing more complex imagery and sounds to be digitally constructed. Computer-generated technologies have increasingly also entered into the domain of mainstream filmmaking, operating within a more fully representational mode, and so making sense of them requires other kinds of knowledge to be mobilized by viewers. For instance, in *Westworld*, produced when the capacity to generate digital effects was comparably limited, a grid effect was shown as the robotic Gunslinger's point of view. Viewers can make sense of this grid from their contextual knowledge of robots, graphics, futuristic genres, as well as their knowledge of point-of-view film language. As the network of knowledge a viewer draws on to interpret an image expands, it begins to encompass effects not as abstract technological constructions, but as representative of narrative elements, as realities within the story-world of the fiction. Looking at the typically cited trajectory of emergent digital effects from *Westworld* and *Futureworld*, in 1973 and 1976 respectively, to *Tron* (1982) and *The Last Starfighter* (1984) and towards *The Abyss* (1989) and *Terminator 2* (1992), each innovation operates within a representational mode that continues today with the release of *War of the Worlds* (2005), *Charlie and the Chocolate Factory* (2005) and *Superman Returns* (2006).

Until relatively recently this move into the representational has often been associated with transparency or presented as symptomatic of an over-investment in the surface of things. However, it can also be seen as an index of ways in which technological imagery is becoming increasingly visible in the world of cinema. Such visibility is emerging in two different ways. The first is through an exponential increase in the circulating discourses around effects, and the second is via watching the sounds and images themselves. Although information about filmmaking has been available for a long time, its presence has more recently expanded through DVDs.[4] As an industry, filmmaking has always had journals where issues or techniques have been discussed, for instance *American Cinematographer* and *Millimeter*, and the more recent addition of *Cinefex*, which is dedicated to effects. Such interests now increasingly cross over into an expansive market of movie buffs through general circulation magazines such as *Total Film*, *SFX* and *DVD Review*, as well as potentially anyone able to play a DVD. The impact of DVDs in extending the discourse of effects is apparent on several levels. Reviews of DVDs in high-circulation magazines are frequently as concerned with the extensiveness and quality of the 'additional materials' as they are about the feature itself. These additional materials range from commentaries by directors, producers and actors, or combinations thereof, to 'making of' segments covering actors, effects, directing, design, including sets and costumes and so forth.

The circulation of information is also mediated by more gimmicky devices. Many DVDs include 'easter eggs', less obvious menu options to click into hidden features.[5] *Memento* (2000) was more unusual in including the option to watch the film backwards, a possibility that only makes sense in the context of the temporal organization of the film itself. While these kinds of materials are available through the menu either on the feature disc or on the second, third or even fourth disc, sometimes the feature disc includes a different kind of interface that can be activated within the feature itself. One of the first films to use this tactic was *The Matrix*, where the DVD included the 'white rabbit' option. When a white rabbit appeared in the corner of the screen a viewer had the option of selecting to interrupt the feature viewing by entering into a commentary on the effect. The *My Little Eye* (2002) 'interactive' DVD takes this further by including an interface for watching the film as though it were through a webcast site, allowing DVD users the possibility of imagining themselves as one of the invisible web-based viewers referred to within the story-world of the film.[6] On the Windows-like interface the feature can be viewed through a smaller frame, with other information becoming accessible as the plot moves on, including extra-die-getic back stories, a choice of different camera views and alternative soundtracks. As even this very brief summary of DVD materials suggests, it is increasingly diffi-cult not to be aware of the technological work behind a film, as well as a range of other kinds of labour involved, including acting, directing, building and design.

The relatively new format of the DVD also alters viewers' film-watching habits. The earlier technology of video equally allowed viewers to exert more control over the temporality of their viewing through the ability to stop and start at will, to fast-forward or backwards, and, if they had a high-quality machine, to look at stills. DVD players also allow these controls, though even the cheaper machines allow for viewing stills and slow stepping forwards or backwards. This capacity to control playback is presented as an instance of technology able to interrupt, in both positive and negative ways, the temporalities of watching films.[7] DVD/video players are, then, instances of the impact of technologies on controlling playback, and DVDs themselves include an extensive discourse around contemporary filmmaking prac-tices and the use of technologies. While both are influential in how we see and hear films, they are only indirectly mobilized in our encounters with digital technologies on the screen itself. Knowledge about an effect or fast-tracking through chapters on a DVD until a particular image is found may well alter how we approach a sequence. Knowing how something was constructed may indeed increase or decrease our pleasure, while seeing a sequence out of sequence can alter the intensity of our engagement, but none of these things change how the elements of the image are themselves organized on the screen and how this organization may or may not reveal something about the impact of technologies on the viewing interface.

Where effects discourse is one of the ways through which contemporary audi-ences have gained knowledge about cinema technologies, the second is through hearing and seeing the sounds and images of the films themselves. To think about the ways in which viewers gain more knowledge about cinema technologies, I explore how digital effects are beginning to become more visible on the interface of the screen, and how these in turn act as digital inscriptions. One means of articu-lating this visibility is through the idea of competing elements, when a viewer's attention is split between two elements on the screen. For instance, in *Dark City* (1998) when John Murdoch is trying to avoid being captured in the transforming cityscape controlled by the aliens' tuning, he runs through buildings that morph, becoming something other even as he runs through them. The figure of the actor is one site of focus, but this has to compete with the second focal point of the changing buildings. In such moments, to what does a viewer pay attention? Although a device familiar to viewers of split-screen works, this phenomenon is returning to mainstream cinema, and represents the emergence of digital inscriptions.

The aim of this chapter is primarily to explore the diverse range of competing elements within digital effects cinema, including *Titanic* (1998), *The Matrix* (1999), *Minority Report* (2002) and *Sin City* (2005). By looking across a number of films, I argue that the appearance of competing elements is having an impact on narrative strategies by expanding narrative space, introducing dynamic spaces, sometimes with what might be called incipient agency. While the idea of competing elements introduced in the following is an innovative approach to effects, it coexists with others that are grounded in questions about spectacle. Before more fully discussing organizations of competing elements it is worth glossing over some of the debates about spectacle as they establish the context from which my idea of competing elements emerges. Although the term 'spectacle' is often used rather straightforwardly, it actually has a number of meanings, including the generalization that cinema is a technology for display, one of a more or less public nature, and usually forming an impressive show.[8] Within cinema studies, this more general usage of spectacle has given way to at least two others. One describes the process by which objects or figures are lingered over, retaining the idea that narrative is interrupted by 'body-spectacle'. The second describes a particular kind of filmmaking variously showcasing technological innovation, extraordinary set building, pyrotechnic displays, stunt action or other kinds of special status action such as dance. This latter usage is associated with 'spectacular cinema', a spectacle within a spectacle. If cinema as a medium is by its very nature spectacle, then spectacular cinema has come to be centred on a more particular display of the latest techniques within any given era.[9]

Since spectacle is a multifaceted object, it follows that no single dominant view will be able articulate the diverse ways it operates within the cinema.[10] The idea that spectacle is a mode of display set outside dramatic development retains quite a strong hold in critical commentaries, where narrative is linked to 'motivated' movement and spectacle halts such motivated movement.[11] This position has been complemented by approaches seeking to address the integration of spectacle and narrative and their co-operation within the organizational whole of a film.[12] Responses to this kind of argument have relied on asserting that spectacle and narrative, at least in mainstream action movies, are not unrelated elements, and that the two together generate reactions to a film, or that digital effects 'continue the practices of realism and illusionism' (Buckland 1999: 187) by intensifying the verisimilitude of an imagined world. Despite these different ways of thinking about spectacle, there remains a history of indebtedness to a dominant theory of spectacle as a visual and/or auditory organization imposing its 'in-the-moment' spatio-temporality on a viewer. Accordingly, a viewer is pulled away from the temporalities of progression towards the inaction of being held captive by sounds and/or images, with a consequent emphasis on surface or the immediate impact of sounds and image. However, if one looks to effects-based imagery as an interface constructed around competing elements, rather than simply a screen into the story-world, it becomes possible to excavate the extent to which effects are embedded in seamless or non-seamless interfaces. By looking at the visible traces on these interfaces we can then look at how they direct attention across the elements of the text, revealing organizations beyond the surface that both orchestrate a viewer's engagement with the story-world and reveal aspects of technological interfaces.

## Beginning to look again: expanding space

Much has been written about contemporary effects regarding whether or not they offer anything new to filmmaking strategies. For some they offer developments of already existing strategies, albeit within transforming economic systems and modes of labour.[13] Digital technologies have indeed changed the nature of effects production, in terms of both the skills base and work-flow organization, altering the practices through which effects are achieved. And while it is also true that many digital effects are versions of previously existing strategies, increasingly different kinds of narrative organizations are becoming visible. A means of beginning to address these emergent narrative organizations is to look more fully at the relationship between character, space and action. The interplay between these different aspects of the image is central in establishing the points of focus for a viewer by generating their competing elements.

As I suggested in Chapter 1, meaning is given to space through character action, and space is therefore often taken to play a supporting role to character, with the latter functioning as a primary point of orientation for a viewer. As in conventional organizations of character-based animation, in mainstream cinema character too remains a key frame of reference for viewer interaction. '[T]he character, figure of the look, is a kind of perspective within the perspective system, regulating the world, orienting space, providing directions – and for the spectator' (Heath 1981: 44). Whether this perspective is activated by issues of representation, as foci of various kinds of identification or as agents that carry the plot forward, the narrative revolves around events caused by individuals of some kind, and while most often human they can equally be animals, robotic machines or aliens. Whatever their apparent nature, a common feature is that their actions as agents have an effect, to lesser and greater degrees, on the flow of events: 'usually agents of cause and effect are characters' (Bordwell and Thompson 2000: 68). Two points arise from this: characters are agents who move narrative forward *and* they provide orientation for the space of the image and the spectator. Both of these definitions place the character at the centre of the narrative. Gilles Deleuze takes a similar approach when discussing one of the three aspects of the movement-image, the action-image. According to Deleuze, the action-image is the relation between a character and the situation in which he or she finds him/herself, where surroundings, other characters and the various ongoing activities define a situation. The emphasis, however, remains on the action of the character: 'The character reacts in his turn (action properly speaking) so as to respond to the situation, to modify the milieu, or his relation with the milieu, with the situation, with other characters' (Deleuze 1992: 141). It seems to follow from this emphasis on characters that elements of the story-world unable to act or react are not seen as contributing to movement through narrative, and therefore they are aligned, implicitly or explicitly, with the background or space. Furthermore, these elements function to support the actions of characters, and many studies of *mise-en-scène* have indeed demonstrated the ways in which set, lighting, costume as well as editing, framing and camera movements have provided support for and emphasis on characters.

Narrative films following the continuity system present tight connections between character, actions and space, so much so that any discontinuities between the elements are displaced in favour of seamless organizations where the actions of characters lead to outcomes and accordingly space is rendered comprehensible. Another way of putting this is to say that space is organized in such a way that it does not compete with characters for a viewer's attention. Although the Hollywood continuity system has been extensively written about in terms of its appearance of transparency, how it hides its own processes of construction and so seems like a 'window on the world', as viewers we nevertheless understand its processes of construction through a familiarity with its conventions. As Richard Maltby comments of spatial conventions:

> Just as generic convention requires the co-operative participation of the viewer, so Hollywood's spatial representations can only transform images into meaningful components of a spectacle or a story if audiences have the necessary experience to enter into the expected conventional relationship with the fiction.
>
> (Maltby and Craven 1995: 189)

Set building, choice of locations, use of deep or flat focused lenses and various kinds of lighting have always enabled the crafting of space for action: 'In a movie designed for a single viewing, the representation of space must be both comprehensible and significant. It must provide the audience with a sense of the relation between characters, and between events unfolding in the fiction' (Maltby and Craven 1995: 193). Key to the comprehensibility of space is its credibility: 'space in cinema is organised both to convince us of the credibility of the world represented ... and to suggest meaning, usually dramatic meaning, by the way characters are placed in relation to both setting and each other' (Blandford *et al.* 2001: 220). This credibility resides not only in terms of a film space in which the world is represented, but also through one that is expressive:

> Much of Hollywood's benevolence towards its audience (or, as some critics would put it, its exercise of control over their perception) consists in the way that it reassures viewers that they have *comprehended* each image as both

a three-dimensional space and the two-dimensional composition in which that space is always framed, both as represented and expressive space.

(Maltby and Craven 1995: 199)

Throughout its history, from the earliest Méliès to the latest Spielberg, effects have also contributed to the credibility of represented and expressive space in fantastic as well as more 'everyday' images. Depending on the needs of the film, whether invisibly extending a set or location, creating an otherworldly place or creature, or shoring up the illusion of a trick or impossible feat of action, effects follow a particular script by constructing spaces with seamless cinematic conventions in place.[14] Although my emphasis is on competing elements and digital technologies, digital effects do not necessarily produce competing spaces. For instance, although the technologies of modelling and filmmaking developed enormously between the making of King Kong (1933) and Jurassic Park (1993), their conventions of spatial organization are very similar.

The release of Jurassic Park was accompanied by a barrage of publicity surrounding the digital effects used in the creation of the dinosaurs. Innovative though these effects were, they followed a tradition evident in the first dinosaur feature made in 1925, The Lost World, and taken much further with King Kong, released only eight years later in 1933. Across the history of special effects embedded in the continuity system, the desire for credibility has taken the form of developing increasingly sophisticated ways of showing that effects and live-action figures are integrated into the same on-screen space. As the effects work of King Kong (1933) demonstrates in the scenes where Kong first collects Anne Darrow or is attacked by planes at the top of the Empire State Building, this integration relies on maintaining character(s), whether live-action or modelled, as the central point of attention for a viewer.[15] The music and sound effects also provide cohesion to all the effects scenes in the film. Although the makers of Jurassic Park aim for greater authenticity in their construction of dinosaurs, effects-based figures and objects are again carefully crafted and embedded within a framed space in which they are fully interactive with the human figures that coexist within the frame.[16]

While there have been innumerable advances in the technologies involved in model animation over more than 100 years of filmmaking, the motivation behind much of the modelling appears to have maintained a desire for credibility in even the most strange of figures and objects, or in the recreation of imagined histories and fictions.[17] And part of this credibility resides in placing the models of creatures or spaceships within a particular organization of narrative elements. Even though there may be extraordinary creatures present across the years between Kong Kong (1933) and the Lord of the Rings trilogy, the space they inhabit remains familiar. It is one in which the interplay between the elements of character, action and space remain integrated so that character (human or creature) actions secure and contain the connections between spaces. Space only gains meaning from the actions of the characters within it, and so is seamlessly embedded within a narrative organization. The remake of King Kong (2005) demonstrates the continued use of these conventions. Although the editing patterns and camera mobility of the 2005 version are very different from those of the 1933 film, the human and creature characters remain the central point of focus for a viewer.

Increasingly, even as these integrated cinematic conventions remain in place they are being joined by a different kind of organization in which space ceases to be only represented or expressive. That is, elements of the image usually taken to be 'space' are operating in a different way, so that they become more active elements within the organization of the interface. Space is beginning to have meaning beyond its supporting role to the characters within any film. And as space develops meanings of its own, the interface of the screen begins to lose its seamlessness, producing competing elements that expand narrative space. Not only do these competing elements expand narrative space, they also reveal some of the ways technologies are framing space, participating in organizing what we see and how it is seen.

## Visible inscriptions and expanding interfaces

As I have been discussing, one of the ways to explore the changing impact of technologies on the interface of the screen is to look at the interplay between character, space and action. In the following section, I work with a number of effects films to consider several ways in which this relationship is changing and look at how these expand narrative space. I begin briefly with a discussion of split-screen and expanded space, before extending this discussion to effects films such as *Titanic*. In *Titanic*, the effects and character-based sequences are configured in such a way that they operate as equivalent sites of interest for a viewer, at least in segments where the effects have been shifted from the background to the foreground of the narration. Following this, I move on to a discussion of more active organizations of space, describing the effects sequences of *Twister* (1996) and *The Matrix* as dynamic spaces, which again expand narrative space or act with incipient agency. Finally I discuss more recent high-profile effects films such as the *Spider-Man* films and *Batman Begins* (2005), before ending with *Minority Report* (2002), as a film with examples of 'performative space', a name I give to a particular interaction of effects and human actors.

The most visibly straightforward example of expanded narrative space is split-screen cinema. *Timecode* (2000) is perhaps the most well-known extended example, and though I discuss it more fully in Chapter 3 it is worth mentioning here. It would be inaccurate to suggest that digital technologies have inaugurated the technique of split-screen, as two early users of the technique were the French and Russian filmmakers Abel Gance, in *Napoleon* (1927), and Dziga Vertov, in *Man With a Movie Camera* (1929). By the mid-1930s it was also used in Hollywood for *Topper* (1937) and *Bringing Up Baby* (1938). These two latter examples, however, do not show the split-screen and so technically do not expand the narrative space. In both films, two segments of action were filmed in the same space and were then spliced together to generate the whole image. In *Topper* the effect was used to allow one of the ghost figures to fade out, while keeping the non-ghost figure visible; in *Bringing Up Baby* its usage was more to do with the practicalities of actor safety, as 'Baby' was not apparently the friendliest of large feline co-stars. This double usage of split-screen technologies has continued, with obvious use of split-screen associated with stylistic choice or even experimentation, while hidden use is part of an embedded effect. In the former the technology is visibly inscribed, and when used in narrative film expands the narrative space by showing parallel actions.

On a screen interface inscribed by split-screen the competing elements are very clear. Whether used in more experimental films such as *Timecode* and *Hotel* or the mainstream *Hulk*, on television shows such as *24* and *Trial and Retribution*, or on news bulletins in which inset pictures, tickertape and the news anchor are all on screen together, each element competes for a viewer's attention. As such, we can begin to see them as examples through which technologies participate in organizing the ways things are seen. While this may appear to be a means through which viewers' engagement with the text is dispersed and dissipated as they are distracted by split-screen devices, it can also be seen as an interface that is open to interpretation in several ways. As I discuss more fully in Chapter 3, it can be taken as an interface at which viewers are required to make a synthesis of meaning between the different elements, make connections between the competing elements for themselves.

In textual organizations where the competing elements are less obvious than those of *Timecode*, where they are more fully embedded within a narrative, thinking about the interplay between characters, space and action exposes the organizations of competing elements. The digitally created elements of *Titanic*, for instance, add additional narrative elements to the human stories of the disaster. Often the additional narrative layer emerges as an effect, or set of effects, which remains on screen for long periods, and as it does so the effects begin to escape the meaning given to them by characters. As the temporal dimension is extended, the space of an effect ceases to be used up as setting and place, becoming instead an additional element within the narrative. A distinctive element introduced by digital technology has been to give live-action filmmakers the capacity to extend their control of space from a process of exchange to one of active transformation, allowing them to generate temporalized space. To make this distinction clearer: through the conventions of editing, space changes from shot to shot through a system of exchange, as one space is replaced by another, and so on. In digitally expanded spaces, a different system of exchange is introduced – one of transformation. As has been true of animation since its beginnings, digital technologies can now be used within live-action cinema to create transforming space.

Even though exchanged space rather than transforming space remains dominant, examples of transforming spaces are becoming more common. For instance, a series of images at the end of *Titanic* temporally shifts from the deck on the underwater wreck to the still pristine RMS *Titanic*. Digital effects give the impression of the camera moving in a single shot along the deck on the wreck even as it also crosses time. The changing temporality is represented as the wreck visibly transforms into its earlier incarnation, which can also be described as expressive of nostalgia for the grandeur of technology in the early twentieth century. The digital morph places particular attention on the spatio-temporal dimensions of the morph since the figure or object literally changes before our eyes.[18] As such the morph is a special category of spatial and temporal transformation that draws attention to the mutability rather than the stasis of space.[19] It also opens up the possibility of spaces actively transformed by a filmmaker, and not simply exchanged from shot to shot. Through morphing, space can change *within* the framing of a shot, whether or not the framing is mobile. This change occurs not only in the more familiar figure-based morph, but also in the spatial morphs acting as temporal shifters in *Titanic* and *Time Machine* (2002).[20]

As temporal shifters these effects do not really operate as competing elements; however, when temporally extended effects are edited in a sequence so that they operate in conjunction with characters, then the narrative can be seen to be expanded to include multiple foci for a viewer. Writing of the effects in *Titanic*, David Lubin states: 'Cinematic special effects . . . [such as] shots of the Titanic as it cuts through the sea or sinks into it, are meant to re-create reality but to do so with such an extravagance of detail as to stun the viewer with the excellence of the simulacrum' (Lubin 1999: 33). Another way of thinking about the effects in *Titanic* is that by 'recreating reality' so effectively a viewer is not so much stunned into implied inactivity as asked to invest some meaning in the object. For instance, the lengthy digital shot of the vessel speeding off into the sunset provides the ship with its own story. As the image stays longer on the screen, it expands into another dimension of the story, placing a particular emphasis on the technological giant as it visually articulates all the dialogue-based praise of the preceding minutes of *Titanic*. Of this emphasis, Stephen Keane comments:

> [I]t could be argued . . . that the main 'character' – or at least element – introduced and developed through the film's overall production values is the ship itself. This is to say that in the first two hours of the film we are given a lot more insight into the workings and majesty of the object of the disaster than any other plane, ship, or building before . . . . From launch to disaster we are on a journey with the ship itself, by turns a lavish set and a convincing, hazy computer-generated illusion carried along by the perceived context of movement.
>
> (Keane 2001: 117)

Keane here only considers the ship, but throughout *Titanic* the ship and humans are important, and the digital effects expand the narrative space by intercutting and combining images, so drawing attention to both the human and technological stories. The narrative of *Titanic*, though reliant on a technologically expanded narrative space, also develops through the more conventional parallel editing of different parts of the plot. The stories of the characters (Rose and Jack, Jack and Fabrizio, Rose and Cal, Cal and Spicer Lovejoy, Bruce Ismay and Captain Smith and so forth) are interwoven with that of the technology. The ability of digital effects in *Titanic* to add another dimension to the narrative relies not only on the extended screen time of any one image on the screen, but also on how they are intercut with images including live-action figures. Such intercutting brings live-action and digital elements into the same narrative space, and if both have been invested with meaning through other strands of the narrative, they have a competing status on the screen. Although intercutting intersperses the computer-generated shots with digitally assisted shots of model and action-based effects, giving them less single-shot screen time, their presence is nonetheless extended as they coexist with reaction shots and with counter shots from different angles including human figures.

Towards the end of *Titanic*, in the moments when the ship splits and the aft sinks, the rupturing vessel is directly shown digitally as well as through reaction shots of human figures. Similarly, overhead shots of the aft falling back and bouncing on the surface of the ocean are interwoven with the reaction of Rose, Jack and other passengers. The intercutting ensures RMS *Titanic* and its passengers coexist in the same space and structure of feeling around the disaster, creating an expanded narrative in which the human figures and technology are inseparable. The impact of this disaster sequence also relies on sound technologies. The dramatic score of the film and its soundscape of human and technological disaster add a cohesive layer to the competing images on the screen. Using a soundscape constructed from manipulated wild sound from ships, docks and water, as well as human voices and music, including that played by the quartet within the diegesis, the sound effects invest more feeling in the sequences of destruction.[21] The groans and creaks of the splitting ship generate as much emotional impact as the voices of human characters.

The competing elements of this interface give viewers two different sets of narrative elements at which to look, a point I return to later. In addition to expanding the narrative space, the presence of these two elements allows a further exploration of questions about technology, deepening our understanding of the articulations of the interface. Where the digital ship obviously stands in as the historical object, it is possible to argue that it equally stands in for the contemporary technologies that made it possible. The technological object of the film exists in an indexical relationship with the cinematic technologies of the era of its making, in the sense that its existence on the screen establishes a direct relationship to the capabilities of image making, which in turn can reveal a whole series of economic and cultural details. The content of the film itself is relevant to thinking about this relationship. The framing story of *Titanic* is about revisiting the past: the character Rose travels out to the Atlantic location of the treasure hunt. The cinematic technology of the film reveals the capacity of technology to enable glimpses of the past, but while doing so it also quite explicitly reveals how the representational strategies of filmmakers surface in imagery created on a computer. Although not all the effects were created through CGI, many were generated using complex modelling programs whose representational possibilities are contingent on the interplay between the modeller and the algorithms of the program, combined with a painstaking eye to authentic detail. These technologies operate as a tool in the hands of the filmmakers, making something more credible than earlier technologies allowed. At another level the images have been saturated with the same structure of feeling as the human characters, and the index visibly carries melodramatic manipulations. From the hubris of technological endeavour, the romance of romance, to the destructive outcome of the disaster, the technology is embedded in an emotional appeal to the viewer. The otherwise incomprehensible 'black box' of CGI technologies is rendered knowable through the interplay of different influences and actions. This is not simply visible in the sun setting romantically as the ship speeds into the distance, or the cold dark water closing over its sinking remnants, but also because of how the competing elements co-operate with each other. The pleasure and fears of the human figures carry over to the RMS Titanic.

Effects in *Titanic* may stun a viewer, but they are equally visible inscriptions of the presence of technologies and their impact on how we see the world. At the level of narrative organization, this impact is manifest in the presence of effects expanding the dimensions of the story-world, allowing the narratives of technology and human disaster to compete for a viewer's attention on the screen, and requiring a more distributed mode of viewing. The competing elements also introduce a paradoxical relationship between the viewer and contemporary cinematic technologies. As the power of computer modelling allows the past to be revisited by viewers as well as characters within a story-world, a doubled relationship becomes apparent. The lost object is revivified on screen, drawing meaning to itself, but in addition the seemingly impenetrable ability of technologies to allow people to see things anew is given substance by its visible index.

## Dynamic inscriptions at the interface

Let us set aside for a moment the idea that the competing elements of the interface directly articulate questions around technologies, in order to spend some more time thinking about the different arrangements of competing elements within the narrative organization of effects cinema. By expanding the narrative organizations of mainstream films, digital technologies demonstrate their capacity to manipulate audio-visual imagery. In this section, I suggest that the specific impact of digital technologies is to create different kinds of narrative organizations, which ultimately speak to the capacity of digital technologies to frame the world. Beyond its story of Rose and Jack, *Titanic*'s claim was to make the ship a character within the film, and in order to do so it mobilized an array of CGI, scale modelling, set designs, costume, along with spatialized sounds. As with other films aiming to recreate a history, whether fictionalized versions of history such as *Saving Private Ryan* (1998), *Pearl Harbor* (2001) and *Alexander* (2004), or fictions such as *Gladiator* (2000) and *Troy* (2004), the effects, precisely because they makes claims to authenticity and credibility, keep in place the physical laws of the world, regardless of whether or not these films include expanded narrative space.

In other effects films a different kind of element competes with the human figures for the attention of the viewer, which can be described as *dynamic space*.[22] In *Industrial Light and Magic* Mark Cotta Vaz comments:

> In the post-*Jurassic Park* era, computer technology has provided filmmakers with the ability to create wholly unique characters or digitally manipulate

composite elements with a freedom not possible with the old photochemical means. As such, the new digital tools provide a corollary freedom for art directors, who are dreaming up the dynamics and visual look of a shot.

(Vaz 1996: 28–30)

The presence of dynamism within a shot yields a different kind of space, one requiring another conceptualization of effects-based elements in the organization of narratives. Like the expanded narrative examples of *Titanic*, dynamic space emerges when digital effects give extended movement to spatial elements, again creating a transforming space, rather than an exchanging one. The images of tornadoes in *Twister* are generated through detailed computer-generated graphics, full of swirling movement and power as the storm races destructively across different tracts of land. The tornadoes exist beyond their roles as a background to the romantic drama of the central characters, since part of the point of *Twister* is the power of these forces of nature, and the digital effects generate that element of the narrative. Because the digital tornadoes are constructed on a computer they can be fully manipulated, and in *Twister* they are given something akin to characterization and exert an impact on narrative progression. Although not agents in the sense of an actor, the tornadoes act as mobile elements, vehicles of the narrative and not simply supportive spaces.[23]

The plot of *Twister* is constructed around a group of scientists who chase tornadoes, and this chase structure necessitates the use of increasingly impressive tornado effects. While showcasing the possibilities of special effects as spectacular elements, this also develops 'characterization' for the tornadoes by demonstrating some of their stranger behaviour. The impact of these scenes, partly based on a cohesive layer of sound effects, depends on the digital crafting of the storm cut together with shots of character reactions as well as those of the storm damage (some of which are also digital). Editing together of the live-action images with digital ones reconfigures the relationship between characters, action and space. The tornadoes are made credible by being integrated with the human figures, but at the same time they compete for a viewer's attention, redistributing it between the character and non-character elements. As spatial objects they have meaning beyond that given to them by character actions.

There are five tornado sequences in *Twister*, and each begins with long-distance images of the tornadoes, which gradually reduce as the tornado nears the human figures. The amount of framed space taken up by the twisters varies with the moment of the plot and the 'character' of the different tornadoes. For instance, in the sister sequence the three funnels are elegant thin white-grey pillars moving over water, two of which gracefully weave around each other, even as they have the power to spin cars at the centre of their convergence. The two final tornadoes present quite distinct characterizations, as they are based not so much on the potential beauty of these phenomena, but around their destructive power. The first, at the movie drive-in, is initially humorous as the encroaching monster forms the backdrop to Jack Nicholson's famous door-chopping scene in *The Shining*. As Jack crashes his axe into the door the drive-in screen begins to disintegrate, giving the impression that the story-world of *The Shining* has escaped the frame. This gives way to a series of more indirect images showing the power of the tornado: roaring on the soundtrack, smashed glass, whizzing hub-caps, ripped-off roof parts and flying cars. More direct digital images of the tornado's destructiveness are retained for *Twister's* barnstorming ending. Unlike the sister sequence where the twisters are pale narrow funnels dancing on water, the funnel, a belligerent deep grey, fills half the screen even in a distance shot. As the film continues, it fills more and more of the screen, with different angles and perspectives used to show its speed and size when it towers above the buildings and human figures.

Throughout *Twister* digital images are intercut with action and reaction shots, but because they are so numerous (47 tornado images are included in the final sequence alone) the effects sequences build into an overall presence within the film. The extended screen presence of the tornado pushes the space of the tornado beyond the place of the narrative in which the figures act and react to events, allowing it to exist as an active narrative dimension about the tornadoes in themselves. The digitally constructed dynamic spaces of the tornadoes evoke them as powerful, destructive elemental forces, which, despite their ability to turn, leap and split, still relentlessly cause havoc until they suddenly evaporate back into a cloud mass. To an extent, these images of tornadoes are spectacle, there to be looked at as effects, even as they form the credible background against which characters act. Crucially, they are also active in their own right. Within the structure of the narrative these phenomena, in giving the characters their rationale, are the driving motivation behind much of the activity of the film. This rationale is also brought into an extended existence on the screen. Instead of trying to envisage what is so distinctive about these things via brief glimpses and the reactions of characters, a viewer is shown them acting in several different ways, and in being shown them given some understanding of them. As objects in their own right, the tornadoes also coexist on screen with the human figures, creating a double point of attention, expanding dimensions of the narrative.

Digitally constructed dynamic elements can be called 'timespaces'. The conflation of the words 'time' and 'space' reiterates the idea that dynamic digital effects introduce a particular kind of spatio-temporal dimension into the narrative.[24] As is well known, narrative temporality is based around an ordering of events into a specific chronology. Even more generally, narrative is a strategy for organizing information or data about the world.[25] In narrative models based around sequences of causality such as 'chains of events', there is little place for time untethered from cause and event linearity. The notion of timespace weakens straightforward linearity by introducing parallel dimensions into the structure of narratives. This parallel dimension, while still embedded in the narrative, reconfigures the interplay of character, action and space by establishing a second active location for the narrative progression. Where it has been usual to see these elements organized so that spaces are contained and secured by the character actions, timespaces are active in themselves, and so the point of action is redistributed across both character and space. *Sky Captain and the World of Tomorrow* (2004) is an example of an effects film in which the space is fully secured by characters. Well publicized as a film in which the actors performed against blue-screen throughout, the computer-generated spaces are non-dynamic. They are imbued with an expressive noir tone, through lighting effects and colour tone, but space otherwise represents, existing as a support for character actions. By contrast, digital effects in *The Mummy* (1999), while used to generate places of action, also produce other kinds of spaces. The opening sequence in the city of Thebes, for instance, is created from a scaled digital model, with digital and composited figures added to bring the place to life. The images recreate the ancient place where the drama of an illicit love affair between Im-ho-tep and Anck-Su-Namun plays out, setting up the 1920s-based plot for the film. At other moments, however, the static spatial elements cross over into timespace. The sandstorm and tidal wave sequences in *The Mummy* and *The Mummy Returns* (2001) are examples of spatial elements – sand and water – dynamized to act as Im-ho-tep's extended reach, allowing these timespace elements to function as vehicles for the narrative, though not quite as agents.

The ability of timespace elements to function as vehicles for narrative is also apparent in *The Matrix* and the subsequent films in the trilogy. As a film about an explicit opposition between different views of reality, the Oscar-winning effects provide an additional dimension for working through this opposition. Although dynamic in a similar sense to the elements of *Twister*, the digital effects in *The Matrix* evoke a different kind of timespace, one in which conventional spatial dimensionality is reconfigured in a way that is more often associated with animations. For instance, digital effects literally dynamize objects, creating micro-dynamic spaces. In the moments after Neo swallows the red pill and begins his great adventure, the mirror into which he is looking turns to liquid. The reconfiguration of this broken mirror from fractured lines to a fluid mass operates as more than a gimmick. It presages Neo's journey. About to break free of the strictures of his alienated existence within the Matrix, Neo moves into a different reality that is as yet uncertain and open to change. The dynamic spaces also form timespace-based elements operating as additional dimensions to the physical actions of the human agents of the story. The presence of these elements is evident at different levels of the narrative, and they are usually mobilized around the theme of conflict between two competing forces, humans and machines, where the agents of this contest are humans (or machines mainly played by humans). Although this emphasis on human agents ensuring change retains the view that action within a narrative is based around the capacity of human figures to alter the environment of either themselves or other figures, some of this action emerges in timespace-based elements as well as the character-based elements.

Morpheus, Trinity and Neo, as agents of the resistance, and the Agents, as representatives of the machines, form the cast of figures across which the conflict is played out. In addition, effects in *The Matrix* produce timespaces where the spatial and temporal co-ordinates are disrupted according to the conflicting demands of the competing forces of the film. In such moments space is reconfigured into timespace, as the 'architecture' of the spatial construction of images is warped beyond the confines of representative space. The story-world of *The Matrix* consists of two apparently distinct spaces – the Matrix, a machine-controlled virtual environment powered by energy produced by human metabolism, and the 'Real World', an alternative grungy space inhabited by the Resistance. Much of the action of the film occurs in the Matrix, and so it is here that the conflict over the spatio-temporal dimensions emerges through the interruptions to the machinic space by the Resistance. This interruption in the machinic space is also visible by the play with the space and time of the images. As the progression of images is slowed, stretched and warped, a sense of shifting phases introduces a dynamic quality to the spaces. And it becomes clear that some of the conflict between the humans and the machines will be at the level of this mutable timespace. Rather than the conflict being simply evident through the actions of the human actors, the manipulation of timespace through digital effects introduces conflict at the level of the organization of the visual images. The sense of a timespace with a manipulable rhythm is not only a feature of digital effects, as it is also a reality for the figures within the narrative, which again creates layers within the narrative progression.

The Trinity chase sequence, which occurs close to the beginning to the film, introduces some of the possibilities of this manipulation of timespace. On the first viewing of *The Matrix*, this sequence may seem just to be a showcase for the cutting-edge special effects the publicity surrounding the release of the film would have led many viewers to expect – effects in which time, space and gravity are defied. The use of 'bullet-time' photography allows Trinity to hang in the air as the policeman, also suspended in inaction, simply gapes at her unwinding kick that sends him at speed into the wall. In addition to allowing Trinity to hang in the air, a combination of conventional filmed action sequences with computer-generated images, wire-work with blue-screen effects, and 'bullet-time' enables her to leap across impossible spaces and be reconfigured from a three-dimensional human figure into a signal on a phone line. With the revelation of Trinity's disappearance from the demolished phone box it becomes fully apparent that this is a world where the conventions of time and space can be disturbed. As the image lingers over the rubble of the phone booth, and the absence of a body, the strangeness of the Matrix becomes inescapable. It is not only Trinity's ability to act on the other human figures that is demonstrated here; so too is her capacity to exert control over timespace. The bullet-time images may give the impression that Trinity can defy gravity, but within the story-world of the film it is her ability to distort the normal timespace of the machine world that is established.

Throughout *The Matrix* bullet-time is used to demonstrate how different groups can exert control over the timespaces, as it allows filmmakers to speed up or slow down a sequence of shots whilst keeping some elements within the same image much slower. During the rescue sequence when Morpheus breaks free of his chains and runs across the room, the trajectory of the bullets from Agent Smith's weapon is marked in the splashes of water. Very briefly there is a disjuncture between Morpheus' movement and that of the bullets. Although Morpheus and the bullets both coexist and are also moving within the same timespace dimension, the construction of the images shows one set of movements to be subordinate to the other. Morpheus is frozen at first in the background, but as the images show the bullets' trace as a disturbance crossing the room he is repositioned in the foreground. In this sequence, the conflict over control of the timespace occurs on two levels: through the interactions of the characters (Morpheus escaping the Agents) and also the timespace of the images themselves (the trajectory of Agent Smith's bullets takes precedence over the movement of Morpheus).

In each of the set-piece conflicts between the Agents and the Resistance – the rooftop bullet-dodging sequence or the battle between Neo and Agent Smith in the underground – the manipulations of the rhythms of the timespace provide an additional narrative dimension to the actions of the characters. In the rooftop sequence, as the Agent avoids Neo's bullets, the hydra-like, overlapping, blurry images of the Agent's head and torso are meant to give the impression of his incredible bullet-dodging speed. A different effect is used to demonstrate Neo's growing ability to control the time and space of his environment. A 360° bullet-time sequence captures a full rotation of both his slow-motion flailing and the bullet trace disturbances. *Swordfish* (2001), another film whose narrative is based around a computer hacker, can be compared with *The Matrix*, as the main explosion set-piece of *Swordfish* is filmed in a similar way to the bullet-time sequences of *The Matrix*. Since questions about controlling time and space are not central to the narrative, the set-piece exists primarily to show the extensiveness of the explosion. By contrast, in *The Matrix* all the ripple effects, the shifting resonances of time and space captured in the timespace-based elements, interact with and expand those centred on character-based actions.

## Narrative agency and digital effects

Though many timespace effects serve the purpose of expanding the dimensionality of the narrative in *The Matrix*, examples from the *Mummy* films hint at the possibility of seeing some degree of narrative agency in the effects. As digitally constructed sandstorms and tidal waves exist as extensions of character actions, they suggest a further distinction between digital images extending the temporality of special effects spaces and those securing the credibility of the story-world. I have discussed how digital effects introduce dynamism, and hence temporality, to spatial elements. While this space is generally active, it can also take on a stronger degree of agency in the sense of having the potential to alter a situation. The timespace of the sandstorm in *The Mummy*, for instance, has a direct effect on the characters in the film. Temporalized space is not only active, but can also have the potential to extend agency from character-based elements into timespace-based elements. The potential for dynamic spatial elements to extend agency depends on how they operate within the narrative whole. *The Perfect Storm* (2000) uses digital effects extensively, at times conventionally, but at other times in ways that give them an extended agency going beyond the examples discussed so far.[26]

In timespace sequences filmmakers can give movement to elements associated with space, and once given movement can be directed to modify a situation and operate as mobile agents of the narrative. Like *Twister*, *The Perfect Storm* uses digital effects to recreate natural phenomena. Unlike the effects of the *Mummy* films, or even the changing cityscape images of *Dark City*, they are not extensions of the will of either individuals or groups; instead, they can be seen as more independent mobile agents. Clearly, they are not the same as human agents, since they are not able to react to situations, but they do act to cause situations that have an impact on the character-based elements of the plot. The structure of *The Perfect Storm* initially holds apart the timespace- and character-based elements, but in the final section of the film the two come together in a way that emphasizes the distinctive organization of competing elements within the film. *The Perfect Storm* dramatizes the events surrounding an extraordinary storm that occurred in 1990, in particular the death of a group of fisherman who crewed the *Andrea-Gail*, a swordboat that was unable to outrun it. The digital images in the film operate as both non-dynamic and dynamic space, and across the course of the film shift from non-dynamic spaces, creating the place where events occur, to timespace elements characterizing the storm.

As non-dynamic narrative location, digital wave images provide a background to scenes that were filmed on a set. For example, the on-boat sequences were filmed in a water tank in which a full-size model of the *Andrea-Gail* was mounted on gimbals that provided motion; the water effects were generated using wave machines, hoses and so on. The skill of the digital work in such scenes is to bring the two kinds of images seamlessly together and maintain the credibility of the story-world. Digital effects in *The Perfect Storm* also, however, create dynamic spaces around the digital images of the storm. Timespace-based elements emerge when images of the storm gain more centrality in the narrative, once they shift from providing a coherent location to becoming instead an additional narrative element about the power of the storm itself.

This shift occurs only gradually within *The Perfect Storm*, as the film gathers together its various narrative elements by following the evolution of the storm. These elements are constituted by a series of events whose only connection to each other is via their interaction with the storm. Rather than using a linear chain of events established around a particular character, the progression of the story is established through the transitions between distinct sets of events. Take, for instance, the 'gathering storm' section of *The Perfect Storm*, the sequence following on from the prologue that sets up the story of the *Andrea-Gail* returning to sea. The gathering storm section emerges across different locations – the *Andrea-Gail* and the seas off Bermuda and Sable Island. As the narrative progresses and the images cut between the locations, several effects occur. First, a relationship is established between the different and distant locations, as it is already known that the *Andrea-Gail* is headed into the storm area; the portentousness of this journey is evident in the different visual rhythms of the locations. About a third of the way into the film, there is a transition between the calm and stormy waters of two separate locations. The images of calm, relatively long shots with smooth movements, are counterpoised with angle-framed shots of water pounding on a yacht, along with rapid cuts between the different figures. The contrast between these two very distinct rhythms inserts a sense of impending crisis into the narrative, as this is the storm, not yet near its full power, which will destroy the calm of the fishermen.

The establishment of a relationship between the different locations is, however, only one effect of the presence of the different spaces. Their presence also adds competing elements to the narrative, competing in the sense of viewers' attention potentially distributed between the sets of events, which they will have to organize for themselves to make sense of progression. The two main elements of the gathering storm sequence revolve around the *Andrea-Gail* and a more disjointed network that connects together into a second element around the three fronts of the storm. The rhythm of the *Andrea-Gail* is established around the work patterns of the fishermen as they go through their activities of waking, eating, sleeping and arguing with each other. The rhythms of the men working, instead of being associated with times of day, are anchored to the routines of fishing – the timing of the activities of the men revolve around the baiting of the lines and hauling in the catch. The rhythm of the work on the *Andrea-Gail* appears self-contained as it is confined to the relatively enclosed area of the vessel – the crew is either inside the small cabin or within the perimeter of the deck. In contrast, the storm establishes another rhythm as the three initially separate weather fronts move towards one another.

The effects of these three fronts are demonstrated via three narrative dimensions established by the satellite image sequences, the yacht rescue sequence and the tankers crashing through waves. Whilst each of these dimensions is separate, especially in terms of geographic location, they are linked through the structuring device of the storm. The storm here exists as a digital entity that provides the cohesion to the different narrative strands. In most films, it is a human, or equivalent, who pulls together the narrative elements, a device essential to the credibility of many effects films. For instance, Maximus in *Gladiator* is the figure through whom viewers encounter all the different locations of the action, placing him as the centre of the narrative. Similarly, in *Pirates of the Caribbean: The Curse of the Black Pearl* (2003) the figures are the focus around whom the different aspects of the narrative cohere. In *The Perfect Storm*, by contrast, the digital storm acts to pull the different parts of the narrative together, making it important that it is a credible presence within the film's organization. In order to achieve this credible presence, the effects work has to shift the storm into the foreground of the narration as a mobile narrative agent.

As the storm operates to pull the different narrative elements together, the images of the sea begin to shift from serving as background to being a more active element within the narrative; in other words, they shift from being used up in the formation of a location to becoming a timespace. For instance, in the sequences with the yacht *Mistral*, the sea is the backdrop against which the drama of the rescue takes place. Put together with the tankers pitching in huge digital waves and the swirling cloud masses of the satellite images, the elements work together to foreground the storm. The storm is not only represented, but also given expression by the growing sense of the accumulating ferocity of the storm and its changing status within the story. The effective rendering of the stormy seas through digital techniques ensures that such images can remain on screen without calling attention to themselves as special effects, a feature that allows them to retain credibility and contributes to their status as elements of the narrative. Just as the extended views of the tornadoes in *Twister* contributed to their status as elements of the narrative, so the views of the sea and waves in *The Perfect Storm* contribute to the narrative about the power of the sea. Because this aspect of the narrative is organized in what might appear to be a disjointed way, it is for the viewer to gather these elements together and to give them sense amongst the other competing elements of the story-world. The storm narrative competes for a viewer's attention, which is already distributed across the story of the threat of the storm against various human characters, and also the more marginal strand of the romance.

For much of the gathering storm section of *The Perfect Storm* the different elements, created through both digital and non-computer-generated effects, serve to generate a sense of both the impending catastrophe and also the increasing wildness of the storm. The progression of the third section of the film is different, as rather than building up possibilities it finally turns towards a demonstration of the collision of different fronts of the storm, a device resulting in digital effects constructing a timespace for the massive power of the combined fronts. The full force of the storm becomes clear as the narrative elements collide in a maelstrom of images. The sequence opens with a digital dive from a satellite cloud swirl right into the eye of the storm. The wild energy of the storm is captured in the rapid cutting between the rescue attempts (still associated with the yacht *Mistral*) and the fishermen battling against the storm, as well as within each of the two spaces, where rapid cuts and angled shots heighten the effect. The images, which at times verge on the chaotic, are linked by music and dialogue to anchor the images to a particular location. On the Coastguard vessel, for example, there is a series of very rapid cuts from one group to another, frequently without any linking figure (beyond the storm), but the whole sequence is held together by the dialogue. The music is also important, as unlike the dialogue, which operates within the confines of a particular location, it provides cohesion across all of the scenes, even though it frequently has to compete with other sounds. As well as the rapid cutting conveying the power of the storm, in this third section the digital effects become visible as central components of the narrative, as the larger waves previously kept in the background take on more of the visual emphasis by filling the screen space, an effect that is extended in time to allow the waves to be seen. The people in the water are tiny dots on the swell of the massive waves, and the boats appear insignificant and lacking in power when confronted by walls of water about to crash down around them. Once the *Andrea-Gail* has sunk, the power of the sea and of nature as an elemental force is triumphant, whilst the human figure of Bobby (one of the *Andrea-Gail's* crew) is small, insignificant and finally lost as he recedes into the distance of the shot. Through these scenes the multiple elements of *The Perfect Storm* come together into a single timespace. As the images of the waves crash over the upturned hull of the swordboat, the narrative about the power of the storm, created through huge digital waves, reaches its apex just as the storm causes the death of the fishermen. The use of digital effects culminates in images of waves that not only generate a narrative about the power of a storm, but also make the storm a mobile agent that devastates the environment of the human figures.

The examples of *Titanic*, *Twister*, *The Matrix* and *The Perfect Storm* provide a means for thinking about the ways in which digital technologies can expand narrative spaces within mainstream cinema. Digital technologies, of course, encompass sound- and image-recording devices as well as computer-based post-production facilities. Generally speaking, as digital technologies become both more available and versatile they are increasingly being used to record, as well as construct and manipulate, the sounds and imagery we see in the cinema. The digital intermediate demonstrates not only the capacity of digital technologies to create and manipulate sounds and imagery, but also their potential impact on the organization of the film-making industries. This expansion of filmmaking technologies is frequently invisible within the final product. For instance, computer-generated or assisted constructions and manipulations often exist on seamless interfaces, either hard to discern or so embedded in the conventions of filmmaking that their presence is not immediately noticeable without knowledge of digital discourses available through DVDs and other media sources. The colour palette of *O Brother, Where Art Thou?* (2000), which is noted as the first film to use a digital intermediate, was digitally manipulated, but not in a way obvious to someone unfamiliar with the limits of filters and lighting. For *Hotel Rwanda* (2004), though the film was traditionally colour timed, digital intermediate technology was also used to improve the transfer from the original film stock to that used in the exhibition of the film.[27] Even in the obviously effects-based film *Hellboy* (2004), where CGI is extensively used, the images are integrated into the story-world to support the actions of the various characters within the film.

Although the interfaces of many films currently being produced in Hollywood remain seamless, these coexist with a smaller number of films where the effects are more visible as competing elements. In the above I have used the interplay of character, action and space to develop a means of thinking about how digital effects can expand narrative space through the notion of competing elements. These elements not only allow us to think through ideas of an expanded narrative space, but also provide a ground for thinking beyond the surface of effects. While it is often more conventional to talk about the immersive potential of effects, the idea of competing elements introduces both a different way of engaging with the images and also another means of 'reading' effects. By creating two or more points of engagement for viewers, competing elements have the potential to place viewers in a position where they have to make choices concerning which elements they pay attention to. In addition to distributing a viewer's attention, a point I discuss fully in Chapter 3, these inscribed interfaces also bring the impact of technologies into the foreground. Digital technologies not only have an impact on the content of a story-world, but also complicate the organization of elements on the interface of the screen.

## Technologies as an interface with the world

My discussion of competing elements in the previous sections has primarily been focused on how digitally assisted or generated imagery opens up the dimensions of narrative organizations. Inscribed interfaces, however, not only expand narrative, but are also articulations of the ways in which moving image technologies frame how we see and what is seen in the world around us. As I suggested in relation to *Titanic*, the CGI of the ship stands in not only for the lost object of the ship, but also as an index for cinematic technologies themselves, making visible something that for many of us is quite incomprehensible. In revealing the ability of technologies to allow glimpses of the past by reconstructing images and sounds of histories, they show how technologies are not transparent tools but are embedded in a series of representational strategies. As the index for technologies is configured within the same structure of feeling as characters within the film, how technologies frame the world becomes more comprehensible. The potential contradiction of competing elements sharing the same structure of feeling is evident in *Twister* and *The Perfect Storm*, and to a lesser extent *The Matrix*. In each of these films, effects create dynamic spatial organizations – timespaces – which allow them to act as more active narrating elements of the film, distributing attention between character and effects-based elements. The problem is the balance between the appearance of an effect as a competing element and the potential for a shared structure of feeling to contain that appearance. For instance, as I describe it above, *The Perfect Storm* is constructed from a series of competing elements, in which the digital effects become an active agent within the narrative organization. In one sense, the place of technology in organizing and manipulating imagery becomes visible. In another, since the film takes its viewers into the heart of what many would probably hope never to experience directly, the impact of technology is quite awesome. The viewer's encounter with the interface of a digital effects film suggests, then, a double articulation of technology: it is both visibly a construction and awe inspiring.

If we take for granted that imaging technologies of all kinds have always interceded, and continue to do so, in the ways that we see, is there a specific intervention invoked by digital effects cinema? My formulation of competing elements as something made possible by digital technologies presents a positive answer to this question. But where does that leave films whose interfaces do not incorporate competing elements? The ideas of immediacy and 'scripted space' point to organizations in which the technology of the interface is obscured, suggesting the familiar idea of transparency, whereby we are only given access to the story-world, and where attention is not drawn to the technology itself.[28] The insistence by directors such as Christopher Nolan that effects should not draw attention to themselves, quoted at the beginning of this chapter, would tend to support this view. However, by stepping back from the story-world and thinking instead about what seamless effects might articulate about cinema technologies it is possible to develop a more general view that looks to the specific intervention of digital effects and to digital technologies more widely.

A film such as *Gladiator*, for instance, uses effects to recreate the story-world of an era of the Roman Empire and draws on a series of influences for its set designs, including both historical facts and fictions. The look of *Gladiator* is embedded in layers of convention derived from a study of Roman artefacts, nineteenth-century paintings depicting Rome, and Hollywood epics from the 1950s and 1960s, as well as *Triumph of the Will*.[29] Taken together, these influences combine into a claim for historical authenticity mixed with a series of representational strategies.[30] The digital effects are also embedded in this mixture of influences, with the addition of figures to the battle and Coliseum scenes, the modelling of the Coliseum and digital mattes of the cityscapes of Rome primarily supporting the actions of the human characters. Throughout, the digital effects remain allied with the movements and actions of the characters, enhancing the illusion of a carefully constructed reality. The seamless interface of *Gladiator* aims to give a viewer an experience of being in a story-world appropriate to both the sweeping panoramas of place and the rapid editing of the battles and the gladiatorial combat set-pieces.[31] *Gladiator* only rarely evokes a more obvious technologized interface, one brief instance being the passing overhead shot of the Coliseum, which owes more to late twentieth-century sports events than earlier examples of epic cinema. In *Gladiator*, where the digital technologies do not draw attention to themselves, it is difficult to see anything distinctive in their articulations as technological interfaces other than that they very effectively operate within a tradition of continuity filmmaking.

By contrast, other films aim to exploit the possibilities of digital technologies by using them to transfer some kind of more direct experience to its viewers, something evident in *Twister* and *The Perfect Storm* as well as *The Matrix*. In making this move we again encounter the notions of immersive spectacle, as indeed such shot sequences often encourage the viewer to sit back and enjoy the 'wow effect' of the array of audiovisual effects. Such moments, however, are equally instances in which we are shown the ability of moving image technologies to exert absolute control over the imagery. When watching effects we are not only caught up by the display of sound and imagery, but become witnesses to the apparent ability of technologies to exert full control over what is seen and heard. In this way the viewer is confronted with an index for technology's capacity to reframe the world beyond our quotidian experience.

In a phenomenological sense our temporal experiences of the world are taken hold of by cinematic technologies. Temporality, and the space we see in any given moment, is marked by objective and subjective relationships, with an objective relationship one of durational time in which we are caught up and which we are unable to control. Our orientation to the world can only occur in a more subjective or partial way since our access to the flow of time and events is limited by the very fact that our bodies only allow us to inhabit the world in specific spatio-temporal locations. Audio-visual technologies exaggerate the contingencies of this position by literally placing a frame around the sounds heard and the images seen, exposing our partiality further by taking control of time. For instance, two different emphases can be encountered in *Batman Begins* (2005) and the *Spider-Man* films. Each of these films employs numerous effects: the on-set scale models of the monastery and Gotham's streets in *Batman Begins*; the Times Square sequences of *Spider-Man* (2002) and Doc Ock's floating laboratory in *Spider-Man 2* (2004). Each also utilizes green- and blue-screen digital compositing effects to bring together live-action and effects sequences (both set-based and digital constructions). In *Batman Begins* the monastery images combine exterior shots in Iceland, which included some buildings, a miniature to increase the scale of the monastery complex and a studio-based exterior set.[32]

These establishing images follow the same emphasis on ensuring illusionism as seen in *Gladiator*, but they coexist with others where the effects technology goes beyond establishing locations to also give a more expressive impression of that location. This is particularly visible in the digital construction of Gotham City that provides Wayne's aerial view of the city when he returns after his period of exile. Seen from an aircraft, the digital Gotham is glimpsed as a vast sprawling place into which Wayne must descend, its greyness suggestive of a fathomless depth sucking away at the spirit of anyone who inhabits the city. The expressive qualities of digital effects are also evident in a more temporally pronounced way. In *Spider-Man 2* computer-controlled 'spidey-cam' shots swoop and swing a viewer through the city, giving Spider-Man's agile point of view; similarly, in *Batman Begins* the digital bats, and the audio accompanying their arrival, give an impression of the impact of being caught in an enclosed space with creatures flying into your face.[33] Embedded and edited within a seamless interface, these effects offer a viewer the passing speed of such moments. But unlike approaches to spectacle that emphasize spatiality, if we think instead about the kind of technological temporality offered, the encounter is with speeding time. As the elements of the interface are embedded behind a series of conventions where storytelling and immersion are paramount, the contingency of viewing remains visible in the rush of images that seems far beyond our control.

In cinema where inscriptions of technology begin to appear on the screen this headlong rush starts to be reconfigured. As the technology becomes more visible, it ceases to exist on its own terms, in a seamless interface in which its temporality seems to bear no relation to anything else around it. As digital technologies are increasingly used to visibly manipulate aspects of sounds and imagery, their presence becomes obvious, at least when embedded in a non-seamless interface. In *Pleasantville* and *Sin City* digital technologies were used to combine black and white with colour. They were both filmed in colour, the former on Eastman film stock and the latter on HD-digital video, then de-colourized prior to the re-addition of colour. In *Pleasantville* the colour changes operate as another level of narration, since when individual characters undergo their transformation it is marked by a change in their colouration.[34] When Betty is first transformed following her discovery of sexual passion, she is seen sitting in the still black and white kitchen of her home. Her pink-toned skin stands out against the grey tones, anticipating her separation from the old ordering of her home, yet her grey dress, which includes dashes of other colours, is more suggestive of her ambivalence at being so visibly transformed.

In *Sin City* the use of black and white and colour works in a different way, as it draws its influences from the *Sin City* comic book series, originally drawn in striking black and white, with some use of colour.[35] Although the use of colour, including characters' eyes or the yellow of 'Yellow Bastard's' body, as well as the numerous flashes of red on costumes and objects, is an important stylistic device, the extensive use of black and white defines the film's look. *Sin City* keeps to the extreme edge of greyscale, aiming for black and white rather than the mid-tones usually seen in black and white cinematography. Such a spare tonal range is combined with various stylizations: blood appears as splashes of white against the dark of Hartigan's coat, and

Marv's array of plasters look as though they have a fluorescent glow.[36] Furthermore, the strong lighting effects, often achieved on camera, give way on occasion to more angular silhouettes of white characters against black, or vice versa.[37]

*Pleasantville* and *Sin City* are double articulations, drawing attention to the ways in which computer technologies have been used in the manipulation of the imagery, while also making it possible for viewers to lose themselves in their unfolding story-worlds. With the former heading towards romance and well-being in the world, and the latter towards the bleakness of anti-heroes who survive only by virtue of being more brutal than the already brutal villains, there is much to be said about how both films work with conventional representations of gender, ethnicity, race and sexuality, pulling them in different directions in order to fit their very different world-views, *Sin City* perhaps being the real underbelly of *Pleasantville*. Nevertheless, there is also something to be said about the impact of having the technologies of the films constantly on display. And as it is on display its visibility, perhaps paradoxically, makes it more accessible. Even if most of us have no sense of how to use the programs the filmmakers use, at least we can see the traces of something done. And in seeing those traces it becomes more possible to see how technologies actively participate in constructing images of the world.

## Performative space: evoking power and control

*Minority Report* (2002) features within its story-world a technology that displays the kinds of competing elements I have been discussing throughout this chapter. This technology is the 'detecting wall' at the centre of the Pre-Crime Department's surveillance facility. Since we see characters within the film working with these elements in a way that is equivalent to our own, though admittedly more physically limited, I use their experience of the wall to think more fully about how technologies can be used to control the ways in which the world is framed. In doing so I first look at the distinctive organization of these competing elements into 'performative space', and then move on to what they might reveal about technologies, both for the characters within the story-world and for us as viewers.

Digital effects are central to constructing the visual and aural dimensions of *Minority Report*, from the creation of a futuristic area of Washington, DC, the maglev highway, and police transports, to the more intimate moments of family album holographic playback.[38] Mostly these are digital versions of the possibilities long offered by special effects work – set extensions, addition of backgrounds and straightforward compositing of human and model elements. A key exception is the detection wall at which the detectives manipulate images; this comes close to being an interactive environment, as the detective, using digital gloves, interacts with the images as they scroll across the curved wall of the screen. With all their attention directed towards the images, detectives manipulate and expose the details of violent actions, taking control and unlocking the secret of the time and place of the crime. Within the story-world, as a demonstration of the process of detection the interaction between detective and detection wall is a powerful visual motif. As an example of digital effects, the detecting wall is structured around competing elements that establish a distinctive spatial organization, and demonstrates technologies having an impact on how the world is seen.

Throughout, the architectural and technological organizations of *Minority Report* manifest the control exerted in making information visible for the process of detection so central to the film's narrative. They represent and express the dimensions of power on which the Pre-Crime System subsists. The role of digital effects in generating these spaces varies between the different sets: the detecting wall relies on digitally manipulated image sequences; the Department of Containment is extended via effects. In the latter case, the effects work to give the impression of the expansiveness of the containment facility, and therefore the effectiveness of the department's ability to control crime. In the former, the effects create the location of the detection wall, but through their interactivity push these spatial components from being representative and expressive of control into also being a different kind of spatial organization, one that 'performs' control. A part of their role within *Minority Report* is to 'enact' the stability and the eventual collapse of the topological structure of the Pre-Crime system.

This role is evident in two scenes, the opening sequence and the revelation that Anderton, the commanding officer of the Pre-Crime Unit, will himself commit a murder. The escalating instability and uncertainty central to *Minority Report*'s narrative progression is established not only through human actions, but also through the intersection of the human figures and the digital interface. The detective–image interface is central to Pre-Crime detection, not only in establishing the transparency of the unsorted images, but also in establishing the objective control central to both the figure of the detective and the technology of the system. The images of a murder replayed and orchestrated by the detective serve the function of demonstrating the ability of a detective to 'scrub the image', but the mobility of the images as snatches of actions, the movement of their manipulation on the perspex 'wall' of the interface, shifts them out of being simply images looked at by a detective. Like many of the effects I have already discussed, they form competing images for the viewer. In looking at the detective–viewer interface, we are confronted with a choice between either looking at the human figure or trying to make sense of the often insubstantial images moving across the perspex screen controlled by the detective. Such competing elements form a different organization from the elements expanding the narratives of *Titanic* or *The Matrix*, or the mobile elements of *The Perfect Storm*. In *Minority Report*, the mobility of the images and the movements of the detective combine into a 'performative unit'.

By performative unit I mean that the moving images of the detecting wall and the gestural actions and the detective *together* establish a site of performance. While the detective's gestures and the movement of the images have meaning on their own, when put together they create a unit that is more than the sum of its parts since the combination of the two is a synthesis. To explain this fully: through the opening sequence of *Minority Report* viewers first encounter the technology of 2054. The plastic boxes of computers and plasma or tube-screens familiar from the late twentieth and early twenty-first centuries have given way to clear perspex curves and flat screens on which the image is visible from either side. Within the dimensional or static space of the detection chamber, camera movements and editing frequently place a screen between camera and actor, or the actor between screen and camera. Whichever way, the final effect is of three competing layers of image: parts of the room, the detective manipulating the image and the images themselves; on occasion this expands further into five layers, to include two human figures and two sets of images. The layering in part relies on a depth focus that allows even the grain of the background panelling to be visible, but also on the demarcation provided by the physical presence of the perspex screens across which the flow of images scrolls. As the camera moves, or there are cuts within the space of action, the different perspectives give the images substance as multiple layers of competing elements. When the detectives step up to the interface, and visibly organize these competing elements, the extensiveness of their control is emphasized. Layered space is not the only visual effect produced in the pre-vision sequences, as equally important is the degree of their mobility. The flat fragments of images scroll horizontally across the curved screen as multiple foci of action, and they are rewound, fast-forwarded, separated, zoomed in on, rotated, enlarged and so on, until they give up their information about the location and time of the crime yet to occur. Under the orchestration of the detective, who takes his place in front of the screen to dimmed lights and music, surface and depth are revealed with equal effect. As a description each element of the set can be taken alone: the static base and the structures inside it; the addition of the digital scrolling images; the presence of the actor; the movement of the camera; and the editing. But as a performative unit the individual components are inseparable.

The performative units created around the pre-vision sequences can be said to perform a role within the narrative, if 'perform' is allowed to stand in a looser sense than is usual. I do not mean a performance in same sense as the skills and interpretations an actor brings to a role, but instead how spatial elements again take on a more 'active role' within the narrative, this time through their intersection with an actor. During the sequences of detection at the screen during *Minority Report*, the detective and pre-visions intersect as a performative unit when the topological flattening from depth to surface and the exchange of mobility for stillness operate as visual instances of control exerted. The temporal dimension of these interactions is also important because of how temporality functions in the film. In the performative unit the character and image elements coincide with, and act out, other elements of the narrative.

Within the story-world of *Minority Report* the ability to carry out actions with effects on a predicted future is central. Most obviously this ability is performed when the Pre-Crime Unit acts to prevent a crime, or as the fragile predictability of the future is put into question when Anderton's actions are given alternative outcomes. This ability to reach into the future is evident in the performative unit of actor and detection wall, as it is in these images that the detective visibly works with elements of the future. Whereas conventionally an actor looking at an image or set of moving images would simply be an actor looking at images, in this instance the images' movements are part of the performative element of the scene. Within the confines of the individual fragments, the digitally manipulated blurry edges and ripples express the trauma of murder as an excision from 'the metaphysical fabric that binds us', but their orchestration by the detective performs the spatio-temporal extension of pulling the future into the present. The mutual movements of image and figure depict the process of accessing another spacetime.

The control of space and time is most compelling in the moment when the triple layers of rotational motion coalesce into one synchronized movement. Anderton, looking again at the opening images of the murder, uses the rotational control on the interface to impose his view on a scrolling set of images. The visual effect is a stacked layer of reinforcing action: the highlighted circle of the control key; the rotation embedded in the content of the original image; and the circular movement applied by Anderton (especially visible from the glowing tips of the data gloves). Taken together, Anderton's gestures and the movements of the images create a performative unit demonstrating the power of the Pre-Crime system. Impressive though it may be as a tool of detection, the apparently transparent spatio-temporal interplay between the detective and the image establishes a view that will be rapidly destabilized within the story of the film. As with the drug that Anderton buys in the Sprawl, 'customary clarity' gives way to a 'new improved kind of clarity' when the illusion of control over the pre-visions shatters. As this occurs, the images, instead of becoming clearer, are paradoxically more obscured once the existence of a minority report is revealed. As the loss of triangulation produces insecure and uncertain revelations, the images are reconfigured from flat and manipulable images to ones that are themselves layered. The revelation that the flow is in fact a composite of *only* reinforcing data leads away from transparency towards obscurity, engendering questions of where to look, what is being seen and how far back these layers really go. Accurately interpreting the images requires attention to depth as well as surface.

It is at this point that we can begin to move beyond the ways in which the competing elements of the detecting wall expand the performance of the spatial elements to think more about what they have to say about technology. As I have just commented in relation to the narrative of *Minority Report*, making sense of the puzzle, both on the detecting wall and more generally within the story-world, requires that we pay attention to depth as well as surface, otherwise we may miss something important. For instance, in the story-world of the film the cohesive surface is in fact only a fragile interlacing of competing elements that hides a materiality of excision, where there is an erasure of mismatching pre-visions. Such is our own experience of the world, which is at best partial; and looking at how technologies can either occlude or expose that partiality is an important aspect of our continuing existence in a world where technologies are increasingly pervasive. Layering, for instance, is a facet of digitally-constructed imagery, in which different elements of an image can be separated from one another, physically disconnected through the operation of a technological system. Green- and blue-screen work disconnects live-action figures from their environment, allowing the two aspects of the image to be manipulated. In a seamless interface these layers are fully reconnected by filmmakers. It is possible to make an analogy between seamless filmmaking in general and the effects work of *Minority Report*. In seamless filmmaking the imagery operates within a heavily regulated environment, and filmmakers are equivalent to the detectives, orchestrating competing elements until they form a unified whole. In more inscribed interfaces the connections between the layers become more visible, and as a consequence the regulating environment that aims to control meaning becomes more explicit.

*Minority Report* is again useful here. The introduction of the detecting wall early in the film's plot is a demonstration of the exercise of control over crime, but equally it is a demonstration of an unquestioning reliance on technologies. However, later in the film this reliance is brought into question, and the competing elements again operate as a performative unit. As in the opening section of the film, Anderton works the images, trying to find out information as on any other case, only to be shocked by the appearance of his own face on the screen. Visually and aurally this moment is distinct from others: the volume of the gunshot is high and there is a marked splash of red amongst otherwise bleached imagery. Anderton's subsequent attempts to scrub the image are frantic, shoving aside the fragments leading up to the murder, making for a chaos that he seems unable to control. As a performative unit, the interplay between actor and images accentuates the disintegrating poise of Anderton's orchestration. The music plays a part in this as well, as it reaches a crescendo when Anderton is confronted with a pre-vision of himself committing a murder. The sequence is also distinctive in exaggerating a collapsing of image layers. Even in the opening sequence of *Minority Report*, when the camera is placed to give a medium frontal image of the detective behind the clear screen there is a collapse of depth, but the images remain in lateral motion, ensuring that detective and pre-visions remain separate. More particularly, the detective's distance from and control over the images are clear. In the final part of the 'Anderton as murderer' sequence, the two images of Anderton coincide in a front view of both the screen and the actor. The coincidence of detective and pre-vision is established by a close framing on the shot and the partial overlap of both images of Anderton's face. The effect on space is a performative one. In a deflated planar coincidence of actor and pre-vision, the visual effect seems to ask the question: to which plane does Anderton belong, that of detective or that of criminal?

The set-up of the detecting wall within the story-world of *Minority Report* reveals more than the duplicities of the characters, as it also demonstrates the capacity for technology to be used in exaggerating the partiality of our engagements with the world. Anderton's consternation could stand in for a more general realization of our lack of understanding of the systems within which we operate. And although our experience of an interface is unlikely ever to be as a dramatic as the fictional Anderton's, we too need to ask questions about what we are looking at. The emergence of competing elements, even when operating with a narrative that seeks to amaze, allows us to begin looking through the surface of digital effects, enabling us to see them as articulations of the ways in which moving image technologies frame the world around us.

# 3

# ENCOUNTERING THE INTERFACE

> Embodiment is the property of our engagement with the
> world that allows us to make it meaningful.
>
> (Dourish 2001: 126)

Whether we are looking at animations, live-action cinema and television or computers, screens are where images make their first appearance, giving access to their
diverse imaginative and intellectual possibilities. We are familiar with the ability of
moving image technologies to create the changing shapes and colours that establish
spaces inhabited by figures, maintaining the spatio-temporalities of an unfolding
story. Many approaches within cinema studies take us beyond the screen into the
world of the film, favouring the myriad possibilities of stars, performance, design
and dramatic actions. The screen, however, is not only a place through which we
enter the fabulous dimensions of story-worlds; it is equally a site that can inform us
about our experiences of technological interfaces, especially in this moment of
proliferating screen technologies. In animations and live-action effects cinema, we
have already seen that the presence of technology is increasingly surfacing, stepping
out from behind the figures inhabiting the story-worlds. This chapter explores
competing elements more fully, as not only do they expand the possibilities for
narration, they alter how we view and experience moving imagery.

Cinema and television, already joined by computer monitors in homes throughout
the 1980s, now coexist with hand-held devices, including mobile phone technologies, games platforms and iPods. Increasingly, these technologies are also visible in
public spaces, with large-scale plasma screens carrying not only adverts, but 24-hour
newscasts in railway stations, while large-crowd sports events or concerts use live
digital projection to provide a view for people not lucky enough to have good
tickets. This proliferation of hardware, which makes audio-visual materials available
to viewers from multiple sites, sometimes several at once, is paralleled by an
increasing tendency to split the image within a single screen, creating more complex
interfaces for a viewer. Although split-screen has been used within cinema since the
1920s, it is becoming more commonplace on television screens, especially in
newscast and children's television formats, while website design takes for granted

split-screen formats mixing words and images as well as hyperlinks across internet pages. This is the fragmented nature of our contemporary media. It also stands as an index for the technological apparatus allowing the circulation of audio-visual imagery, as well as the written word. Electronic and digital networks have facilitated an expanded domain of information flow, materialized at the multiplying interfaces of proliferating screen technologies. The impact of these networks has been to expand and diversify points of access for viewers who inhabit environments where such a network exists. This expanded network does not simply alter our access to audio-visual information, but also represents the technological interface through which we increasingly come face to face with the world. There have been many responses to this expanding technological landscape, but recent approaches have set aside use/abuse debates, opting instead for a perspective which takes technologies to be embedded in people's everyday lives: 'We don't just use or admire technology; we live with it. Whether we are charmed or indifferent, technology is deeply embedded in our everyday experience' (McCarthy and Wright 2004: 2).

The consequences of technologies being embedded in our everyday lives have provoked two trains of thinking about these encounters: as losses or gains to human experience. A potential loss in encounters with an expanded network is distraction from engagements with the world, as the technological system individuates and separates viewers through the illusion of an alternative communion via the machine.[1] Furthermore, networks and informational flows disperse viewers who access fragmentary interfaces, their ability to engage, identify with and take up a subject position compromised in the absence of a centralizing, unified and embodied presence.[2] Although it is indeed possible to argue that some elements of this loss may occur in encountering networks, in the same way that ideas of an interpellated subject suffered from the assumption that individuals are unable to negotiate a subject position, both the distracted and the dispersed viewer are presented as passive captives, the network a web holding on to viewers before they eventually dissolve away in the jaws of a determining system, denying the possibility that 'people adapt to perturbation in their own way' (McCarthy and Wright 2004: 31). My argument, in contrast, is that a viewer's engagement with fragmented interfaces can be more productively understood by giving consideration to the range of agencies available in such an engagement, and seeing in them a generative potential rather than only losses. Since viewers are always enmeshed within the structures within which they view, the situation is without doubt compromised, but not necessarily in the most negative sense of that word. Negotiation involves give and take, being resistant as well as acquiescent to the conditions that impinge on our lives.

The technological interface of moving images can be viewed as both a place of negotiated agency and as an experience of technology. The negotiations of a viewer are, therefore, also a negotiation with technology. To flesh out this perspective, developing a bridge between the competing elements of digital effects cinema and my later chapters on digital games (Chapter 4) and gallery installations (Chapter 5), here I build on the idea introduced in my discussion of *Titanic* in Chapter 2, namely that a digital effect acts as an index for a more direct technological experience. The spatio-temporal organizations of competing elements have the potential to evoke the impact of technologies on how we see the world, by creating a tension in which a viewer's illusion of omniscience is countered by having to make a decision about which element is given attention. When the television programme *24* shifts into split-screen, for instance, viewers have also to shift from their encounter with a seamless interface based primarily on the unifying actions of a single figure or linked group of protagonists. Instead, they are offered a series of viewing options, established by three or four panels, each depicting one of the parallel threads of the narrative. Rather than only taking in the already complex details of a unified seamless interface, a viewer has to scan across an interface inscribed by multiple perspectives.

While proliferating hardware is part of the context for the argument presented in this study, the approach presented in this chapter follows on from my interest in the ways in which technological presence is inscribed on the interfaces of animation and digital effects cinema or television programmes such as *24*. Though less physically dispersed than the hardware I have mentioned, as they appear within a space defined by either single or multiple screens in the case of gallery installations, the multiple perspectives created through competing elements also offer a system of fragmented materiality to a viewer, but again this does not necessarily engender a distracted or dispersed viewer. Instead, as in the case of viewers of *24*, they scan across a series of images and make a synthesis of those elements as they gain an understanding.

Throughout this chapter, I explore this process further in order to consider how agency can be encountered in such a process. To do this, I begin by discussing more fully the impact of competing elements on a viewer's attention, a point made through a discussion of *Timecode*. Having established what I mean by distributed attention, I use the work of Vivian Sobchack, Lois McNay and Pierre Bourdieu to move on to the question of how embodied viewers gain agency through the act of making sense of competing elements in their encounter with the interface. To provide the ground for agency, I also give an account of textual organizations that moves away from familiar linear models of narrative towards more complex spatio-temporal systems. Through making this move, it becomes possible to connect the competing elements found in many cinematic examples with those of digital games and gallery installations, both of which I discuss in the final chapters of the book.

## Distributed attention: encountering the interface

By stepping back from the familiar world of a film, television or digital game, we can restage our encounter with the screen, revealing its importance as an interface where technologies of image construction and viewers come into contact, where the inscriptions of digital technologies are becoming increasingly apparent as they generate competing elements. To briefly recap on the ideas presented earlier, throughout its history the cinema has been a site for continuing technological developments – recording devices for sounds and images, projection technologies, film-processing techniques and a whole array of technologies used in various effects, including lighting, set design, as well as special and visual effects. Between them, many of these technologies have created the elements making up the whole of the image. That is, lighting effects, set designs and optical compositing techniques all generate constitutive elements of an image which, within the traditions of a continuity system, are organized as an assembly where the interplay of characters, space and action tend to privilege the character as the singular point of focus. The character moves in space, which in turn acts to support the actions of characters. In the current era of emergent digital technologies this convention continues, but is joined by a second that reconfigures the interplay between character, space and action. Rather than only providing the space for action, effects are often employed to create elements that compete with characters for a viewer's attention.

Generating moving elements that compete for a viewer's attention is not a particular facet of digital technologies, but as digital technologies become more pervasive competing elements are increasingly visible within different media. Two particularly strong examples of competing elements are television news broadcasts and webpages, in which words and images compete for a viewer's attention. Although the presence of competing elements in television, news bulletins and webpages has been noted by a variety of critics within media and communication studies, their potential as sites of agency has not been fully considered. While responding to debates within cinema studies, the following discussion also engages with others from within (new) media and technology studies. Although theories relying on the notion of a unifocal gaze may remain appropriate to thinking about films assembled around a seamless continuity system, other kinds of textual organizations call for a different approach. My discussion begins with the split-screen film *Timecode* (2000), as the obviousness of its competing elements makes it a useful point of departure through which to ground the meaning of the terms 'distributed' and 'attention'. Following an initial explanation of these terms, my argument moves towards an articulation of how distributed attention represents a material encounter with the screen. From these encounters we can begin to see the surfacing of agency in the form of an embodied viewer, since 'embodiment is not just a state of being but an emergent quality of interactions' (McCullogh 2004: 27).

It is not conventional to talk of the screen as an interface, though theories of spectatorship take for granted its place as an interface through which different kinds of engagements occur. Psychoanalytic approaches, apparatus theory and cognitive theories all see the screen as the means through which viewers become active participants in the paradigm established within their theoretical parameters. Taking the screen as an interface which orchestrates such participation requires looking at it more closely, and seeing not only that it can be constructed from competing elements such as those seen in effects-based films, including *The Matrix*, *Pleasantville* and *Sin City*, but also that these elements act to distribute a viewer's attention. For instance, split-screen is used in *Hulk*, and though it follows split-screen conventions by showing parallel moments in space and time, it does so with an unusual degree of visual urgency. In the scenes of the failed frog experiment, multiple inserts are used both simply to show the actions carried out and to split a viewer's attention across the different objects and figures on the screen. As the appearance of the inserts speeds up, the viewer's attention is rapidly distributed across the different elements as the tension of the experiment increases. At such points in *Hulk* the interface of the screen visibly intercedes in a viewer's ability to engage with the story of the film.

The idea of distribution used above draws on Edwin Hutchins' study of human and technological networks, *Cognition in the Wild* (1995). While Hutchins discusses the actual situation of naval navigation, his point can be illustrated by referring to a film example. In *The Day After Tomorrow* (2004), a group of environmental scientists located in different continents assemble an account of imminent apocalypse. The detail of their account is generated across a network of technologies (monitoring devices in multiple locations around the world, computer and telecommunications systems) and a social network. Following Hutchins, the cognitive activity of the scientists is distributed across a technologized system *and* across a social network, generating an extended view of the world that mobilizes both human and techno-logical systems. Of particular relevance is the way a human sense of being in the world is modified by an interaction with technology. This interaction is not a les-sening of experience, but a reconfiguration of it through a technological interface. As N. Katherine Hayles remarks:

> By contrast, in the model that Hutchins presents . . . human functionality expands because the parameters of the cognitive system it inhabits expand. In this model, it is not a question of leaving the body behind but rather of extending embodied awareness in highly specific, local and material ways that would be impossible without electronic prosthesis.
>
> (Hayles 1999: 290–91)

Drawing explicitly on Hutchins, Hayles sees technologies as more fully dis tributing the spatial parameters of the human body through extensions of the cog-nitive system.

While this model would be particularly appropriate for thinking about how an individual's encounters with the world are modified by the proliferation of screen hardware, viewing a screen clearly does not operate in the same way, as it is not an encounter in real time with activities and events occurring elsewhere, and the spa-tial distributions are more imagined than actual. But as different kinds of cinematic technologies or televisual and games technologies create screens inscribed with multi-focal elements competing for a viewer's attention, a viewer's initial means of engagement – attention – is similarly distributed across the different elements of the image. As such, the activity of viewing emerges in the context of an attention that is distributed. Rather than occurring across a network of technologies, this occurs at an interface of elements generated by the organizing capacities of cine-matic technologies. Attention is understood here as a process by which individuals attend to particular elements within their perceptual field.[3] The process is an active one, as it involves selection, choosing to pay attention to something, as well as establishing a constraint on what is attended to. As attention is paid to spatial and temporal elements in the perceptual field, cueing occurs, a kind of 'pointing to' which draws the attendee towards particular aspects of the perceptual field while at the same time pulling them away from others. Although cognitive approaches to attention refer to visual acuity in the actual world, the idea of attention and cueing is equally relevant to the cinema. Cinema technologies organize time and space, whatever the kind of film. Taken straightforwardly, all cinema cues attention, continuity editing seamlessly, jump cuts and other kinds of disruptive techniques jaggedly, disposing a viewer in different ways to what is occurring on the screen. The tactics of textual organization influence the viewing experience, intercepting engagements with characters, genres and so on.

*Timecode*, with its four-way split-screen organization, moves beyond cueing to also distribute attention. Cueing of attention follows from the plotting and a growing awareness by the viewer of the potential connections between the different characters. For instance, at the beginning of the film, after a series of images of filmmaking technologies, the upper right-hand quadrant shows two women, one who takes a key role in the plot (Emma) and another who does not (her therapist). For several minutes these two women are the only human figures visible, with the sound of their voices fading in and out against a background of instrumental blues. Cueing is achieved both visually and aurally by using what might be called a fading counterpoint. The relatively simple set-up of sound and image is manipulated through the changing sound levels and depth of focus, which cue a viewer to pay attention to the spoken words, to the music or to one or other of the women. Once a second screen becomes active, the cueing becomes more complex, as sounds and images begin to more fully distribute the attention of a viewer.

On the second active screen, the top left, after a pause in action, a woman (Lauren) descends steps. As she comes forward in the image, passing by the camera, the scene is energized by camera movements that follow her to a parked car, where intriguingly she lets air out of the tyres. At this moment a third window is activated, the bottom left, which is itself divided into a four-way view of security camera footage, mostly empty. Finally, as the action in the upper segment is reframed from Lauren to a second woman (Rosa), the fourth screen also becomes active. Within two minutes the complexity of the screen has expanded exponentially. The emphatic cueing of music and focus-shifting of the single quadrant have given way to the establishment of a dramatic intrigue between two women, all the while slowly introducing other points of potential interest. The opening sequence of *Timecode*, because it builds from relative simplicity to a more complex organization, demonstrates the generation of the higher order of cueing that I mean by distributed attention. The shifting sound and image-scapes of the first quadrant show the simple yet effective cueing of a single screen. But as the images and sounds build across the four segments, as camera movements catch the eye and as dramatic tension builds within a frame, attention is not only cued but distributed across a range of competing elements.

## Digital imagery: an absence of materiality?

The interfaces of *Timecode* and digital effects films such as *Hulk*, in their different ways, are contingent on emergent digital technologies. To make *Timecode* the director Mike Figgis exploited various innovations in digital technologies such as sound editing packages, light DV cameras and tape lengths.[4] For *Hulk* digital editing techniques were used to generate split-screens and the more unusual temporal and spatial cuts on action seen throughout the film. In each film, digital technologies were used to inscribe the interface and therefore have a role in distributing a viewer's attention. In the section that follows, I take this idea further, arguing that in distributing a viewer's attention these interfaces establish the ground from which it is possible to think about the materiality of digital imagery, and also an embodied viewer.

My discussion engages with Vivian Sobchack's phenomenological study of cinematic and digital imagery. In her influential essay 'The Scene of the Screen' she compares digital (and electronic) imagery less favourably with the cinematic, because the latter represents a dislocated material experience for a viewer: 'unlike cinematic representation, electronic representation by its very structure phenomenologically diffuses the fleshly presence of the human body and the dimensions of that body's material world' (Sobchack 2004: 161). Sobchack's argument resonates with other recent writings expressing reservations about digital technologies. Within film studies this has frequently taken the form of concerns about a loss of indexicality. For instance, Winston Wheeler Dixon states: 'The veracity of the moving image has been hopelessly compromised; the demarcation line between the real and the engineered (both aurally and visually) has been obliterated. All is construction and fabulation. All is predetermined; nothing natural remains' (Wheeler Dixon 2001: 359). Wheeler Dixon's articulation of the loss of indexicality is clearly applicable to films making use of CGI, such as *War of the Worlds* or *The Day After Tomorrow*, but Sobchack's version of this argument unusually extends to incorporate all kinds of digital technology.

To more fully understand Sobchack's perspective on digital and electronic technologies we need to see it in the context of her study of cinematic technologies, *The Address of the Eye* (1992). Drawing on Martin Heidegger's famous statement that '[t]he essence of technology is by no means anything technological', Sobchack sees our encounters with cinematic technologies as embodying perceiving subjects as 'beings in the world'. In this view the link between perception and the cinematic emerges through the viewing subject. As perceiving subjects in the world we select and combine what we see, shifting our attention simultaneously away from and towards objects in the world. Our bodily orientation, our directionality of looking and hearing, expresses the intentionality of our perception. And as this is an embodied facet – orientation is defined in time and space – so it follows that our perceptions are equally always grounded in a particular spatio-temporal moment. As a specific example of a technology, Sobchack argues, cinema reveals our processes of perception, since it both enacts perception in an equivalent way to a human viewing subject and presents that act of perception in the duration of a film:

As the multiplicity and discontinuity of time are synthesized and centered and cohere as the experience of a specific lived-body, so are multiple and discontiguous spaces synopsized and located in the spatial and material synthesis of a particular body. That is, articulated as separate shots and scenes, discontiguous spaces and discontinuous times are synthetically gathered together in a coherence that is the cinematic lived-body.

(Sobchack 2004: 152)

From the quotation above, Sobchack's view of indexicality becomes clear. If an indexical relationship is one of existential contiguity, then the cinema is an index for perception as it constitutes a bond between perception and the world – the cinema not only presents the world, but points to a perceiving relationship with that world. Fundamental to this cinematic lived-body is both spatio-temporal embodiment and also continuity, and it is the displacement of these in the digital that troubles Sobchack: 'electronic presence randomly disperses its being *across* a network, its kinetic gestures describing and lighting on the surface of the screen rather than inscribing it with bodily dimension (a function of centered and intentional projection)' (Sobchack 2004: 159).

It is at this point that I find myself deviating from Sobchack. For Sobchack, indexical equivalence between the cinematic lived-body and the lived-body of a being-in-the-world relies on seeing the technology of cinema as something that stands in the place of a perceiving subject, to some extent mimicking rather than interrupting processes of perception. My perspective, by contrast, takes for granted that technologies change how we inhabit the world, and so aims for an account of those transformations. So, while I agree with Sobchack's view that devices such as DVD and video players alter how we experience films, and that digital information is dispersed across networks, and, unlike analogue, is compressible, manipulable, encoded and decoded by the processors of different interfaces, this view of digital information strikes me as a curiously machinic one that does not fully represent a viewer's visual or aural experience of engaging with digital interfaces.[5]

Rather than looking only to the digital as a dispersed form or as offering different control options in viewing, we can pay attention instead to the interfaces at which digital technologies are *experienced* as audio-visual media. Although the spatio-temporally embodied experiences of the world brought into being through the competing elements, whether textual or as proliferating hardware, may indeed be disrupted by these different uses of technologies, diffusion and dispersal (even disembodiment) are not necessarily taking their place. Instead we find a range of interfaces exposing other relationships, and it is necessary to excavate them as sites of embodied experiences by viewers. As Hayles argues: 'information, like humanity, cannot exist apart from the embodiment that brings it into being as a material entity in the world; and embodiment is always instantiated, local and specific' (Hayles 1999: 41). Rather than generalizing about digital interfaces, we might look more closely at their specificities and reveal the possibilities of the embodied encounters they offer.

## Digital embodiments: the emergence of agency

Technologies of all kinds reconfigure our relationships with the world by enabling us to inhabit it differently, and technological interfaces can be taken as articulations of a multiplicity of habitations. A striking facet of digital interfaces inscribed by competing elements is the level to which the image is fragmented rather than continuous. The idea of such an interface may indeed seem to resonate with the notions of fragmentation and disembodiment sometimes used to characterize an experience of digital information. It does not follow, however, that when confronted with a more distributed world we become mere ghostly presences, caught up and wholly determined by the operations of a technology. Neither does it follow that we become distracted. The competing elements of interfaces offer a different mode of experience and perception, one in which agency can be gained through the process of making sense of the fragmented images. The need for a viewer to make a synthesis of the competing elements of an image, rather than simply be directed by them, affords agency to that viewer.[6]

Maurice Merleau-Ponty's writing on the concept of freedom is useful in thinking about agency:

> The world is already constituted, but also never completely constituted; in the first case we are acted upon, in the second we are open to an infinite number of possibilities. But this analysis is still abstract, for we exist in both ways *at once*. There is, therefore, never determinism and never absolute choice.
>
> (Merleau-Ponty 2002: 527)

Following on from this, engagements with interfaces constructed around competing elements can be seen as an encounter between determinism and absolute choice, and different kinds of interfaces offer different kinds of encounters. This point can be made more fully by returning again to *Timecode*. Making sense of this film revolves around working between the four screens on which dramatic action occurs. The sound is a limit case unless one is viewing the film through the option of the 'interactive audio mix' on the DVD interface. Although the images remain constant in the four corners of the screen, viewers can perceptually fade them in and out, shifting them between the periphery and centre of their attention according to how they are engaged by the flow of images. This freedom of engagement is qualified by varying degrees of determinism as the relationship between the four screens motivates how the flow is tracked. What one sees in *Timecode* emerges through our embodied attention as we encounter the interface of the four-way screen, taking up an orientation that moves between the determinism of the pre-established organizations of the text and individual choices. *Timecode*'s distribution of attention has the potential to be generative rather than dispersive. It opens the viewing interface to a diversity of possible viewing positions.

*Timecode*'s more durational distribution of attention opens the viewing interface, and it is in negotiating these diverse positions that a viewer's agency begins to become apparent. The argument presented here does not involve agency in the sense of a fully articulated social agency, but notions of agency developed in the social sciences do have relevance here. Lois McNay has argued for the idea of generative agency, and, although beginning as a criticism of agency only established through a negative relation, the following statement points towards ways of revealing agency with generative potential:

> [T]he negative paradigm ... tends to think of action mainly through the residual categories of resistance to or dislocation of dominant norms .... This is not to deny the efficacy of all forms of resistance, but it is to suggest that a more precise and varied account of agency is required to explain the differing motivations and ways in which individuals and groups struggle over, appropriate and transform cultural meanings and resources.
>
> (McNay 2000: 3–4)

McNay goes on to describe the gradually increasing movement of women into social fields previously confined to men as changing traditional gender norms through generative agency. Accordingly, different kinds of agency emerge from the intersections between the particularities of gender norms (for women and men) and the particularities of the social fields. McNay's notion of agency draws on Pierre Bourdieu's concepts of habitus and field.[7] Habitus is the site where the person-in-action exists, refining his or her identity through dynamic intersections of structure and action, society and the individual. It is a strategy-generating principle that allows individuals to cope with ever-changing situations. Put more fully, habitus is 'a system of lasting and transposable dispositions which, integrating past experiences, functions at every moment as a matrix of perceptions, appreciations and actions and makes possible the achievement of infinitely diversified tasks' (Bourdieu 1977: 95). It is a twofold organization:

> [Habitus] expresses first the *result of an organizing action*, with a meaning close to that of words such as structure; it also designates a *way of being*, [an] *habitual state* (especially of the body) and, in particular, a *disposition*, *tendency*, *propensity*, or *inclination*.
>
> (Bourdieu 1977: 251; emphasis in original)

In the context of the more delimited agency involved in the process of embodied viewing, I make an analogy between Bourdieu's description of the habitus and the interface established by competing elements. The competing elements are structures in the sense that they pre-exist and are visible to any viewer, but equally they are open to the ways of being of viewers as their disposition influences how they make sense of images. The synthesis of meaning through the process of attention distributed across competing elements also bears some comparison to Bourdieu's notion of the field. The field expresses the idea that individuals exist within an array of intersecting influences so that a category set up in the habitus can be reconfigured or deformed as lived through any given field:

> [A] field may be defined as a network, or a configuration, of objective relations between positions. These positions are objectively defined, in their existence and in the determinations they impose on their occupants, agents or institutions, by their present and potential situation (*situs*) in the structure of the distribution of species of power (or capital) whose possession commands access to the specific profits that are at stake in the field.
>
> (Bourdieu 1992: 97)

The field is a multidimensional space of positions and the position-taking of agents. As the logic of one set of influences intersects with the logic of another, the two are transformed. Thus, as a viewer makes a synthesis of meaning across a series of elements the relationships between the elements become transformed by an individual's viewing. The diversity of transformations varies with the organization of the text, in that some offer more or fewer opportunities for viewing differences than others. Agency emerges between structure and action in the habitus, just as it emerges between the organization of the texts and the viewer's synthesis of meaning.

McNay's generative agency is, then, relevant to my discussion of the agency in play during the complexities of making sense of a text. Viewers distribute attention across the interface, and making sense is contingent on the cueing of the textual elements and the distribution of one's attention. In addition, viewers' dispositions, based variously on their own histories of viewing and on their personal and cultural histories, can be brought to bear on the text.[8] For instance, throughout *Timecode* the impact of Alex and Rosa's affair on their respective partners has developed, leading to Alex's murder by Lauren and Emma's truncated encounter with the woman she meets in the bookstore. Lauren might easily be placed in the long line of lesbian murder narratives, in which a spurned lover wreaks revenge by murdering or attempting to murder the new lover. Indeed, this is an interpretation that stands but can be qualified by other responses to the film made possible by its competing elements. The final images of *Timecode* are of Lauren and Emma walking in the street, Lauren away from the scene of her crime, and Emma apparently wandering as Skin is heard singing *The Comfort of Strangers* on the soundtrack. As these two women walk away from their respective partners – duplicitous and dying Alex, Rosa attempting only to reach Lauren via a mobile phone – the latter images end, leaving the two women alone together, contained within their separate quadrants on the screen. The images of the two continue almost throughout the credits, until finally only that of Emma remains.

Because of this extended counterpoint, my sense of disappointment that Lauren's trajectory has been leading towards an inevitable incarceration mingles with a curiosity about where Emma's life will lead once she discovers that Alex is dead: will she carry on seeing women, men or both; will she get herself together or fall apart?

This interest in Emma does not alter the fact of Lauren's fate, but it does place me in the position of constructing an alternative route of engagement with *Timecode*. I want to resist the determining narrative thread of Lauren's murderous actions, so I become engaged with Emma, asking questions of the character, even as I also watch Lauren's frequent over the shoulder glances, checking for the police or maybe Rosa. As the competing elements of the two screens distribute attention between the two narrative strands, there is scope for agency in the balance of creating a more generative reading of the film.

The opportunities for agency available to a viewer depend on the different ways interfaces distribute a viewer's attention. In discussing technological interactions with the world more generally, Paul Dourish remarks: 'the ways in which we experience the world are through directly interacting with it, and . . . we act in the world by exploring the opportunities for action that it provides to us' (Dourish 2001: 17–18). In an equivalent way, different interfaces offer a range of opportunities through which a viewer can interact with textual organizations. In *Timecode* the organization of the elements on the screen allows an extended distribution of attention across four panels, offering high degrees of freedom. Although the dispersed audio-visual competing elements of *Timecode* may initially disorient a viewer, dissemble their engagements with the text, its lengthy duration gives viewers a temporal axis along which they can explore the opportunities to work towards making sense of the elements. The tendency towards fragmentation is countered by this temporal axis, creating an interface which, though inscribed by technology's ability to reframe the world through an expanded multiple view of events, is organized so that the viewer's encounter is a generative one.

## Interface textualities: structures and organizations

*Timecode* points to the way that competing elements have the potential to form the ground through which a viewer can interact with images, allowing an embodied encounter to emerge. My discussion has primarily focused on competing elements, almost in isolation from the other organizing factors of a text. While it is clear that competing elements exist as a structure that can orchestrate how a viewer engages, an engagement further mediated by the particular dispositions of an individual, they exist within overarching organizations which equally have a role to play in generating different kinds of engagement for a viewer. As used so far, then, the concept of competing elements has remained a quite general way of thinking about textual structures, and in order to more directly address the ways in which different overarching organizations reveal how technologies frame the world a more detailed way of talking about these structures is necessary. Briefly outlined, this argument will encompass an innovative model for thinking about textual organizations as architectures, and introduce the idea of an attractor, a temporal element within a system that exerts a particular influence over how a viewer engages with a text. Anyone who has encountered pop-ups on websites will recognize these as an attractor that draws attention away from other words and images. My aim here is to argue for the idea of an attractor as central to our understanding of how competing elements operate to distribute our attention.

Making this claim for the centrality of an attractor necessitates building a different view of how we think about narrative organizations and their structures. The most familiar example of an overarching organization is that of a character-driven, plot-based structure. In such a case, the primary functions of all of the elements that constitute an image are determined by the need for clear explication and the need to move the plot forward. This is as true of *Timecode* and *Hulk* as it is of either of the *King Kong* films. Although the former include competing elements, just like the latter their momentum is driven by plot, and so the spatial dispersal of the competing elements needs to be also understood within the context of changing temporalities. The temporality of moving imagery is only, however, partly contingent on plot, since by their very nature moving images move and so have a temporal existence driven by the technology of both production and exhibition. While the term 'competing elements' might very well be applied to paintings or tapestries that combine multiple activities and points of attention for a viewer – for instance, the Devonshire Hunting Tapestries depict events based around multiple actions that each draw a viewer's eye – since these are not moving images a viewer's engagement is not subject to any kind of temporalizing technology.[9] A similar point is true about works that are constructed from multiple still images. In Tacita Dean's seven-piece work *Roaring Forties: Seven Boards in Seven Days* (1997), even as it requires a viewer to turn around to piece the whole together and implies a temporality in its organization by days of the week, the images themselves are without motion, and so do not exert a temporal pressure on the viewer.[10]

## Singular and complex linearities

I have argued through *Timecode* and *Hulk* that the construction of an interface intercedes by distributing viewers' attention, and that this occurs before they even begin to engage with their readings of the text. The extent to which an interface intercedes is contingent not only on the relationship between a viewer and the particular structures of a text, but also on the relationship between that structure and the overarching organization of a text. The soundscape of *Timecode* is useful to clarify this point. The soundscape of the film, especially that created by the dialogue and ambient noise, exists as a structure that aims to determine a viewer's interactions almost throughout. There are only a few moments when the four panels exist in an exact aural balance, and therefore fully competing for a viewer's attention. Instead, the sound is more usually managed so that it draws attention to a single screen. In this way, while viewers may be free to exert control over their choices of which panel to pay attention to, this is restricted by the soundscape. The structure of the soundscape, therefore, closes off the more open potential of a film based on four competing elements and functions according to the higher level of narrative organization. Although the visual competing elements exist for the duration of *Timecode*, the organization of the plot, mediated through the soundscape, imposes some constraint on the ways in which viewers distribute their attention.

A more generalized point emerges from this idea. Familiar terms used to describe organizations include 'animation', 'narrative film', 'non-narrative film', 'digital games' and 'gallery installations'. While there are many ways of establishing the similarities between these organizations, they are accepted in practice to be different, functioning as shorthand descriptors. Under each of these organizational umbrella terms there exists a range of structures that operate under the restraint of the organization, generating what I am going to call the architecture of the interface through which viewers engage. 'Narrative film', for instance, is a general term used to characterize a film whose momentum is driven by a series of events that befall various characters, where the chain of events is the plot. Such a broad definition covers films from the earliest examples of characterization, such as *The Great Train Robbery* (1903), to the most recently released examples of digitally manipulated cinema, including *Superman Returns* (2006).

Within studies of narration, a typical description of such an event-driven organization is that of a linear chain of cause and effect. In the terminology I used above, in which the character or equivalent central figure is the primary point of focus, with space acting to support and give location to character actions, the unified interplay of character, space and action creates the structure through which the linearity of the organization is maintained within a seamless interface. The character drives the plot, and the architecture of the interface is transparent. A non-seamless interface in a narrative film can equally maintain the linearity of the overarching organization, though the more disaggregated interplay of competing elements distributes a viewer's attention in a different way, creating a more complex architecture in which both character and effects-based elements drive the plot. Returning to films I discussed in Chapter 2, a comparison between *O Brother, Where Art Thou?* and *Pleasantville* makes this difference clearer. Both films make use of the capacity of digital technologies to manipulate the colour spectrum of the image, yet do so in very different ways.[11] Stephen Prince suggests that the difference between the two films reveals two distinct effects conventions, one that is naturalistic and the other showy or gaudy (Prince 2004). These two examples also, however, reveal a differing relationship between structures and organization. The more naturalistic colour techniques of *O Brother, Where Art Thou?* keep in place the unified interplay of character, space and action, with the colour manipulation kept to the background in order to evoke a sense of a mythologized history. Throughout the seamless structure, the characters and their actions keep the momentum of the events flowing and are the primary point of attention. In *Pleasantville*, by contrast, the gaudy use of colour creates a non-seamless structure, in which colour elements compete for a viewer's attention with characters – at key moments in the film, a colour change carries the narrative momentum as much as the character. At any moment of such an active colour transformation, a viewer's eye is drawn away from character action towards the colour 'action'. This splitting, or distribution, of attention results in a more complicated engagement with the imagery through the addition of another point of focus.

One way of envisaging this expanded view of a text is to think of it as a transparent architecture that becomes dimensionally deformed. Where the cause and effects elements of a seamless text are usually understood in terms of a singular linearity, competing elements lead to a more complex linearity.[12] If we imagine a singular linearity to involve an already complicated mode of engagement, in that viewers' dispositions bring their particular interests and histories into proximity with the structures of the text, the addition of competing elements brings another dimension to the engagement. Each time a competing element appears on the screen the singular linearity is deformed, as the competing element's ability to distribute attention puts pressure on the linear engagement of a viewer. This can be illustrated by looking again at *O Brother, Where Art Thou?* and *Pleasantville*. In the former film, the manipulated images present a seamless interface in which the colour scheme supports the nostalgic qualities of the story-world. As Prince remarks: 'The dustbowl look, the hand tinted postcard quality of *O Brother*, are, of course, effects, but they do not advertise themselves as such' (Prince 2004: 28). Returning to *Pleasantville*, there are two modes through which the images are colourized, only one of which generates competing elements.

An example of colourization without the introduction of a competing element can be seen in the 'fire, fire … cat' scene, in which an orange reflection is used on the greyscale fire truck to ensure that the effect of the orange-coloured fire of the blazing tree sits within the otherwise black and white imagery of the story. That is, the colour effect of the fire is blended into the image as a whole so that it does not stand away from the other aspects of the image. This mode of colourization aims to keep in place the seamlessness of an image constructed around two very distinct colour palettes – the greyscale of the black and white and the orange tones of the blazing tree.[13] By contrast, at other moments within *Pleasantville* the colour change is striking since it actively occurs on screen. Although frequently cited, the scenes in which Betty's skin tones are changed are worth mentioning. In both scenes the colour scale of Betty's skin is seemingly altered by the addition or wiping off of make-up. In the first scene with Bud, grey is added to cover up her colour; in the second, grey is wiped off by Mr Johnson to expose her colour. The fascination of these two scenes lies not only in how they establish the tenderness in the relationship between the mother and fake son, and also the potential love affair between Betty and Mr Johnson, but also in seeing colour removed or added in the movement of a gesture. These moments make explicit a process of masking and unmasking, of the performance of identities in context; in addition, the colour change competes for a viewer's attention with the expressions and body language of the actors. In terms of narration, these two colour changes carry meaning. With Betty unable yet to take control or be comfortable with the possibilities of her new life, the covering over of her vibrancy with grey allows her to remain hidden behind the duties of her role of running the home for her husband and children. By contrast, in the later scene with Mr Johnson the re-emergence of her colour occurs at a moment when she begins to explore the pleasures of the new opportunities opening up for her.

These contrasting examples demonstrate two ways of using effects. When the colour effect remains in the background, primarily serving to support the actions of characters, it secures location, as indeed many films use effects more generally to secure their locations. Where *O Brother, Where Art Thou?* relied on manipulations of a digital intermediate to create its nostalgic colour palette, other films use digital methods to generate or extend the locations for action. For instance, *The Aviator* (2004), most noted for its historically accurate colour processing via a digital intermediate, also used effects to recreate the dogfight footage of Hughes' *Hell's Angels*, originally released in 1930; and in *War of the Worlds* effects were used to create Martians, their crafts and the scenes of devastation. In securing the location of action as a seamless interface, these keep in place a simple linearity. By contrast, when effects are visible on screen in a way that competes for a viewer's attention their impact is different, generating both a spatial and time-based engagement where watching one thing means not watching another. The extent to which this deforms the linearity of engagement depends on the extent to which the competing elements deform the narrative trajectory of a film. In most effects-based cinema, including many films discussed in Chapter 2, such as *The Matrix* and *Dark City*, competing elements only briefly appear on screen, and their truncated temporality does not offer the same scope for agency as a film such as *Timecode*. The temporal duration of competing elements, then, is central in understanding how they might deform the architecture of the simple linearity of a narrative film, and consequently how the text opens towards agency.

## Interface as architecture

The idea of an interface as an architecture is most useful when it is used to make sense of the potential complexity of a viewer's encounter with interfaces that have a more intricate structure, even though it also has the capacity to describe encounters with simpler ones. As interfaces begin to be structured around more complex arrays of competing elements, which are not necessarily embedded in narrative, such as digital games or gallery installations, an emphasis on linearity becomes less productive because the connections established by viewers as they negotiate their way between competing elements of the texts may be more elliptical, routed across an array of elements rather than along a series of elements. To address the intricacies of this process of negotiation I take the idea of an architecture further.

'Architecture' is most commonly used to describe buildings in a given space, but I use the term here in a more expanded way. Taken at a glance, there is a direct correlation between architecture as a physical spatial organization and the structural relations of competing elements, since like buildings they fill a space as they are organized within the dimensions of a screen. The problem with such a view is that it only approaches the spatial structure of the textual elements, saying nothing about the temporalities of a viewer's encounter. The idea of architecture can be expanded to include all the potential interactions a viewer may have with a structure, allowing viewing to be understood as a process by which an encounter occurs with the architecture of an interface and emerges out of a complex entity combining virtual and actual possibilities. For instance, in any of the multiple split-screen sequences of *Hulk* there are many ways through which a viewer may look at the competing elements, but out of all these virtual possibilities in each viewing there will only be one actual encounter. Defining an interface as an architecture constituted by both the virtual and actual connections allows links to be made between a viewer's encounters of animations, digital effects cinema and the more complex organizations of digital games and gallery installations. As I have argued so far, these intersections are influenced by the different organizations of competing elements as well as the dispositions of individual viewers. To more fully excavate how these offer agency I introduce the notion of an attractor. In this chapter I maintain my focus on film interfaces, but the concepts will also be applied to digital games and gallery installations.

I have suggested that complex arrays of competing elements be seen as architectures defined by virtual and actual possibilities. While theoretically this implies that the combinations and permutations of the competing elements define the numbers of virtual possibilities, in reality a system of competing elements will only favour particular routes of engagement. An attractor is a significant influence in establishing these routes. For instance, in a seamless interface organized around a singular linearity the architecture is relatively straightforward, since the dimensions created from the virtual possibilities are minimal. That is, encountering this linearity involves a reading mode that shifts between two key spheres of overlapping influences: the structure of the text and the dispositions of the individual viewer. The way viewers engage with the structure will depend in part on their disposition and in part on the interplay of elements within the structure of the organization. Following the logic of a seamless interface, the structure can be defined in terms of the unified interplay of character, space and action, with the character the primary point of focus, and space being defined and contained by the actions of that character.

Another way of stating this is that a character acts as an attractor within the system of the narrative organization.[14] That is, the character draws particular attention within the textual system constructed around a figure, sets, costumes, lighting, colour, camera movement and framings, as well as patterns of editing. While each of these aspects of the system may draw attention, the principal point of focus is the character, something that is evident in the flying sequences of *The Aviator*. The background images, computer-generated recreations of the original footage from *Hell's Angels* of swooping and looping bi-planes, were digitally composited with the figure of Leonardo DiCaprio as Howard Hughes working the camera and seeming to dodge potential collisions. The figure of Hughes operates as an attractor, a perturbative influence that takes attention away from the other constituent elements of the structure, limiting and flattening out the range of potential encounters: as viewers we are encouraged by the image's organization to pay attention to the actor rather than the fighting planes. As the character attracts attention, viewers' agency in bringing their dispositions to bear on making a meaning of the film is gathered around that character rather than the other constituent elements of the images and sounds. In a non-seamless interface structured around competing elements, the character's position as an attractor is no longer singular as each competing element has the potential to exist as an attractor within any given system. With more than one attractor the possibilities for agency begin to expand.

This way of thinking about the architecture of a text holds true for animations, digital games, television, webpages and gallery installations, each of which includes numerous structures and, depending on whether they include competing elements, contains a number of potential attractors. The extent of the agencies emerging in encounters with these architectures depends on how they play off each other, opening up or closing down the meanings that may be synthesized by a viewer. The animator Paul Driessen has recently been working with split-screen formats in *The End of the World in Four Seasons* (1995) and *The Boy Who Saw the Iceberg* (2000).[15] These animations are narrative based, yet their structures are organized around competing elements, and I use them here to give more substance to my notion of architecture and attractors.

The architecture of potential encounters with *The Boy Who Saw the Iceberg* is set up by its split-screen format as well as through the interplay of other elements making up the audio-visual imagery of the piece. Each of these aspects can also act as an attractor. Throughout its duration of 11 minutes, *The Boy Who Saw the Iceberg* uses a split-screen based on a roughly equal vertical division. The film opens with two almost identical images on either side of the screen – a young boy asleep in his bed in a large room with toys on the floor and an alarm clock on a table near the bed. The narration begins as the boy sleepily moves his head, but the head squashes inwards, as though sucked down into his body. As this deformation of volume occurs, the boy's head on the left panel changes colour, going from the white/pink to grey to green. During the repetition of this strange head movement, the colour palette of the right-hand side panel changes from a green-toned spectrum to a pink-toned one, and there is an appropriate squishing sound on the soundtrack. In the pink panel the alarm clock rings, the little boy leaps out of bed and pummels the clock into a pile of debris with his feet. Still in the pink panel, as the boy turns to get back into bed a figure enters the room through the door, and the framing shifts as the boy forces him back out of the door. This shift in framing accentuates the focus on action in the right-hand panel, but as the boy returns to bed the framing shifts back so that left and right sides match. As the animation continues, and the boy on the left panel gets up, the actions on the left panel begin more obviously to compete for the viewer's attention with those on the right-hand side, which often remain in a grey-blue tone for the duration of the animation. Indeed, it quickly becomes clear that the left-hand screen represents the ordinary everyday of the boy's life, while the right-hand one represents his daydreaming. An example of this can be seen in a still from *The Boy Who Saw the Iceberg* (see Figure 3.1). On the left hand panel the adult servant of the household is asking the little boy to get up, while in the right hand panel the boy imagines himself to be tortured.

Despite the complexity of the competing panels of action, there are quite clear shifters, which direct a viewer's attention throughout. Whenever the daydream sequence is running in competition with the 'ordinary' one, the sound cues tend toward the daydream panel, though occasionally they also function either to expand or close down the relationship between the competing elements and their meanings, as occurred in *Timecode*. An example of expansion can be found in the breakfast

*Figure 3.1* The left-hand panel shows the boy getting up; the right-hand panel shows his imaginary alternative reality. Still from *The Boy Who Saw the Iceberg* (directed by Paul Driessen © 2000 National Film Board of Canada). Courtesy of National Film Board of Canada.

scenes, where the clatter of a spoon fits both set of images, though with different meanings. In the ordinary sequence, the clatter is the boy's spoon against his porridge bowl at the breakfast table; in the daydream, a cruel gaoler holds the spoon as he stirs some porridge in a large pot, while the boy, who is tied to a chair, looks on anxiously before the gaoler shoves the food down the boy's throat. Similarly, when the school bus screeches to a halt, in the ordinary sequence all the other kids tumble off the bus, with the boy dragging along behind lost in his daydream, where the screech is incorporated into a car chase. By contrast, at other moments the sound signals a closing down through the collapse of the daydream: the arrival of the school bus ends a fantasy of escape, and the school bell signals the end of a torture scenario. In both of these latter instances, the soundscape closes off the distributing impact of the competing elements, while in the former the distribution of attention across the images remains active.

To return to some of the more abstract language that I was using earlier, the competing elements generated by the two-screen format constitute the materiality of the structure, with the two screens constructing the visual and aural aspects of the actualized architecture of the interface. The overarching two-screen structure splits viewers' attention, giving them reason to look between the two screens. Initially, it seems as though each screen is an attractor exerting an equal pull on a viewer's attention. However, the presence of more subtle shifters means that the pull between the two screens is not equal. In engaging with the animation, viewers work their way into a relationship between the audio-visual imagery, deciphering the operations of the animation: the unfolding narrative, the audio and visual shifters, the micro daydream narratives embedded within the macro narrative of the boy's life, as well as the changing colour schemes. The numerous virtual connections of the interface's architecture are established by this range of potential points of engagement, and these are in turn perturbed by the impact of the attractors, which act in conjunction with an individual's dispositions as they gather around the numerous aspects of the image.

The location at which agency gathers in this complex system is contingent on the degrees of freedom which exist around different elements of the texts, but most particularly around the attractors. Attractors exert power over the ways the system is negotiated, but some systems offer more opportunities in the routes of that negotiation than others.[16] For instance, in *The Boy Who Saw the Iceberg*, on many occasions the daydream sequence plays off the ordinary sequences, making their interplay a central attractor that seems to direct viewers towards a relatively straightforward understanding of the animation. The boy dislikes the mundane routines of his life, so he escapes by imagining more exciting alternatives: glumly eating porridge he imagines being force-fed by an evil captor; he turns his journey to school into an abduction; and he imagines he is being tortured while bored in a school lesson. However, reading the cartoon as a criticism of losing oneself to daydreams is probably too simplistic, because it assumes a clear narration of that perspective, and the cartoon only *might* be said to offer this meaning.

Such equivocation also exists in the 'cry wolf' section on the ocean liner, where the boy, who is desperately telling his parents about the approaching iceberg, is not believed, possibly because he has too often talked about his imaginary existence as though it was real (see Figure 3.2). The apparent didacticism of these observations is undermined by the final moments of the animation. Once the iceberg has struck and the ocean-going liner has sunk, only the daydream panel remains active. The images return to the beginning, with the grey/blue boy lying in bed. Looking around, he realizes something is not right, and tries to rouse the oddly crumpled figure by the window and pull open the door leading out of the bedroom. Having failed in both of these activities, he goes back to bed and the panel changes to mirror that on the left hand – a ripple on the surface of the water where the liner had been. The oddity of this ending is that, having seemingly avoided his life by daydreaming, the boy is able to comprehend his death through daydreaming. Without the left-hand panel, there is no objective account of what has happened, beyond the fact that the liner has sunk. Instead, the boy's imaginative reaction to the events is playing out on the panel that has always been associated with his escapist imaginings. Yet the images are far from escapist, articulating a growing awareness of an inability to act that goes with dying. It is tempting to suggest that the boy has always been more alive in his imaginary world, and so can only give meaning to his mortality in that world. The final panels, then, insert another attractor into the system, one that

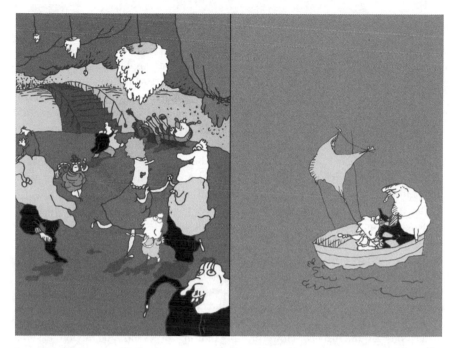

*Figure 3.2* The boy is ignored in his attempts to tell his parents about the iceberg (left panel). In his alternative reality he is adrift on a small craft in the ocean. Still from *The Boy Who Saw the Iceberg* (directed by Paul Driessen © 2000 National Film Board of Canada). Courtesy of National Film Board of Canada.

perturbs the symmetry of reading the meaning through an interplay of right versus left panels. This perturbation is not simply a question of losing the symmetry of interplay, but the distinct shift in the status of the images in the right-hand panel also skews the meanings that might be attributed to the animation throughout.

The above encounter with *The Boy Who Saw the Iceberg* represents my negotiations with the competing elements of the text, which emerge in viewing the animation and also the dispositions I bring with me to that encounter. Through the idea of an attractor and its place in more complex textual organizations, we can begin to see how attractors are elements within a given structure, a virtual architecture of possible interactions, which exert some influence on our engagements with those organizations. The potential for agency emerges through the extent to which the attractor determines the choices of reading. At any given moment within the narrative of the boy's death the shifting attractors distribute my attention in different directions, seeming to strongly determine how I might make a meaning. But since the relationships between these different elements are quite open there is scope for choice in my readings.

Attractors indeed pull a viewer's attention, but the extent of their determinative influence varies according to their specific location within the competing elements of the texts. In the same way that Bourdieu's notions of field and habitus take into account the ways that social forces exert power over the ways individuals take up positions of agency, an attractor operates within any textual system to deform the ways a viewer may interact with the interface. It is not simply that competing elements add attractors to a system, but rather that all systems contain attractors – an actor is an attractor within a textual organization – and how they exert an influence within any system determines the degrees of agency for a viewer. As the virtual architecture of a system increases in complexity, the influence exerted by attractors also becomes more complex, with different elements exerting more or less power at any given moment. Instead of an attractor being a particular object throughout the text, different elements take on varying degrees of attraction, allowing their push and pull effects to flow between structures and organizations.

The concept of attractors is relevant to a discussion of *Timecode*, in which the influences of an attractor shift between the soundscape, the plotting of events and also the emotional tenor that determines the ways in which the competing elements might be engaged with. Watching, for instance, involves a sifting process through which a viewer makes sense of the plotting and establishes connections to individual characters. Since *Timecode* exists in four panels, a viewer's intention to follow a particular thread may cause them to resist the cueing of the dialogue or soundtrack, or the movements in another panel as they attempt to follow the dramatic impetus in any one of the panels. However, the plotting of events and action has the potential to exert an influence over their viewing – a relatively slow segment exerts less visual attraction over a more active one, as action and dialogue tends to take more attention than silence. In a system in which the plotting of events in one segment goes into abeyance as another begins to take precedence through the soundscape, the movements and action reiterate the attractor of the sound. Taken together, these two elements tend to close down the viewer's agency in making choices in viewing the different panels; as attractors they deform the potential for openness. Other aspects of *Timecode*'s organization also counter a viewer's ability to freely engage with the images by pre-establishing connections across the panels through reinforcing images. As in any narrative film, there is an emotional pacing within *Timecode*, and this can overreach the actions in a single frame to pull the four together within a single emotional register. This emotional register, though not an object within the film, acts as an attractor channelling the ways in which viewers make meanings of the four panels. The strongest example of such reinforcement occurs in the quake sequences, where camera shake and sound effects combine with the actors' movements to give the overall impression of an earthquake.

Emotional registers can privilege particular panels, especially when they compete with the sometimes more mundane actions of other characters. The sequences involving Q, for instance, draw attention away from the other panels by using humour, as the business of a film production company goes on as normal while various figures in the room are manipulated by the masseur. Similarly, suspense reinforces connections across panels. In the screening room scenes, during which the Red Mullet executives view screen tests as Rosa and Alex are having sex behind the screen, connections across the other panels contribute to the suspense as to whether they will be seen or heard. The sequence begins with each of the four characters – Lauren, Rosa, Alex and Emma – listening and/or talking on either mobile phones or eavesdropping devices. Alex and Rosa talk on mobiles as he walks towards her location. Once Alex and Rosa are together (lower right-hand panel) the music changes from the orchestration of Gustav Mahler's Fifth Symphony to a rhythmic guitar score, and as they begin to have sex the camera on the lower left panel starts to shift around the edge of the projection screen. Just at the moment when the lower right panel reframes to show the studio executives watching the screen, inviting the possibility that they may become aware of Alex and Rosa behind it, the two upper panels also become active in the generation of suspense. The woman who has been talking on a mobile outside Lauren's limousine suddenly raps on the car's window. This rap, heard as a sudden crack on the soundtrack, makes Lauren jump as though she has been caught eavesdropping. Lauren's anxiety around being caught seems also to pervade the two lower screens: will the studio executives catch on to the actual sex behind the act projected on the screen? Although not fully determining, such conjoined emotional cadences act as an attractor, drawing together particular combinations of images, favouring a synthesis of meaning that follows through paths of connectivity already established within the organization of the text.

My discussion of *The Boy Who Saw the Iceberg* and *Timecode* points to the means by which attractors intersect with a viewer's engagement with an interface. An attractor always influences how a viewer reads a text, and opens up or closes off meaning to different degrees. The presence of competing elements has the potential to distribute a viewer's attention, elements with the capacity to capture their focus exerting an influence over where a viewer will attend or not attend. Competing elements never offer complete freedom as they are part of a structure whose organizations perturb contact, and within these organizations attractors are points around which agency can collect, allowing viewers to generate their synthesis of meaning.

## Temporalities and interfaces

Throughout I have stated that screens are not only places where images appear, but also interfaces on which technologies are inscribed. Moving image technologies of any era present information in distinctive ways, and the impact of competing elements in all the texts I have discussed has been to introduce an alternative way of managing information, in terms of both narration and viewing, through a different organization of space. Commenting on the move towards graphical interfaces in computers, Paul Dourish remarks:

> [G]raphical interaction is characterised by its use of space; information is spread over a larger screen area, so that the locus of action and attention can move around the screen from place to place or can even be in multiple

places simultaneously. The task of managing information becomes one of managing space.

(Dourish 2001: 11)

While it is no surprise to anyone working with moving images that information can be spread over the width of a screen area, Dourish's remarks are pertinent to the introduction of competing elements as an instance of a distinct system of managing information on a screen. However, given that moving images have a temporality, space is not the only aspect of a competing element that needs to be considered. The spatio-temporal organization of an interface is therefore important to under-standing the management of information.

As I have argued, the visibility of technologies depends on the extent to which competing elements are present. Accordingly, agency emerges in our encounters with competing elements because they offer choices in viewing by making us establish connections between the elements in ways not fully determined by the structures of any given text. Within such a system, attractors exert a degree of influence over the directionality of those choices, deforming the openness of struc-tures of competing elements and so altering the possibilities for agency, narrowing down the vast array of virtual encounters to actual ones. Another way of thinking about the impact of an attractor is that it intercedes in our progression within a given spatio-temporal organization. By progression I mean the way in which we establish linearity in our sense-making by connecting up different elements, includ-ing and excluding various pieces of information as we go along. Potentially, any spacetime is open to many progressions, but only a limited number occur, and attractors exert an influence over which progressions tend most frequently to occur. In the actual world, technologies intersect with our lives in equivalent ways, as they can literally deform our journeys to other places and spaces, altering our spatio-temporal interactions with physical space.

The ability of technology to relocate us spatially and its impact on our temporal experiences of the world have been extensively documented. By contrast, it is more rare to find accounts of how moving image technologies materialize such experi-ences for viewers. There is an extensive literature on cinema's ability to represent technology, with films from the science fiction and horror genres often cited as works exploring the impact of technologies on human experience.[17] While these accounts draw out the ways cinema has depicted the changing terrains of know-ledge, as well as representations of gender and to a lesser extent race, in the con-text of technologies, they do not look to the cinema as a technology in itself. Mary Ann Doane's work *The Emergence of Cinematic Time* (2002) is an exception as it places the emergent technology of cinema in the context of prevailing contemporary dis-courses on temporality in the late nineteenth and early twentieth century. Doane considers how the irreversibility of time emerges as a central issue and suggests that 'the significance of cinema ... lies in its apparent capacity to perfectly *represent* the contingent, to provide a pure record of time' (Doane 2002: 22). Doane's view of cinematic technology articulates it as part of a moment of technoscientific and philosophical transformation in which temporality became a site of contestation. As different meanings for the concept of temporality emerged, especially those based on contingency, transformation and duration, cinematic technologies were able to generate the illusion of a 'pure record of time' in which the nature of temporal irreversibility is paradoxically captured. Even though cinema is a mechanistic illusion, it appears to also carry something of the actuality of temporality:

> The cinema presents us with a simulacrum of time. Nevertheless, knowledge of the indexicality of the cinematic image sustains a belief that something of time, something of the movement or its imprint, or, at the very least, its adequate representation is there.
>
> (Doane 2002: 172)

Doane's work demonstrates how cinema as a technology is not simply an emergent art form, one which would quickly become a vehicle for mass entertainment, but can also be placed at an intersection with discourses about time. Although Doane's argument particularly focuses on the temporal status of the cinema, it also points to the ability of technology to generate its own spatio-temporal organizations, as 'the cinematic production of temporality, which for the most part goes unseen, is naturalised through a logic of "real" time' (Doane 2002: 190). To put it another way, the technology of cinema took hold of time and then re-presented it to a viewer, imposing a machine time, but since the pacing created by the recording and projection devices of the era seemed to match what is seen in the actual world, its status as machine time is rendered invisible. Even though viewers are confronted with a technological system as they watch moving images, that system is transparent. This transparency effect was furthered from very early on with the emergence of narrative forms, as these distracted attention away from the technological interface.

The emergence of competing elements begins to break down the transparency of this technological interface, so engendering an experience of a technology and the distinct temporalities a technology can introduce. As Manuel de Landa comments, there are many kinds of temporal scales, but individuals experience a 'lived present', a temporal scale relevant to their perceptive abilities: 'certain cycles are simply too slow for them to appear as changing ... certain oscillations are far too fast' (de Landa 2002: 11). Temporal scales of this kind refer to extrinsic or measured articulations of time, rather than intrinsic or durational time. The lived present is not only defined by those temporalities that impinge on a person's presence in the world, as it also represents the qualities of being in a particular present. That is, a lived present does not simply refer to different ways of measuring time passing, but also articulates something about the experience of a passing of time marked in specific ways.

Temporalities that impinge on our presence in the world include such obvious examples as the time of day, month or year, workplace schedules, transport timetables and so forth. Engaging with each of these temporal structures is a contingent process, in which our experience of passing time depends both on which temporal organization we are connecting with and on the context within which this occurs. For instance, our anticipation of events at the end of a journey can determine whether we think a transport schedule is too fast or too slow; the fullness of our lives outside the workplace can determine our response to work timetables, making work a place to bolster self-esteem or somewhere that keeps us from better things. In each of these examples the temporal structure is not natural, but the consequence of an organization, and we take up different attitudes to it according to how we see it limiting or enhancing our lives. Our lived present, and in particular our perception of our temporal existence, is, in this sense, a series of negotiations with temporal structures that both mark the passing of time and articulate an experience of those temporal organizations. Again, the question of choice and agency emerges here, since, though these organizations more usually than not exist beyond our control, they are not fully determining. Instead, they operate as structures around which we can take up various orientations, and these orientations are contingent on a diverse range of influences, including the restrictions imposed by the time of day or week, as well as more diffuse influences to do with emotional well-being.

The interfaces of moving image technologies present a particular kind of temporal experience to a viewer, and so intercede in the already complex dynamic through which temporalities make sense. It is precisely this temporal aspect that generates the experience of a technology; since moving image technologies present temporalities determined by the mechanism of recording and projection, they are a technological intervention mediating our negotiations with an ongoing lived present. Yet this mediation is not in itself determining. Just as our sense of a lived present emerges as a consequence of an ongoing negotiation with a series of contingent temporal markers, the mediating presence of a technology involves an ongoing process of negotiation, which may be visible or invisible. My analysis suggests that moving image technologies are not only sites of entertainment, but also a means through which we can understand our complex negotiations with the temporalities of technological interfaces. In arguing that competing elements inscribe a viewing interface, and therefore reveal a ground from which an embodied agency has the potential to emerge, I also implicitly assume a negotiation with the temporalizing aspects of moving image technology. But the question of temporality must be made more explicit in order to draw out what our encounters with moving image technologies can tell us about our encounters with technologies more generally.

In intersecting with the world through a technological interface, viewers can be both aware and unaware of the impact of technologies on how they see. In the simplest instance of watching a film with a seamless interface, viewers sit and watch an audio-visual interface. In allowing themselves to co-operate with a text's organization, whether it is a narrative film or a more experimental one such as *Blue*, viewers participate via the temporalities established within the interface. I do not mean this in the sense of entering into the temporal world of a story, which can place us in a past, present or future, but in the sense that the images are experienced via the temporality established by the technological devices of the interface. Someone sitting inside a moving vehicle over which they have no control may find external objects taking their attention, but they can only watch in passing, as the technology takes them forward according to its momentum. Such is the interface of cinema – images are offered and seen from its temporal perspective. And even though watching moving images in the home through VHS or DVD is commonplace, and we can control the speeds and directional flow of the imagery, we are indebted to the technology of display as it remains ultimately in control through default options and standard settings. The sense of things being beyond our control might lead us towards the view that technology is determining, and in a seamless interface in which the technology is transparent it is relatively easy to reach such a conclusion. In watching a film viewers usually enter into its story-world, or other narrational strategies, setting aside any awareness of its technological status. I want to stress here that I do not mean that viewers give up their interpretative capabilities, as all these remain active. Instead, I am suggesting that they set to one side their awareness of the technological status of the fiction, a setting aside that is especially encouraged within the traditions of narrative cinema.

As I argued in relation to animation, in the early days of cinema, whether animated or live action, cinema's status as a recording or animating technology was an aspect of the entertainment, but this reflexive view was quickly superseded by the establishment of narrative conventions. Only in moments of technological innovation does the display of technology again become evident, showing off the possibilities of sound, colour, widescreen, rear projection, stop-motion modelling and CGI as they each become the latest thing. And though it is true to argue that discourses circulating in cinema maintain an emphasis on the technological work of effects, within films themselves the technological status of an effect is more fluid. Filmmaking practices in any era shift between displaying the innovation, both as a sophisticated technology and as a narratively important element, exploiting an innovation to bring in an audience and, finally, allowing the technology to settle as one of the many devices available to filmmakers. Across this movement, the visibility of the technology within the story-world of the film gradually fades, partly because it is familiar, but also because of how it is narratively embedded. As competing elements begin to appear on the screen, the presence of technology is reinscribed on the interface. I have argued in Chapter 2 that one of the consequences of the appearance of competing elements is a distinct narrative organization in digital effects cinema.

The impact of competing elements does not fall only on narrative and the aesthetics of the image, but also on our awareness of technological interfaces, and in particular on how these interfaces bring to attention the temporalizing organizations of a technology. Moving images by their very nature are in perpetual motion – even apparently static images move through the apparatus – but for viewers familiar with this movement it is taken for granted. Keeping pace with the movement involves a process of quick scanning, with focus placed on those particular aspects giving the most relevant information for an individual viewer – the actor, the creature, the moving object and so forth. Viewers have different degrees of competence in this scanning process, which is in turn dependent on their familiarity with editing patterns and framing devices. For instance, the fast edits combined with a rapidly shifting camera in both live-action and computer-generated sequences of the remake of *King Kong* provide a fast flow-through of narrative information. For someone used to watching this kind of film, this is a comfortable interface in which the story unfolds, opening out to the range of interpretations viewers may bring to it through their dispositions. The feeling that something is being missed, or that the flow of sound and motion is too fast or overwhelming, is not at the forefront of such a viewer's experience. For another viewer, less familiar with fast editing and reframing, the opposite is true and the technological interface can be experienced as too fast, too fragmented and 'busy'. Underlying these two opposing examples of viewing moving images is an encounter with the temporality of a technology. In the first case, the viewer feels able to 'read off' enough audio-visual information to allow him or her to make sense of what they see; in the second, the viewer is unable to do so and so feels as though he or she is missing something.

These two facets underpin experiences of many kinds of technology, whether cinematic or digital or not. Mainstream cinema has tended to rely on creating a comfortable interface, while more experimental works aim to disrupt this comfort. While such a view is familiar and longstanding from commentaries on the readerly/writerly text or enunciation and *discours*, the tendency has been to draw attention to narrational strategies in order to investigate their cultural politics. A consequence of the current proliferation of media, and media form, is that it allows the question of technology to become more active in these debates. The appearance of more interfaces, especially ones structured around competing elements, reveals more fully how viewers both co-opt and are co-opted by a technological interface as they negotiate their ways through its structures.

## Encountering the interface

I have argued that competing elements distribute viewers' attention and so create the ground on which viewers can generate degrees of agency as they synthesize meaning from an embodied position. I have also suggested that this ground is not one of absolute freedom, but that a viewer's intersection with the structures of a text is further mediated by an attractor, a particular aspect of a text that perturbs the relationship between textual elements, so that they draw attention and so gather agency. A complex text is a composite architecture of virtual and actual connections, with attractors limiting access to the virtual, favouring instead particular actualizations. My final point is to argue that attractors, as well as being textual elements that mesh with others to generate meaning, are sites where the presence of a technology not only becomes visible, but reveals the different ways in which viewers encounter technology. In the following, I want to look more directly at how this encounter is often experienced in terms of spatio-temporal relations, and therefore as a form of embodiment.

Encountering *Timecode* and *The Boy Who Saw the Iceberg* involves an embodied mode of viewing, where agency emerges in the opportunities presented to viewers as they synthesize a meaning across the spatial configurations of competing elements; however, the relations between these elements are limited by the temporalizing presence of attractors. Although different in many ways, *Timecode* and *The Boy Who Saw the Iceberg* share a quality of long duration in the presence of their competing elements. As I argued in Chapter 2 digital effects films equally contain competing elements, but their duration is usually only for short bursts. The quality of emergent agency is consequently more limited, but these films nevertheless offer an insight to our encounters with technological interfaces. For instance, the competing elements of actors and effects used in *Titanic*, especially when the vessel steams across the ocean at sunset and during the sinking sequence, expand the narrative space and allow for a range of possible engagements, where viewers can pay more or less attention to the human or mechanical protagonists across the temporal flow of the plot, though equally they can distribute their attention between both. Such examples demonstrate the capacity of effects to be vehicles of the narrative and, in these particular instances, to compete with the actors for a viewer's attention. At other points in *Titanic* the effects, though not necessarily structured as competing elements, act as indices for the experience of technology. The morphing technology seamlessly takes viewers across a temporal chasm of 80 or so years, showing the capacity of technologies to intercede in our sense of time.

In other films, the competing elements themselves can also be seen to act as more direct expressions of the impact of technologies. In *Hulk*, the spatial and temporal distortions introduced through digital editing techniques become encounters with the effect itself, a more direct experience of the sudden shifts enabled by technology. A feature of *Hulk* was the use of a non-linear editing system to stylize the look of the film. Tim Squyres and Ang Lee experimented with digital manipulations on an AVID system, before handing them on to Industrial Light and Magic for finishing into the high-end imagery of the final version of the film.[18] Much of the editing in *Hulk* is seamless and relatively conventional, but some spatial and temporal constructions do confront the viewer with the ability of digital technology to manipulate space as well as time. A number of these manipulations are equivalent to quite straightforward cuts between location, but use instead visual echoes as a bridging shot: the pattern of foliage at dusk connects to a pattern of stars; the green plume of a chemical explosion connects to the green iris of Hulk, forming a specific temporal bridge between Banner's past and his present.

Other manipulations more deliberately play with the cinematic conventions of spatial and temporal continuity, disturbing them by excising space between characters, placing them together in a frame when the previous or subsequent shots show them in distinct locations within a room. This occurs when Edie Banner tells her husband David she is pregnant. Initially the two are both standing on one side of the kitchen, and the shot cuts to David moving into the far space of the kitchen, with Edie no longer visible. As she is heard saying, 'David I have wonderful news', he begins to turn back towards her. At this moment, with David's movement still partially visible in the background, an insert moves up from the bottom of the screen, showing a closer view of David's turning back; at the same time, a second insert drops down, placing Edie into the framed space, as she is also turning towards David. The overall effect is to 'pull out' the space between the two characters even as the temporal continuity is maintained through the soundscape of the dialogue. The spatial and temporal distortions break a straightforward viewing by introducing moments of a more unexpected encounter with the text, but as these occur abruptly and change again with equal rapidity, little opportunity exists to make a synthesis from the competing elements. As there is little time to generate a synthesis of the different elements on the screen, an encounter instead occurs with the effect itself, a more direct experience of the sudden shifts enabled by technology disturbing our easy engagement with the imagery, alerting us to its organization.

The editing strategies of *Hulk* present a different kind of attractor to the ones discussed in relation to *Timecode* and *The Boy Who Saw the Iceberg*. Where those placed pressure on the how a viewer made a synthesis of the competing elements, in *Hulk* the attractor draws attention to the condition of technology itself: the ability to transform the experience of space and time. This capacity is given further substance when allied with the story of *Hulk*. The two examples of spatio-temporal distortion discussed above occur within the opening six minutes of the film, including the credit sequence, during which images of the transformative experimentation at the centre of *Hulk* progress from invertebrates to lower vertebrates and primates, with David Banner finally using himself as an experimental subject in a radical technoscientific intervention. The organization of elements on the interface invokes an equivalent encounter with transformed time and space. Just as the content of *Hulk* will tell the story of Bruce Banner's transformations because of his father's scientific hubris, the attractor established by the disruptive interface enables a viewer's identifications with the transformative potential of technology.

These comments on *Hulk* point to the ways that the attractive impact of competing elements pulls in two directions, which in turn has an impact on the site at which a viewer's agency can emerge. They evoke the experience of technologies interceding with our viewing experience, but at the same time this experience is located within the structure of a plot, so that the direct address of the interface is woven into the narrative strategies of a film. In *Titanic* and *Hulk*, as well as *Flatworld*, *The Matrix* and *Dark City*, the effects are embedded within a plot about technology, creating a tight fit between the effect and the narrative; in *The Street*, *Twister*, *The Perfect Storm* and *Pleasantville* the fit is looser, but nevertheless the effects-based competing element narrates transformation. An outcome of this balance is that, even as a technological experience is evoked through the process of splitting a viewer's attention, these experiences are masked through the interplay of a system's attractors. Competing elements inscribe the interface, making the technological intervention more evident, but this set of attractors coexists with another established by the plot structure of the text. The complex linearity of these examples of digital effects cinema, with their brief bursts of competing elements, therefore presents a particular mode of engagement with technologies. Technologies, through how they are mobilized by filmmakers and other moving images, have the capacity to transform things, but our encounter with these transformations does not always offer an opportunity for reflection in the process of our engagement. This is not to restate an argument in which digital effects create a passive viewing experience, as viewers are still capable of bringing all their interpretive and critical capacities to bear on their reading of the film. Instead, in addition to the dispositions they bring to their interpretation of a text, viewers enter into a negotiation with the organization of an interface. How they manage the information on an interface is contingent on the spatio-temporal organization of its architecture and the extent to which opportunities for agency are present. In a film offering only brief encounters with competing elements, and where the attractors of the system tend towards enabling agency via making a synthesis of the competing elements generating plot-based information, the more direct encounter with the interface is set aside.

By contrast, the more complex interfaces of *Timecode* and *The End of the World in Four Seasons* allow a viewer to encounter competing temporalities of a technological interface for longer durations, and so offer a different mode of encounter for a viewer. Although both films still have a plot-based structure, this attractor has to compete more fully with those generated by the multiple screens on which the moving images and sounds appear. The eight-panel organization of *The End of the World in Four Seasons* pushes this to an extreme. The 13-minute animation is split into four sections, spring, summer, autumn and winter, and in each section the eight panels show the various activities of figures just prior to the end of their world (see Figure 3.3). On first watching the animation it is easy to feel anxious about missing something in one or other of the panels, recreating a sense of absolute disorientation with a technological interface. However, as the animation continues viewers begin to adjust to its strategies, making choices about which panels to attend to, which panels are more or less relevant to their engagement in the animation.

Taken as an architecture of virtual and actual potentials, *The End of the World in Four Seasons* is a very complex system. The spatial spread of information over eight panels constantly transforms as each panel continues, and therefore the connections between the panels are never static. Each of the eight panels acts as an attractor, but the degree to which they draw attention, and influence a viewer's reading of the animation, is contingent on their content and the impact of its shifters, on the dispositions of the viewer and on the previous record of viewing this interface. For instance, in the opening spring segment three panels appear to be connected (see Figure 3.4). A bird in a tree lays an egg that drops directly into the eggcup of a man seated at a table in the panel below. In the adjacent panel, the egg cracks open in close-up. It quickly becomes apparent, however, that the egg in close-up is not the same as the one in the eggcup, and from it another thread of the plot opens out: the battle between a cat and a bird. In watching the sequence again, the viewer already knows about the falling egg and so can instead watch the beginning of the thread about the cat and the bird. Throughout, all the other panels are playing out scenarios: for instance, in a single panel, two dogs take turns sniffing each other; in adjoining panels, a man rings on a doorbell as he holds a spring flower and a woman lies in

*Figure 3.3 The End of the World in Four Seasons* is constructed around eight panels. Each depicts an element of the story-world. Still from *The End of the World in Four Seasons* (directed by Paul Driessen © 1995 National Film Board of Canada). Courtesy of National Film Board of Canada.

bed thinking the doorbell is her alarm clock. Making sense of the actions both in and across each of the panels relies on a viewer making a choice between which panels to follow and then negotiating the system's attractors: the shifting cues of the sound, action and movements in the individual panels. For instance, the man at the table and the dogs are relatively uninteresting, both because they do little and also because they are not cued through the sounds.

In watching this animation, my attention is distributed to other panels by action, movements and sounds, with the greatest activity occurring in the cat and bird chase. However, even as I choose to focus on this panel, I am aware of activities in the other panels, and so have the sensation of missing something, and consequently having to decide if I will remain focused on my chosen panels or briefly divert my attention elsewhere. The experience of this animation is further framed by whether one is seeing it with or without access to a remote control. Overall, making my way through the panels and their micro-plots requires me not only to become aware of the narrative threads, but to also assess how each panel on the interface contributes to the whole of the story.

By looking at *Hulk* and *The End of the World in Four Seasons* it is possible to reveal two versions of an embodied engagement with technological interfaces. Like many

*Figure 3.4* The spring sequence of *The End of the World in Four Seasons*. Still from *The End of the World in Four Seasons* (directed by Paul Driessen © 1995 National Film Board of Canada). Courtesy of National Film Board of Canada.

digital effects films containing competing elements, the narrative organization of *Hulk* privileges an engagement with the narrative elements of the interface. Therefore, even in those segments of the film structured around competing elements, such as the split-screen or the moving inserts of *Hulk*, the attractors perturb the system towards an understanding of the narrative. Since this emphasizes agency emerging through making sense of the narrative across the competing elements, the associated agency gained from encountering the interface, though present, is less strong. The direct experience of the transformative properties of technologies evoked by an effect is turned more towards narrative information.

By contrast, in *The End of the World in Four Seasons*, the process of negotiating with the distinct elements of the interface reveals two routes through which a viewer's agency occurs: making sense of the narrative and making sense of the interface. If embodiment can be understood as an emergent attribute of interaction, the different architectures of these films introduce two different modes of embodied engagement. Each text is a spatio-temporal architecture of virtual connections, in which attractors perturb the freedom of an individual to generate a meaning. In making an embodied reading viewers reduce all the possible readings into the actual one, bringing all their dispositions and their viewing histories to bear on the text. In a film such as *Hulk* the embodied encounter privileges narration. In *The End of the*

*World in Four Seasons*, the embodied encounter reveals the intricacies of an individual's negotiation with the structures of the interface.

*Hulk* and *The End of World in Four Seasons* reveal both the possibilities and limits of agency in our encounters with technological interfaces. The technological interfaces framing the world are multiplying, and there remain many questions to be asked about who creates those interfaces and for what reasons. In an environment populated by interfaces constructed around competing elements, a viewer cannot attend to everything, and this is the reality of our exposure to the competing temporalities of technologies. The outcome is, however, a more generative compromise than this latter point suggests, as it is generated from the relational negotiations of an individual with the structures of a system. In a world-view where contingencies reign it is possible to speak of this negotiation as a dispersal or distraction, but how we make that choice, how we judge and interrogate an interface, is partly within our grasp.

# 4

# DIGITAL GAMES

## Fatal attractors

Meaning is not embedded within the game, but rather is
revealed through use.

(Newman 2004: 6)

Digital games are played instead of watched, requiring gamers to provoke an effect that
has meaning within a game. In doing so they step 'out of "real" life into a temporary
sphere of activity with a disposition all of its own' (Huizinga 1971: 103). Although
Johan Huizinga is referring to play in general, his statement is also true of digital
games, where gamers enter into a temporary sphere of activity regulated by the rules
of the game as well as the performance of the hardware and software of a game's
technology. Digital games can be further described as 'socially constructed artefacts
that emerge from a complex process of negotiation between various human and non-
human actors', a view that places them in the wider conditions of their creation:
their technological, cultural and economic context (Kerr 2006: 4). Although I take a
narrower view, the idea that digital games involve a process of negotiation between
human and non-human actors is central to my argument. Digital games are another
mode of digital encounter, one in which gamers create a visible mark of their presence within spheres of activity that have spatio-temporal dispositions all of their own.

Digital games are a relatively new phenomenon, certainly when placed in the
context of animation and the cinema.[1] Unlike the former two media, the existence
of digital games has always relied on digital and electronic media, and so their
developments parallel the changing possibilities of those media. As with all developments, technological ones intersect with other influences placing pressure on the
routes taken in harnessing emergent possibilities. Two such intersections have been
important in the appearance of the current array of 3-D off-line games. The
expanding market of home computing in the UK coincided with the rising interest
in computer games, as production emphasis also shifted from arcade games to early
computer games.[2] With the increasing sophistication and power of home computers
as well as console systems, another key change occurred, as the construction of the
image moved from the flatter perspective of 2-D games to that of a more cinematic
3-D animation (see Figure 4.1). This aspect continues to be fully exploited by the

*Figure 4.1* A piece of artwork from *Tomb Raider: Legend* depicting the three-dimensional construction of Lara Croft. *Lara Croft Tomb Raider: Legend* © 2006 Core Design Ltd. Lara Croft, Tomb Raider and the Tomb Raider logo are trademarks of Core Design Ltd.

tendency to bring out a digital game complementing action-based films; even *The Da Vinci Code* (2006) marketing included a game released in parallel with the film. Despite the aesthetic convergence evident between cinema, animation and digital games, the latter nevertheless retain a distinctive mode of engagement that is based on the scope offered for play.[3]

My first experience of a digital game was peering over the shoulders of colleagues as they flew a fighter through a simulated terrain, egging each other on with taunts of incompetence or 'oohs' of admiration at some well-executed move. Very much on the periphery, I never 'got it', and retained a rather haughty view of games until I discovered *Tetris* a number of years later. While it would be possible to track my exclusion through a number of different contexts, including gender, age, peer group allegiances, what strikes me is the extent to which it was also self-determined by my lack of understanding of the pleasures the game gave to my then colleagues. Digital games only became appealing once I had had a go and experienced the 'pull of the play': wanting to do better next time, aiming to master the skills of playing the game, and of building my score higher and higher. Although I do not wish to assume that this motivates everyone's engagement with digital games, since their appeal, both generally and generically, is as individual as someone's taste in animation or cinema, this perspective provides my way into a discussion of what is an increasingly debated field of interest. Given the subject of this book, my perspective is integrated with the ideas introduced in the previous chapters. Just like live-action cinema and animation, digital games are a form of entertainment, yet they are equally a technological interface. In the following I weave these two arguments together, taking the ideas of competing elements, textual architecture and attractors, and use them to model a description of interacting with a game and to place that interaction as a particular kind of technological experience.

Although there is some debate over which was the first, it is probably safe to say that digital games have been in existence since the late 1960s, becoming available to a public audience initially as arcade games and then through the first wave of home machines in the 1970s.[4] The discussion that follows primarily focuses on games developed from the 1990s onwards, a period in which the increased power of games processors allowed the construction of game-worlds drawing on cinematic visual conventions.[5] While games have also expanded to include massive multiplayer online role-playing games such as *EverQuest*, my discussion mainly addresses those played on home platform formats such as PC and Playstation 2 (PS2). As was true of my earlier chapters, I do not aim here for an exhaustive overview of digital games, seeking instead to capture a sense of how a game can be encountered, both as something to play and as a technological interface. A term that is frequently used to describe encounters with games is 'interaction'. Often a loosely used word, interactivity means, or is taken to mean, that a player is able to make something happen within the game-world. Commenting on this, Janet Murray states:

> The interactor is not the author of the digital narrative, although the interactor can experience one of the most exciting aspects of artistic

creation – the thrill of exerting power over enticing and plastic materials. This is not authorship but agency.

(Murray 1997: 153)

In this view, interaction involves agency. It exists in the processes through which a player or gamer exerts power over the digital materiality of the game: the characters and objects created within a digital environment, and which form the substance of a game's interface with a player. By employing the ideas I have already introduced, we can expand the notion of 'exerting power' to give more substance to the places where agency might gather within a digital game. In playing a game, gamers can make the avatar move within the game space to create substantive actions, which can lead to success or failure within the scheme of play. In doing so they are not only evoking the evident actions of the avatar, but are also in the process of negotiating with the structures of the game, actualizing only some of the numerous possibilities immanent within its virtual architecture.

The substance of the architecture of a digital game is constructed from different elements, many of which can be described as competing, in a similar way to those of digital effects films. These elements include the landscape in which action occurs, which can be a complex 3-D environment like that seen in *Enter the Matrix* or a series of 2-D levels, as in the *Pokémon* games. Elements also include puzzles, AI characters, as well as all the status bars. Although gamers negotiate their way through an architecture generated from competing elements, there remains a linearity to a game since playing a game involves progressing through a series of levels, usually of increasing complexity and often through different kinds of landscapes. In *Enter the Matrix* a player moves across a series of locations beginning at the Post Office and arriving at the Logos via the Airport, Power Plant and Chinatown. Nevertheless, this linearity is traversed and transected by gamers, who, via a cycle of failure and repetition, progress through each level by engaging with its array of competing elements, gaining different skills as they go along, until they finally reach an end. A more substantial description of exerting power, then, is that a gamer maintains a high level of concentration to ensure engagement with the different elements of the game – exploration, combat, health, character traits and so forth. And during game-play, the competing elements of the game, variously leading to action and exploration, work together to intensify this engagement with the game, which in turn expands and contracts the limits of agency for a viewer.

To begin to understand the implications of this intensification for thinking about games as technological interfaces as well as sites of agency, I draw out the idea of an architecture defined by virtual connections.[6] If, in a general sense, agency is achieved by negotiating a way through a structure, players can achieve agency as they negotiate their route through the various competing elements of the game. These competing elements primarily include the game-world environment and the AI agents and their actions, with which the gamer can interact in a number of ways.[7] Again, while many virtual interactions are possible, only some will be actualized, and the idea of an attractor is useful in thinking through how the structure of the game promotes some actualizations more than others. It also gives rise to an understanding of a game as a multiply articulated spatio-temporal encounter. As in the example of split-screen cinema, a description of competing elements based solely on their dispersal across the screen interface only gives a sense of the spatial dispersion of a gamer's attention, but if we include the attractor we also acquire an understanding of its strong or weak temporal influence.

In *Half-Life 2* there is a section in which Freeman enters a turret in which the avatar can interact with four competing elements: a canal lock mechanism which must be activated for him to progress through the waterways, two combines and the helicopter which had been attacking him outside the turret.[8] Taken as a static description, there are four competing elements across which a gamer's attention can be distributed. In play, however, the gamer has first to deal with the combines or Freeman will die, and the lock mechanism may be investigated at any point, but at great cost to Freeman's health if an AI agent is still able to attack. Without an account of competing elements as attractors with temporal pressures, we miss their impact on the strategies of a player. In the turret sequence, opening the lock gate mechanism is essential for progression, but in the moment that Freeman enters the turret it intersects with other competing elements whose status as temporal attractors is more aggressive. Giving an account of the architecture of competing elements and their status as attractors is, therefore, essential in understanding the degrees of agency in any sequence of the game.

## Digital games

Increasingly, digital games are the site for a wide range of discussions. Questions about digital game violence coexist with commentaries on their constructions of race, gender and sexuality, their potential for providing a means for learning, as well as their economic histories.[9] There is also a rich and often conflictual discussion about interactivity and digital games, with the arguments characterized as falling into the two camps of narratology and ludology, or narrative space and play.[10] While drawing on the insights provided by these approaches to games studies, I want to begin from the perspective of digital games as an interaction with a technological system. Other scholars working on digital games share this perspective. Writing in 1993, Brenda Laurel made the following comment:

> They [designers] regarded the computer as a machine naturally suited for representing things that you could see, control, and play with. Its interesting potential lay not in its ability to perform calculations but in its capacity to represent action in which humans could participate.
>
> (Laurel 1993: 1)

The capacity for a computer to represent action in which humans can participate is the basis for digital games. But what is the nature of this participation? It is useful at this point to briefly trace two other approaches to the question of participation, as they reveal ideas that form both the context and the jumping-off point for my notion of game architecture. In their influential work on remediation, Jay David Bolter and Richard Grusin wrote of digital games:

> Action games in arcades, on video units, and on computers have continued to require the user's intimate involvement with the interface. Some developers have created more visually complicated games without showing any particular concern to pursue transparency. Others have worked toward a three-dimensional transparency, toward producing in the user a feeling of immersion through linear perspective and a first person point of view.
>
> (Bolter and Grusin 1999: 91)

Bolter and Grusin's comments draw attention to the way the gamer must have an involvement with the interface, though the nature of that involvement remains relatively opaque. Writing more recently, Martti Lahti places a different emphasis on the game interface, seeing it as a site from which technology can be experienced in multiple ways rather than a singular one: 'video games ... [are] ... a paradigmatic site for producing, imagining, and testing different kinds of relations between the body and technology in contemporary culture' (Lahti 2003: 158). Lahti goes on to suggest:

> [Games offer] ... a simultaneous experience of disembodied perception and yet an embodied relation to technology.... On the one hand, various games emphasize an immaterial and disembodied vision that explores a virtual landscape with relative freedom and liberates perception (and the body) in some fashion from its normal limitations of placement and movement in daily life. On the other hand, games respond to this liberated vision and out-of-body experience by locating knowledge firmly in the familiar terrain of the body.
>
> (Lahti 2003: 168)

Lahti suggests that a gamer's engagement with an interface is split between two aspects of a technologized experience: virtual exploration via the terrain of the body as a gamer uses controls to access the game-world. I later challenge the view that exploring a virtual landscape is a disembodied activity, but useful here is the claim that knowledge is located in the terrain of the body.

Although they are quite different, both of these remarks begin to gesture towards the complexity of a game interface, a complexity that I more fully articulate by modelling it as an architecture. Bolter and Grusin's hypermediate interfaces, for instance, are inscribed by the presence of media technologies, but hypermediacy remains more a question of aesthetic influences or histories than of competing elements that have an impact on a gamer's experience and agency. In Chapter 3 I argued that competing elements distribute a viewer's attention, and, in making sense of those elements by synthesizing a meaning from them, the viewer is both embodied and gains agency. This idea can equally bear on the interface of digital games, as these are constructed around competing elements that form an architecture with which a gamer interacts. As I outlined above, a key distinction I make is that the virtual space of a game is constructed from competing elements, and engaging with that space provides the ground for embodiment and agency, within the terms of an encounter with a digital interface. In the following I argue that the digital space of a game is complex and multifaceted, constructed both from spaces within the play space of the game-world and also from the information spaces of the game.[11] To understand how agency and embodiment emerge, we first need to understand how a gamer encounters these spaces, and to challenge an overly simplified notion of immersion.

## Entering the game

Entering a game involves encountering not just a single spatio-temporal organization but a series of organizations, each of which offers agency and embodiment for a gamer. How a gamer enters into these organizations depends partly on the experience and dispositions a player brings to the game, but also on the state of the game. A game can be described as a state machine since it exists in a number of states triggered into action via the interactions of the gamer. Many of these transitions in turn alter the spatio-temporal experiences for a gamer, as various competing elements impinge in different ways on the game-world. I argue later that this view challenges a simple view of spatial immersion, but, before doing so, I address how a gamer first enters a game.

To be able to alter the state of the game, gamers first need to set in place the means through which they will enter the game, literally to get to grips with the hardware of a game's system. Although perhaps not an enticing place to start, and indeed most analyses do jump straight into the more exciting possibilities of the game-world, the hardware of a game is still part of its broader architecture, and one that importantly distinguishes playing a game from watching cinema. In sitting, or lying, or standing in front a game system, we are beginning the process of encountering the game as we connect into a technological system. Once the game is active it requires that we stay there otherwise it will simply hang. This is different from watching a DVD, since once that is active it plays until the end, regardless of whether anyone is watching or not. Such a seemingly obvious difference reveals the centrality of the player in the architecture of a game.

It is widely understood that watching a film is an active process in which a viewer engages with the text, making interpretations and hopefully taking pleasure from that process. How this occurs relies on an interplay between the text's form, content and the viewer's dispositions. In the previous chapters I have argued that competing elements add another layer to this process, interceding in the ways in which a viewer achieves a synthesis of meaning. Encountering a game involves gamers interceding in a different way. Their pleasure remains partly reliant on their prior knowledge and dispositions, their skill in game play, but also on their situatedness within the game. Although it is taken for granted, to be situated involves not only a gamer's place in the level or how they distribute their attention across the competing elements of the game, but also being there to provoke a reaction in the game's state: without the gamer there is no game.

To begin laying out an encounter with games I first briefly consider how we enter the architecture of a game by starting from the perspective of operating a system. If playing a game on a PC, I put the DVD in the drive, wait for some moments while the graphics display reconfigures, and then wait a little more as the interface settles to offer me various loading options. Usually I load a saved game and pick up where I left off, moving the avatar through the game-world using keystrokes, battling and puzzling my way through the obstacles set before me, or rather my avatar. As this short outline begins to make clear, even as I more obviously operate within a game-world, alternating between making my avatar drive the boat, pick up ammunition and health packs, explore the terrain and fight the enemies in the water hazards of Black Mesa in *Half-Life 2*, I am also actively engaged with a technological interface. Entering a game involves embedding oneself within an architecture that is defined both by the competing elements of a game-world created by the software of the game and also by the hardware of the system.

Other writers have used the term 'architecture' in relation to games, but more usually they confine it to the structure of the program: 'Architecture is the structure of a program. Architecture also encompasses the structures and flow of data, and it defines the interactions between all the components of the system' (Rollings and Morris 2000: 497). As this quotation makes explicit, an architecture refers not only to the components of a system, but also to the ways they interact with each other. This description, however, need not only refer to a program. The extension of the term I make here is motivated by an emphasis on the status of gaming as an engagement with a technological interface, and the additional elements in this extended system include the hardware of the system, as well as the gamer, who acts as a nexus through which components of the system interact with each other.

Entering any digital architecture involves interacting with a complex interface defined by the structures set in place by both the software and hardware of the technological interface, and those structures are the elements with which a gamer negotiates to generate agency. Because the hardware of a digital game includes components allowing a gamer to evoke a response within the game-world, they too are important to the system's structure. Having said this, only some components are active in offering degrees of freedom, and therefore agency, during interaction. For instance, in addition to the competing elements on the screen interface, when one sits down to play a standalone game on a PS2 other components contribute its architecture: the PS2 box, the controller, a television screen and possibly a sound system.[12] Although this chapter focuses primarily on PC as well as PS2 games, any system has an architecture. And just as arcade games are different to ones played on a Gameboy, those played on a mobile, PSP (or Playstation Portable) or a laptop each has a distinct physical architecture defined by its construction. Similarly, older cartridge games, X-Boxes and PS2s are distinct from each other. Online games add a whole other set of dimensions to the architecture of a system, which includes the game itself, as well as chat rooms and various sites through which gamers model their characters skins and trade weapons, skills and potions.[13]

Having stated that the architecture of a system involves both hardware and software, it is also necessary to indicate that the some of these components operate in the background, while others move between foreground and background. Those in the background offer no points for negotiated interactions, while those in the foreground often do. For instance, in an off-line PS2 experience, the PS2 box, the television screen and controller are each examples of architectural elements that expose a gamer to different kinds of technological experiences. Although essential, the PS2 box remains a background technology, the place to put in the disc and memory cards and then play the game. For most of us, beyond a rudimentary knowledge that PS2s use a DVD-compatible technology, it is a 'black-box system', and like a computer can be used without a detailed knowledge of how it works. The PS2 hardware is not at the forefront of our awareness during a game, unless, of course, the system breaks down, or perhaps during a save, leaving the PS2 box inactive in an experiential sense. The controller represents a different kind of interaction with the technology of the system since it is the means through which a gamer causes actions within the game space. In initially learning to play on a PS2 gamers are very aware of the controls, as they have not simply to make an avatar move, but also to develop skills in using a multiple range of buttons and toggles, both alone and in various combinations. Once their play becomes more sophisticated, gamers develop a repertoire of moves and strategies. More experienced gamers are less conscious of the controls, but nevertheless are in constant interaction with them, and their ease may break down as they get closer to the limits of their repertoire. The dual shock PS2 controller has the added element of vibration to jar gamers when their avatar is injured in some way. 'Joysticks, game controllers, pedals, and various steering systems further foreground haptic interaction and simultaneously encapsulate players in a game world complete with bodily sensation' (Lahti 2003: 168–69). From the perspective of seeing the controller as a component of a game architecture, it slips in and out of activity, moves between foreground and background of the interface.

The screen interface represents a further aspect of the architecture of a game, and is the aspect of off-line games most fully considered within games studies, an emphasis I follow here, even as I also include references to moments in which the controller or keyboard is a more active component. Before moving on to this, however, I want to comment about my use of the term 'interface'. Throughout this book, I have used the term 'interface' in a very specific way, one that aims to step back from our encounter with the story-world via a transparent screen and to see the screen itself as an interface that is more or less inscribed with the presence of technologies. A seamless interface, for instance, does not draw attention to its status as a technological interface, but one marked by competing elements does. Out of the presence of competing elements I develop the idea of an architecture of virtual and actual connections, with the actual ones generated by viewers' synthesis of meaning at the interface, how they negotiated their way through *The End of the World in Four Seasons*, for instance.

This definition can be extended in relation to digital games, where the actual architecture of the game emerges out of the numerous different elements that vie for a viewer's attentions, although the capacity for a gamer to have agency in these actualizations is actually quite variable. The hardware elements of the architecture prompt a limited number of actualizable connections between different elements of the architecture, while the interface of the game offers numerous ones. Although it is obvious to say, a PS2 will only work if connected up in a particular way, and though the controller offers 14 buttons to press and two toggles to swivel, there remains a small number of effective combinations, as unskilled gamers often discover at the cost of their avatar's health status. The moves that button and toggle combinations make, how an avatar manipulates tools and fires weapons, how low he or she can duck, how high he or she jumps, and so forth, are 'above discussion'.[14] As such, though active through a gamer's manipulation, the range of actions enabled by a controller are non-negotiable since the hardwiring of the controller pre-actualizes the connectivities for a gamer.

The architecture of a digital game becomes far more complex when the myriad of virtual and actual connections between the competing elements of the screen interface is taken into account. At this juncture, the pre-actualized connections of the controller expand into a multiplicity of possibilities, out of which emerge all the pleasures and frustration of play. It is at this point that my use of the term 'interface' begins to come into potential conflict with its more usual usage in digital games studies, where writing about digital games interfaces conventionally describes the interface between the players and the digital game in the following way:

> [T]he interface occurs at the boundary between the player and the video game itself, and can include such things as the screen, speakers (and microphones), input devices (such as a keyboard, mouse, joystick, trak ball, paddles, steering wheels, light guns, etc.), as well as onscreen graphical elements such as buttons, sliders, scroll bars, cursors and so forth. The interface, then, is really a junction point between input and output, hardware and software, and the player and the material game itself, and the portal through which player activity occurs.
>
> (Wolf and Perron 2003: 15)

Useful in catching the diversity of gaming interfaces, this view nevertheless refers to a junction that is of more limited scope than the one introduced in the previous chapters and expanded on here. The interface is indeed the portal through which player activity occurs, but in limiting descriptions of the interface to being between input and output, hardware and software, player and the material game, it misses out the competing elements of a game's screen interface, and how these structure and shape a gamer's experience and agency.

As I have begun to suggest, the overall architecture of a game is more materially and physically dispersed than that of a digital effects film or a split-screen animation. It is equally true to state that the interface of competing elements appearing on the screen is more dispersed than much of the moving imagery already encountered in this book. The extensiveness of the architecture to which this contributes only progressively appears for a gamer, and varies according to the kind of game being played and the format through which the game is played. A brief glimpse at what I mean by the architecture of the interface can be made clearer by referring to a specific scene from *Half-Life 2*. Taking the scene in terms of a progression through the game-world, gamers, having realized that they need to flood a chamber to get from one side of a barrier to another, do so and then follow through the logic by swimming underwater through a tunnel. Emerging on the other side, they find themselves only able to climb onto the ledge that does not give access to the next stage of the level. To reach that stage they must solve a puzzle.

Looking more closely at the process of puzzle-solving reveals the various competing elements of the scenario. In keeping with the tendency for digital games to generate spaces for exploration, gamers can visually take in the space through the first-person perspective of Freeman, their avatar in *Half-Life 2*, and seek the clues to how to get onto the ledge from the water. In the absence of any threats, gamers can give their full attention to the location. The competing elements of Freeman's various status bars – health, HEV suit and weapons – are of a little importance in this sequence, assuming that Freeman is healthy enough to progress, as they remain unchanging in the absence of any attacks or actions. Having got used to the game's logic, the gamer will notice at the bottom of the now underwater space that there is another textual layer, one showing planks of wood and wooden cable spools. As the gamer's attention gathers around these planks they become the primary focus of the scenario, and given Freeman's crowbar the gamer will be alert to the possibilities of planks and dive under the water to take a closer look. Once Freeman is underwater another status bar appears, that of Freeman's oxygen capacity. Since Freeman can only be held underwater for short periods, the oxygen bar becomes an active element, an attractor, within the architecture of the game – it both structures the decisions of the gamer and competes for the gamer's attention. Throughout this segment, Freeman's exploration of the space has been important, but the competing element of the oxygen status bar reconfigures Freeman's relationship with the space, channelling his actions through the pressure of time, as gamers have to gauge how quickly they need to work Freeman and his crowbar by looking between the status bar and controlling Freeman, allowing them both to break the planks and get back to the surface before the oxygen runs out. There are two potential outcomes to these actions. First, the cable spools float to the surface and, once all three are released, make a platform for Freeman to jump onto the ledge. Second, Freeman gets too far inside the new space and is trapped by the remaining planks and spools. Having discovered this pitfall, gamers need to be aware of the potential hazard of their spatial environment, especially in the context of their oxygen status bar. If they do find themselves unable to get Freeman to the surface before he dies, then gamers may again become keenly aware of the control keys they are using to move their avatar, as he ceases to respond if about to drown. Once the screen has become too red, pushing the 'w'-key is to no avail.

In this segment of *Half-Life 2*, the puzzle, actually quite simple, is made more complex as the different elements of the interface become active, working with or against each other to create the play environment. To put this in terms of an architecture, many elements are present within this sequence, but to progress through the level all the virtual possibilities open to a gamer have to give way to actualizations allowing the puzzle to be solved. As part of this giving way, different elements of the architecture are active to different extents, and so compete for the gamer's attention to varying degrees. In the sequence described above, the clues to the puzzle, the temporal pressure of the oxygen status bar and the spatial pressure of the hazard all combine as competing elements forming the architecture through which gamers gain agency in their interaction with the game. In the following I consider more fully the relationship between the spatial and temporal elements of a game's architecture, and how these structure the gamer's interaction with it.

## Game architectures: spatial and temporal attractions

To be embodied involves taking on a spatio-temporal orientation in the world that is experienced as an ability to act directly and meaningfully on that world. Although the digital realm is often taken to be disembodied, offering as it does perspectives untied from the grounded consequences of action in and on the actual world, it too exists as something to be experienced. Technologies of all kinds can be interacted with, and if the 'the ways in which we experience the world are through directly interacting with it, and ... we act in the world by exploring the opportunities for action that it provides to us' (Dourish 2001: 17–18), then digital technologies can be included in such a perspective. At first sight, playing a game by beginning over and over again, in a cycle of repetition and failure, does not seem to offer many opportunities for meaningful action. But if we take a closer look it is possible to see a number of ways in which a game offers a mode of embodiment, and these in turn give insights into how we become engaged with technological interfaces.

The first of these actions is, very simply, the gaining of experience through repetition. Anyone who has let their avatar fall from a great height because they lack the skill to control a rightward leap from one ledge to another eventually learns the moves, and so each time they bring something different to that moment of the game. In the end, however, such experience belongs to the realm of dispositions a gamer brings to the game, and players with very good skills would not even notice themselves thinking about the process of playing. A game's architecture offers stronger ground for thinking about the ways in which gamers can become embodied through their spatio-temporal orientation within a digital interface, but the kinds of actions available vary according to the responsiveness of the programming.

The greater the sophistication of a game's AI, the more effective the game's environment is at creating the impression of changeability, which in turn gives a stronger impression of the spatio-temporal conditions of being embodied. For instance, if in any of the *Tomb Raider* games I miscue a leap by Lara as she is climbing around ruins in order to solve a mechanical puzzle, and she dies in the fall, I simply have to repeat the movements to progress; nothing is different about the puzzle, only my ability to solve it. By contrast, if AI agents are present, the game can be triggered in different ways, so every time I fail and re-enter, my encounter may be slightly different: the possibility for an exact repetition denied by the game's AI. Commenting on this aspect of games Espen Aarseth states: 'Ergodic phenomena are produced by some kind of cybernetic system, i.e. a machine (or a human) that operates as an information feedback loop, which will generate a different semiotic sequence each time it is engaged' (Aarseth 1999: 32–33). This feedback loop, or state transition, only occurs in certain elements of a game's architecture, making visible the different kinds of spatio-temporal structures that exist within a game. Making sense of these is a way of understanding the architecture of the game, and how it in turn constitutes ground on which agency and embodiment may be generated.

The two examples from *Tomb Raider: Legend* briefly cited above point to two modes of engagement for a viewer, both of which can occur within the game-world, the location in which much of the play action occurs. That the game-world can offer complex modes of engagement is not necessarily articulated by the simple use of the term 'immersion', especially if it is accompanied by a claim for disembodiment. This is not to say, however, that commentaries on games have been unaware of the multiple ways in which a gamer interacts with a game. For instance, the spaces of a digital game can be described as 'more than simply the sum of their code – they are experiential spaces generated through code and the player's interaction with the execution of that code . . . [with the player operating] . . . both *on* the game space and *within* the game space' (Taylor 2003: 1). This observation points to the multiple presence of the gamer in relation to digital games, something already noted for new media in general.[15] Jesper Juul also points to the temporality of this doubling:

> In *Tomb Raider*, we click on the keyboard, but we are also moving Lara Croft. In these examples, the *actions* that we perform have the duality of being real events and being assigned another meaning in a fictional world. Additionally, since our actions take place in time, that time shares the duality of being real time *and* fictional world time.
>
> (Juul 2005: 141)

Entering a game's architecture, then, involves a complex negotiation with its spatial and temporal elements, each of which occurs in a multiplicity of levels. The following starts with examples of competing spatial and temporal elements from within the game world in order to give a sense of the complexities of its contribution to a game's interface, before moving on to other parts of a game's architecture.

Although *mise-en-scène* analysis can be brought to bear on digital games, their spaces are different from those of cinema and animations, primarily because a gamer is able to occupy the space of a game in ways not possible in these two media. In one sense this occupation occurs via a gamer's literal interaction with the controller, the keyboard, joystick or trak ball, etc. In another sense, it occurs via a more indirect interaction with a virtual space where the movements of the controller are evoked as actions within a game space. How a gamer occupies the space of a game has been a source of much debate within games studies, leading to a number of different perspectives, including immersion, interactivity and agency, as well as narratology and ludology. 'Immersion' is an early and still widely used term, expressing how a gamer engages with a game-world, and it is useful to begin with the frequently cited definition found in Janet Murray's *Hamlet on the Holdeck*, in which she succinctly defines immersion as 'the sensation of being surrounded by a completely other reality' (Murray 1997: 98). The idea of being surrounded is immediately suggestive of a smooth spatial immersion, but a closer look at Murray reveals the presence of more than one mode of immersion:

> [T]here is almost nothing to distract you in *Myst* from the densely textured visual and aural environment, but this intense immersion in visiting the place comes at the cost of a diminished immersion in an unfolding story.
> (Murray 1997: 109)

This quotation points to two kinds of engagements that may be variably active within any game – the exploration of space and the following through of a story, both of which can be termed an immersion. Although the capacity for gamers to be immersed in an unfolding story has been a hotly debated topic in games studies, what is particularly useful is Murray's gesture toward a player's involvement being invested in more than one attribute of the game. Jesper Juul's perspective rounds this out. While making play a central aspect of engagement, he again stakes a claim around the multifaceted nature of a player's engagement in commenting that a gamer has 'a choice between imagining the world of the game and seeing the representation as a mere placeholder for information about the rules of game' (Juul 2005: 2). As both Murray's and Juul's remarks reveal, understanding how gamers engage with a game requires an awareness of the simultaneous activities being undertaken, or, to use a different terminology, their multiple presences. However, this in turn requires an understanding of the shifting pattern between those presences, since playing a game involves moving between sets of simultaneous activities. By more fully using the notion of architecture, and giving an account of the place of competing elements as attractors, the dynamic quality of shifting activities experienced by a gamer can be exposed as a response to the appearance of attractors within the game-world.

The vocabulary used in discussing space in games draws to some extent on cinema studies, but has also brought into the arena a newer discourse around navigable space. The cinematic discourse is most evident around the questions of point of view and how the perspectives operating in games offer different views and therefore structure modes of engagement. Many of the games discussed here are either first- or third-person games, which structure the game through a linear perspective grounded through the location of the avatar. These two perspectives are particularly suited to exploiting the imagery of a 3-D environment.[16] The *Half-Life* games are first person, as are *Halo* and *Red Faction*, allowing gamers to see everything through the eyes of their avatar, while the *Lara Croft* series, as well as *Primal* and *Enter the Matrix*, is structured around third-person perspectives, which allows the gamer to see the avatar's movements in addition to the space.[17] The primacy of first- and third-person linear perspectives structures not only a gamer's encounter with the game-world as a space that emerges through a series of progressions, but also discussions of space. For instance, perspective is central to the approach to space introduced to describe the distinctive organization of a play space – that is, the concept of navigable space. Lev Manovich has suggested that, 'instead of narration and description, we may be better off thinking about games in terms of narrative actions and exploration . . . [since] . . . movement through the game world is one of the main narrative actions' (Manovich 2001: 247). Marsha Kinder's response to Manovich offers a cinematic precedent to digital space, arguing that Bunuel's radical films require the same kind of attentiveness as 'exploratory computer games like *Myst*' (Kinder 2002a: 10).

Influential though Manovich's and Kinder's comments have become, these kinds of commentaries only take us so far into the space of the game-world. The emphasis on exploration relies on the limited view provided by an avatar's perspective, when in fact a gamer's view of space is often more extensive than that of the avatar, and so the location for action exists only beyond their engagement with an avatar. This can be made clear by briefly considering the opening sequence of *Half-Life 2*. It begins with a voiceover to a darkened screen, telling Freeman to 'wake up and smell the ashes'. Once the image becomes visible it is obvious we are seeing the inside of a train carriage from the first-person perspective of the avatar – Gordon Freeman, the game's hero. This sequence continues as a mini-tutorial in which a gamer learns how to move Freeman and avoid being shot. It ends with an interactive cut-scene in which Freeman is given his HEV suit. Up until this point the gamer's perspective on the game-world of *Half-Life 2* has been in line with the avatar's, but once the HEV suit is added two additional elements appear on the screen: health and HEV status bars. The view of these is not grounded in the first-person perspective of the avatar and, in offering a different spatial view on the game environment, also distributes the gamer's attention. The health bar, for instance, though always important to monitor, only becomes determining when health is too limited and a means of replenishment is required. As I demonstrate more fully below, a gamer's view of space is, therefore, constructed from a range of perspectives and, while a point of view grounded in the perspective of the avatar is important, other spaces also make up the architecture of the game. Part of the shifting pattern of activities that constitute play involves not only being immersed in space, but moving in and out of different kinds of space.

The architecture of a digital game is already beginning to become apparent. A player enters a game and interacts with it via particular hardware, and the screen interface slowly opens out, shifting between spaces that offer greater or lesser degrees of freedom in which to gain agency. As the interface develops, different kinds of space appear within the digital environment of the game, including both the game-world where play occurs and also the 'non-play' spaces. In the same way that narrative organizations in a film impose a structure on the competing elements of the film, in digital games the rules act as equivalent overarching organization. The rules governing play act as the organization within which a game's architecture is embedded. For instance, there are now a number of game genres: in addition to the first- and third-person shooters, there are, for example, fight and sport simulations of many kinds, strategy, action and driving games. Each of these genres operate through a roughly equivalent organization. First- and third-person shooters will involve armed combat and puzzle-solving, whereas sport simulations will be organized around particular sports and their more individual skills. Whatever the kind of organization, the architecture of competing elements is constructed to make playing to the rules possible. The rules of the game therefore structure the architecture of the game, and that in turn offers degrees of agency to the gamer: 'the Rules of a Game also *set up potential actions*, actions that are meaningful inside the game' (Juul 2005: 58). Jesper Juul's words here echo those of Paul Dourish, who links action to embodiment when stating that 'embodiment is the property of our engagement with the world that allows us to make it meaningful' (Dourish 2001: 126). Actions in a digital game can be of many kinds, and offer a mode a digital embodiment to a gamer as they exert control over the spaces of play.

As I suggested above, the idea of navigable space does not really address the various modes of engagement a gamer has with space. A means of beginning to tease out the complexities of this engagement is to revisit the relationship between character, action and space, something I have utilized earlier in this book to interrogate the potential disruption of the unity of these three aspects of an image introduced by competing elements. Writing in the 1970s about space more generally, Yi-Fu Tuan has commented that 'the body imposes a schema on space' (Tuan 2001: 36). This is also true of digital games, and especially of those structured around first- and third-person perspectives, in which the body of the avatar grounds the perspective of the game-world offered to the gamer. By looking at the specific interactions of character, action and space in digital games we can begin to see a different way of looking at the spatio-temporal organizations which are experienced by a gamer. In doing so, we can build up a sense of where possibilities for agency gather within a game. When introducing the concept of competing elements, I argued that as these emerge in digital effects cinema there is no longer a unity of character, space and action. That is, once space is no longer used up through the process of giving meaning to character actions it becomes active within the narrative. In a digital game such as *Half-Life 2* or *Tomb Raider: Legend*, both of which rely on 3-D representational spaces, another means of thinking about the relationship between character and space is required, as there is again a different kind of organization of character, space and action, one which in turn is distinct from that discussed in digital effects cinema and animation.

To take the first-person perspective of *Half-Life 2* as an example, Freeman is fully embedded within the space, with the gamer able to 'see' via Freeman's point of view (see Figure 4.2). Yet, paradoxically, this occupation of space does not unify character, action and space. This is clearer if we look at a third-person perspective game such as *Tomb Raider*. In the third-person game the avatar is visible in a way that might seem equivalent to a character in a film; however, they are only 'properly' embedded when active within a space available to interventions by the gamer. To be properly 'in space' within a game-world requires not just the visible or audible presence of the avatar, or for that matter their point of view, but that the avatar can be made to act on that space at the behest of the gamer. A similar argument holds for 2-D games where a gamer's involvement in the spatial organization of a 2-D game is also pre-dicated on their ability to make something happen within that space. For instance, a gamer can sit and watch the Tetris blocks accumulate, but these blocks are dis-connected from the game, operating under the unimpeded gravity of the game's algorithm. This situation changes once the gamer has become embroiled in the task of orienting the blocks to create complete horizontal lines, as the blocks themselves have become embedded in the space of the game.

For an avatar to be properly embedded, then, means that it is part of a relay through which a gamer's manipulations of the controls achieve on-screen action. Just as stated earlier in relation to the hardware connections of a game system, a game is only a game when it is being played. This relay is clear in some aspects of *Tomb Raider: Legend*. When a gamer is not using the PS2 controls Lara may turn her head, make a larger movement such as the adjustment of a strap or pull up her

*Figure 4.2* The first-person perspective of *Half-Life*® *2* orients the gamer within the game-world element of the game's architecture. *Half-Life*® *2* image courtesy of Valve.

121

socks, or the voice of Zip or Alister, her support team, may be heard on the soundtrack. Given the third-person perspective of the *Tomb Raider* games, Lara is fully visible to anyone looking at the screen, but the moments just described are not instances of her being properly embedded within the game-world; rather, they signal the gamer's lack of involvement in the relay. Lara is not 'in space', since her actions are not in the process of being modified by a gamer; those visible on screen are instead created by the software of the program, ones prompted by Lara's in-action. The relationship between character, space and action is only unified through the interventions of a gamer – by operating the avatar the gamer becomes the nexus through which the actions of a character can have meaning within the space. This statement can be made of any game, and, whatever the perspective offered, or whatever the nature of the avatar, space becomes unified through actions controlled by the gamer.

This formulation of character, space and action allows us to go further than simply describing how a gamer interacts with space because it also reveals the multiple presences that exist in the interplay between avatar-space and AI-space.[18] Exploring the distinction between these two spaces, as well as their interactions, gives greater access to the different ways a gamer may encounter the complex spaces of the game-world. Avatar-space and AI-space offer different organizations of character, space and action, which in turn expose more about the complexities of a game's architecture. Briefly stated, an avatar-space is one within which gamers have the freedom to move the avatar where they want to, but this is circumscribed by the AI-space. As the game's software registers the presence of a gamer, the AI-space becomes increasingly active, throwing up obstacles in the form of AI agents (non-player characters, or NPCs), as well as puzzles and other objects threatening the life of the avatar. Gaining agency for a player can be described as the process through which a gamer exerts increasing control over the space, causing the balance of control to shift from the AI-space to the avatar-space. How this negotiation is achieved depends on the extent to which the competing elements of a game act as temporal attractors perturbing the route taken by the player through the game-world.

To make the process of negotiation clearer, I begin with avatar-space at its simplest – that is, the physical space of the game-world within which a character moves. How gamers engage with the world through their avatar depends in part on the nature or genre of the game and the kinds of attractors they offer to the gamer. *Myst* is a game often cited in the earlier literature, which was concerned primarily with immersion, exploration and navigable space.[19] The *Myst* family of games remains unrivalled for the extent to which they offer complex visual environments, with play revolving around the piecing together of clues whilst passing through a carefully constructed series of linked environments.[20] In these games temporal progression remains in the possession of gamers, as it is primarily determined by their decisions about whether to explore the spaces or solve the puzzles. The avatar-space is uninterrupted by the insistent temporal pressures of AI-space attractors so often encountered in action games. In the absence of in-game temporal pressure, the aesthetic quality of the environment becomes paramount in keeping the gamer engaged, therefore placing an unusual emphasis on spatial immersion as the mode through which a gamer engages with the game-world. A particular facet of the *Myst* series is a credible and variable 3-D environment. For instance, *Myst III: Exile* had four game environments, J'nanin, Voltaic, Amateria and Edanna, each representing an Age to be worked through by the player. The look of each Age is distinct: J'nanin involves the exploration of an Island perimeter and Tower structures, whilst activities in Edanna occur within a world constructed around lush plant life. Steven Poole comments that the visual density of *Myst*, while disliked by action gamers, is what made them so popular:

> Games like *Myst* and *Riven* were rightly derided by the videogame cog-noscenti for having tediously simplistic gameplay properties, yet they sold in their millions precisely because they are rather beautifully pure exploration games. The player wanders around gorgeously designed virtual environments with fabulously detailed landscapes, water lapping against jetties and mysterious dark buildings.
>
> (Poole 2000: 99)

Poole's comments stress the ability of gamers to wander within virtual environments, and are suggestive of the way the temporality of being in these worlds is in the possession of the player. Nevertheless, even in a spatially immersive game such as *Myst*, the gamer is not given absolute freedom to wander throughout the architecture. Although the pathways within stages of the levels can be traversed in whatever ways the player chooses, progression requires that puzzles are solved to open doorways between levels and the different worlds of the game. While these puzzles offer little in the way of temporal pressure, they present specific elements of the environment for a gamer's interaction. As competing elements they remain active as devices that distribute a viewer's attention. Since the *Myst* games are essentially puzzle-based, these include objects that the avatar can touch and move to progress through the game. Access to books, central devices within the game logic, often requires a player to move objects, further enhancing the dimensionality of the game-world. The addition of appropriate sounds for these activities deepens immersion in the game-world. There are also brief moments of interactions with the AI-space as NPCs appear to the gamer, and these elements also provide verbal clues to the solutions of the game. Overall, the *Myst* games present a game-world in which the avatar-space, while channelled at key points by puzzles, remains unimpeded by the temporal restrictions of an AI-space.

The architecture of the interface, though it contains the competing elements of the game's explorable environment and puzzles, is relatively unmarked by temporal attractors. As such, gamers are relatively free to establish their own routes within the space, drawing on their dispositions in engaging with the environment. Agency is available to the gamer, since the relatively open structure of predominantly spa-tialized competing elements leaves many choices to gamers, giving them a high degree of control. In terms of an embodied experience, the competing elements of explorable space and the solving of puzzles create a location in which the avatar can be made to act. Paul Dourish describes embodied interaction as 'the creation, manipulation, and sharing of meaning through engaged interaction with artefacts' (Dourish 2001: 126). In *Myst*, gamers are able to act within the game-world as they explore it, and even if the physicality of this exploration is different from its equivalent in the actual world, in enacting the process of exploration the world becomes meaningful. Any gamer who is enticed into the *Myst* world takes pleasure in moving through the world, in solving the mechanical puzzles, but also in piecing together the various clues to the puzzle at the heart of the game-world. The meaning resides in acting at the intersection of those elements in the experience of playing a game.

*Myst* is dominated by a strong avatar-space in which a gamer does not often have to negotiate an intersection between avatar-space and AI-space in order to generate some agency. The space is more simply available to them to exploit as they wish. By contrast, in many other games the degree of temporal freedom is more limited, which in turn has a consequence on how a player is able to occupy the game's space. In *Tomb Raider* or *Half-Life* games, avatar-space is less available to the gamer as it is constantly restricted by AI-space through the appearance of AI agents. As a result, the process through which a gamer achieves the possibility for agency is also restricted by the AI-space through the temporal pressures exerted by AI-space attractors. However, the extent to which these exert pressure emerges only gradually in each game, with pressure slowly increasing as the game continues and the gamer is expected to become more skilled at dealing with the devices of a game strategy. This strategy gives gamers the capacity to learn how to act within the game-world, to generate the skills to battle against the AI-space before they are fully engaged within it. Like many games, the opening of *Tomb Raider: Legend* takes time to shift from an avatar-space to AI-space, and includes the convention of an opening cut-scene, which is neither avatar-space nor AI-space, but a seamless interface where gamers gain both context and back story. The opening of *Legend* begins with a moment from Lara's life, in which as a young girl she looks fear in the face by refusing to close her eyes as the plane she is in with her parents crash lands. This is followed by a temporal shift to the era of the game, in which the grown Lara is seen rock-climbing in a sequence that clearly rips off the live-action sheer rock face climbing opening of *Mission: Impossible 2* (2000).

Having used this sequence to also indicate the presence of Lara's support crew, the interface shifts into a game space initially dominated by avatar-space. In this avatar-space the gamer is able to get used to controlling Lara, getting her to run, jump, climb, swim on the surface of water, pick up objects and figure out how to move through the space without temporal pressure. Once she has reached the waterway leading to the temple, the Lara avatar triggers the AI-space to generate temporal attractors that impinge on the avatar-space. A rolling rock means Lara has to leap out of the way, and various enemies begin to appear, who Lara has to shoot before she can continue. While the enemies are still alive, Lara's ability to move through the game is limited, and she is under threat, an element that builds in complexity as the gamer progresses through the levels. When under attack, whether from gun-toting human enemies or patrolling jaguars who will maul Lara, a gamer's interaction with AI-space is determined not simply by their ability to lock on to a target, but also by Lara's health status, which adds another competing element into the game space. As gamers encounter an enemy, they have to shift from being in avatar-space to an avatar–AI-space, where the AI enforces a particular series of actions and the gamer is under greater temporal pressure to act.

The architecture of the game still offers degrees of freedom, since, unlike puzzles, at such moments the gamer's actions do not need to occur in a particular order. Nevertheless, the game's devices impinge upon the player's strategies as attractors push the players towards particular routes and actions. Once inside this sequence, the avatar has to be oriented towards an interaction with the AI, and using all of the devices available through the key pad, such as aiming, shooting, moving. The increasing difficulty, in the sense of their spatial intricacy, of these encounters is evident by making a brief comparison between a fight in the Bolivia and Peru levels. In the Bolivia level, Lara progresses from encounters with single AI characters to multiple ones, with the AI characters arrayed for a frontal view. In the Peru level, Lara again encounters multiple AI characters, but these are arrayed in a 360° scatter around the avatar. In such an arrangement, the avatar is again able to encounter the visual sweep of the game-world, but under conditions is which the gamer's attention is distributed between a number of different elements: operating the controls effectively, responding to the gunplay of the enemies, with some attention also being paid to the health bar and ammunition.

In this kind of intersection between avatar- and AI-spaces, the spatio-temporal organization of the architecture is constructed from a set of elements that aggressively compete for the gamer's attention. As they distribute the gamer's attention across many areas of the screen, the latter can achieve agency by working to take control of the space, gradually imposing order on the competing elements. This gradual imposition of order is visible if we look at an early part of the Peru level. Lara has a series of mercenary encounters in the village, and at one point emerges onto a roof only to find herself under attack. There are a number of ways gamers might play out this sequence, but it is likely that they will find their avatar being damaged from gunshot fire from all around her, and at different heights. To survive this moment of the game, though the avatar is under attack from all sides, with their attention pulled in all directions, gamers can most effectively gain control by focusing their attention on the individual AI characters. Their agency, therefore, emerges in how they choose to negotiate their avatar through the gun battle sequence, which involves a set of attractors that each has an impact on the avatar. In this sequence, then, the architecture is defined by the detailed location of the action – a village street with overlooking windows and low roofs, all containing a potential hazard. In addition, the AI-space is populated by five AI characters that can each separately attack Lara, leaving her very little time for respite. Once Lara's movement triggers an AI fight, that fight has to be worked through, establishing a temporality to her spatial engagement. A similar argument is true of *Half-Life 2*. If the presence of an avatar triggers an AI agent to appear, he or she has to be dealt with or the avatar will be damaged (see Figure 4.3).

According to the logic of the *Tomb Raider* games, these points of contact between AI-space and avatar-space are interspersed with a series of interludes during which Lara can move forward through the game, puzzling her way through the space. In *Tomb Raider: Legend*, there is the additional device of puzzles being solvable in more than one way. Solve them through the simplest method, though, and the gamer will likely lose out on some of the game's rewards. At such moments, the gamer's interaction reverts to an explorative one within avatar-space. A gamer's interaction with *Tomb Raider: Legend* is determined by the architecture on display at any given moment. In avatar-space, the player interacts with the location of the temple and its various puzzles. The agency is here derived from the possibilities for exploration and the gathering of awards hidden in different parts of the location. As in *Myst*, there are competing elements present, but many of these are without temporal pressure:

> *Tomb Raider* has more dimensions. It gives the player greater freedom, within the constraints of its basic mechanism, including freedom to explore the on-screen world to some extent beyond the immediate requirements of advancement through the game. It creates a stronger impression of occupying the game-world, even if at one remove.
>
> (King and Kryzwinska 2006: 3)

*Figure 4.3* The zombies and drone act as AI-controlled competing elements that exert temporal pressure on the actions of the gamer. Alyx is also under the control of the AI, but is an aid to the Freeman-avatar. *Half-Life*® *2* image courtesy of Valve.

Though *Tomb Raider* games do not compare with *Myst* in the sense that they do not offer a gamer the extensively textured environments of the latter series, they nevertheless are constructed around puzzles and environments which are complex enough to be a challenge to the gamer's skills in moving the avatar.

Even in games where a gamer experiences a more intense engagement with the AI-space and its attractors, the construction of the game-world aims towards a strong degree of credible construction. Barry Atkins, for instance, in comparing *Half-Life* with *Tomb Raider*, suggests that 'survival, and not exploration, is the core principle that drives *Half-Life*' (Atkins 2003: 63). However, as he goes on to remark, the environment of *Half-Life* remains a credible one that is marked by the consequences of their actions, in that bodies lie on the ground, splashes of blood and bullet pockmarks disfigure the structures of the environment, and sometimes in going to a room a gamer discovers a body marked by violence which disturbs the easy drive forward through the game.[21] Similarly, 'the soundtrack of *Half-Life* features scuttling movements, strange screams and wails, the crackle of electrical shorting, and the grinding and crunching of machinery' (Atkins 2003: 69). All these observations are equally true of *Half-Life 2*, and reveal the outcome of the approach of the game's creators: 'our basic theory was that if the world ignores the player, the player won't care about the world' (Birdwell 2006: 215).[22] As the following excerpt from a game review of *Half-Life 2* suggests, the environment of a game matters, even if it is action-based:

> The level design is awe-inspiring. The amount of stuff that you figure out by yourself and the way the level guides you and shows you information is amazing, as is the use of verticality. What I found impressive in both Half-Life 1 and 2 is how the game leads you on a very heterogeneous path through a very homogeneous environment. You have this feeling of there being, say, an office building with ten identical floors, but the path you take through it will involve elevator shafts (in Half-Life 1), service corridors, ordinary rooms, outside sections, broken down parts, air vents, etc. creating a very rich experience. Re-traversing the same level at a different height felt great too, e.g. walking the streets of Ravenholm, going into a building, working your way up, traversing the rooftops, going through more buildings.
>
> (Hunicke 2006)[23]

In action-based games the location of the gamer in the game space is contingent on the interplay of the avatar-space and the AI-space, which in turn defines the architecture of the interface. Games, however, also contain other kinds of spatial organizations, which reveal a more multifaceted construction of space. In first- and third-person perspective games, there are two additional spaces, the cut-scene and what I call info-space; the latter, especially, demonstrates a game space that is not always grounded through the body of the avatar, invoking another aspect to the architecture of the game.

Until *Half-Life* introduced interactive cut-scenes, all cut-scenes were non-interactive sequences whose pre-rendered full-motion video playback further marked their difference from the playspaces of the game-world. As such, they operate as elements within a game's architecture whose spatio-temporal structure is not accessible to a gamer. Cut-scenes in most games are initially encountered as introductions, and conventionally aim for a cinematic appeal. I have already described the opening of *Tomb Raider: Legend* and its referencing of *Mission: Impossible 2*. Earlier examples of this tendency include the role-playing game *Arcanum*, which opens with a dirigible crash, manipulated to look like a scratched piece of film, and *Grand Theft Auto III*, also released in 2001, which incorporated full credits and music. In games linked to films the cinematic appeal is more direct if imagery from the film is invoked in the opening sequences, as occurs in *Enter the Matrix* and *Spiderman*. Such cut-scenes only play out the first time a game is loaded, and a gamer much more frequently encounters them as elements in the game indicating a level change.

Given that gamers are usually unable to intercede within a cut-scene, they have often been the objects of derision, even though they contain parts of a game's back story or information about the subsequent level or encounter. Whatever kind of information they contain, they exist as a different kind of competing element within a game's architecture. Jesper Juul remarks that 'cut-scenes are not a parallel time or an extra level, but a different way of projecting fictional time' (Juul 2005: 145). Although this is an interesting way of thinking about the different temporalities of a game, it does not make clear that in cut-scenes character, action and space are already unified, as they do not need the gamer to be active to be played out. The cut-scene, therefore, is an element in the architecture reducing the degree of agency for gamers, relocating them as viewers who are able to actively excavate it for relevant narrative information. The interactive cut-scene, first introduced in *Half-Life* and found in both *Half-Life 2* and *Tomb Raider: Legend*, introduces a more in-between space. The cut-scene gives information, but Lara must also react at the right moment or she will die.

In interactive cut-scenes the point of view given to the gamer is either omniscient or retains the perspective of the gamer, maintaining the focus on the game-world view of the gamer. Info-spaces break with such a point of view, making the competing elements of the architecture more apparent. Info-spaces are rarely commented on in discussions of digital games, although they do form an integral part of the game's environment. This is perhaps because, like the hardware of a system, the info-spaces are not where the action is, as that is located in the spaces where the avatar is made to act. However, info-spaces do exist as elements of a game architecture, and form another dimension within the multiplicity of spaces available to a viewer, albeit it one untied from the avatar. The competing elements of AI- and avatar-space, for instance, coexist, and they are both embedded within the game-world according to the same avatar-grounded perspective, first or third person. In info-space, by contrast, a gamer is presented with an additional view that cannot be attributed to the avatar first- or third-person perspective.

The most obvious of these info-spaces is the status bars which give the gamers all the information they need to know about the health of their avatar, as well as which options they have available to them for how to fight. Although not active in the same sense as the avatar, these status bars operate within the game's architecture as attractors which can determine the choice of action available to a gamer. If there are no grenades, then that strategy is unavailable; if there is no oxygen, then the avatar cannot remain underwater; if the bullet-time egg timer turns yellow, time is slowing down further. While not as aggressive as other attractors under the control of the AI-space, status bars nevertheless have the ability to alter the strategies of the gamer, especially when they need something to top up their health, weapons, battery power and so forth.[24] Even on smaller screen formats such as the PSP, screens are inscribed with the competing elements of status bars. The driving game *Midnight Club 3*, for instance, includes, in addition to the streets through which the car is driven, a map (lower left side), speed and rev. gauges (lower right side), game time and position in game (upper right, and a direction arrow upper middle).

Other competing elements within info-space more indirectly inform gamers about their choices, though the information they contain may often not be consequential or also available from other sources within the game. Nevertheless, they exist as elements gamers may activate to help with some aspect of their strategies. Again, these spaces separate off the gamer from their avatar. *Tomb Raider: Legend* includes a PDA that can be accessed via the controller and includes information about weapons, health, awards gained, time within the game level, as well as the basic instructions and back story of the level. Many other games include versions of this kind of space. *Primal*, for instance, includes a series of maps within its info-space, which can be accessed in order to help locate the avatar(s) within the game-world. Role-play games often use the info-space to keep a tally of the characters' monies, potions and weapons, which has relevance for the game play. Perhaps the most unusual and rich info-spaces are those of *Max Payne* and *Max Payne 2*. These present Max's back story in the form of a graphic novel, which is also narrated in the hard-boiled style that permeates the whole of the game. These info-spaces are unusual in that they form a cohesive narrative that can be viewed by the gamer yet also contains information relevant to the play.

To understand how a gamer encounters a game involves looking beyond the ideas of a simple immersion. Games have a complex architecture of competing elements constructed from avatar-space, AI-space, info-space as well as the hardware through which a player evokes all the actions within the game. The intersections between these different spaces are formed under the influence of a range of spatio-temporal attractors which promote some connectivities more than others. In terms of playing a game the attractors operate according to the rules of the game, ensuring that the avatar-space is continually under the constraint of the AI-space and its agents. In *Half-Life 2*, the AI agents can restrict agency for both positive and negative reasons. Friendly AI agents such as Alyx and Barney direct Freeman safely through spaces, while all the enemies aim to kill the avatar. Both of these interventions impede the choices of the gamer. Operating within such a restricted space in an action game is a primary mode of engagement, and entertainment resides in the thrill of moving through an ambush with increasing skill, while more secondary modes of engagement lie in looking around the game-world without triggering the next onslaught, as well as distributing attention between the various status bars of the avatar, seeking hidden caches of health and weapons. Playing the game allows a gamer to shift between and inhabit a number of spatio-temporal organizations.

## Games as digital encounters

What insights does playing a digital game give us about digital encounters? Andrew Darley comments:

> Computer games are machine-like: they solicit intense concentration from the player who is caught up in their mechanisms, trying to fathom and master their workings. Leaving little room for reflection other than an instrumental type of thinking that is more or less commensurate with their own workings, they offer little scope for independent initiative or deviation.
>
> (Darley 2000: 164)

Though is it true that a game elicits intense concentration from the player, in the absence of the kind of reflection that Darley privileges digital games do offer an engagement with a temporary sphere that has a disposition of its own.[25] Digital games are precisely games, and as such they are played rather reflected upon. Although the meaningfulness of this encounter may have little obvious meaning outside of the world of the game, playing a game is not without importance or meaning. As Johan Huizinga comments:

> Play is distinct from 'ordinary' life both as to locality and duration. This is the third main characteristic of play: its secludedness, its limitedness. It is 'played out' within certain limits of time and place. It contains its own course and meaning.
>
> (Huizinga 2006: 104)

If we understand play in general to be distinct from ordinary life, then play within a digital game is distinct from ordinary life as well. Although the secludedness of a game, and how its rules set limits of time and place, do appear to offer little scope for independent initiative or deviation, as I have argued above digital games offer a structure within which agency can be gained by players through the actions they evoke within the game as they engage with its architecture. But even as play within a digital game apparently operates within terms distinct from those of the actual world, it informs us about the experience of technologies more generally.

In an equivalent manner to which a game's architecture is constructed around competing elements, proliferating media create elements within the world that compete for our attention. It is a cliché to argue that the contemporary world, of every era, represents a hastening of our technologized experiences of that world, but clichés often have some element of truth embedded within them. Technologies do speed up our experience of the world and reconfigure our spatial awareness of that world, but our encounter with these processes is as multifaceted as a gamer's encounters with the architecture of a game. In the above account, I have argued that there are different kinds of spatio-temporal interfaces to be encountered by a gamer. A game is constructed from a number of competing elements, and connecting across those elements, between avatar- and AI-space, between avatar- and info-space, and so forth, is the means through which a gamer can achieve agency. The extensive virtual possibilities suggested by the numerous spatializing elements that distribute a viewer's attention are constrained by the temporal elements of the architecture. A gamer may have time to make choices as in *Myst* and part of *Tomb Raider: Legend*; they may have to work within specific time constraints established by the rules of the game (oxygen limits, hazardous materials, a motorbike ride against time); or aggressive attractors may insist on certain courses of action. All these operate against the virtual possibilities for creating connections, narrowing them down to fewer actualization pathways. An AI agent, for instance, tells Freeman to drive the boat along the water feature of *Half-Life 2*, but within those narrowed-down routes there still remain possibilities for choice and agency in reaching the endpoints. The negotiation may not be about deeper meaning, or meaningful within the world, but it is a process of engagement with a technological interface. The embodiment on offer is a multifaceted one, achieved by intersection with a number of spatio-temporal architectures, in which gamers exert as much control as they can within a system designed to limit their actions. Even the increasingly sophisticated feedback loops of game AIs only create the illusion of a reactive game. The enemy will come, no matter what a gamer does, but the pleasure lies in gaining ascendancy within the world of the game.

Although I have made a similar argument about agency in relation to competing elements in Chapter 3, encounters with games are distinctive because of the nature of the interaction between the gamer and the interface. The relationship between character, space and action is an important device for thinking through the particularities of a technological interaction. In a gaming situation, the relationship becomes unified through the presence of the gamer. The temporal conditions of a game sometimes only make sense if attended to by a gamer; for instance, an internal clock limiting a timed task in *Grand Theft Auto* becomes meaningful to the avatar and gamer through their intersection with the game-world. A character can only inhabit space, and act upon it, through the presence of the gamer at the controls of the system. In many first- and third-person games, the body of the avatar imposes the perspectival schema through which the interface is viewed.

However, when we think about those elements of the architecture existing beyond the game-world as info-spaces and hardware, we move away from the body-based perspective so familiar in western art forms. Gamers sit in front of an interface engaging with elements untied from a perspective grounded in their point of view. Yet, nevertheless, these elements are presented to gamers, available to be acted upon by them. What becomes clear here is that being ungrounded from a perspective organized around a body-centric gaze is only disembodied if that embodiment is understood to be guaranteed by a perspective based on the three-dimensionality of binocular vision, human or otherwise. The technologized vision of an interface constructed around competing elements presents an alternative perspective on the world, one in which a capacity for seeing is distributed across elements with diverse spatio-temporal compositions. Technology is deeply implicated in generating both the competing elements and our ability to be distributed through them. Competing elements in the cinema have this effect, too, but in the encounter with competing elements in the game-world the player is embedded more fully as an active component of that distributed interface.[26] The digital encounter of games is one not so much of immersion within a virtual environment, but of having their attention distributed across different spatio-temporal structures within which attractors operate to both limit and expand the possibilities of agency for gamers. And as their agency is constituted, they too become embedded as an element within the architecture of the game. They are not simply viewers in an ongoing world, but active elements in the construction of that world.

# 5

# GALLERY SPACE / TEMPORAL ZONING

> The benefit in disclosing the means with which I am working is
> that it enables the viewer to understand the experience itself as
> a construction and so, to a higher extent, allow [sic] them to
> question and evaluate the impact this experience has on them.
>
> (Olafur Eliasson, quoted in an interview with
> Susan May in May 2003: 4)

My first recollection of encountering an installation in a major art gallery is of entering a darkened space and gradually making sense of the various different components of shining lights, mirrors and models that constituted this particular exhibit. The model was of a multi-layered building edged by beams of light carefully arranged to cut across the dark space, catching at the textures, revealing depth and hinting at colours. My favourite moment was turning my head and being surprised to discover a spatial extension created by a small recess into which was projected a miniature view of part of the model that mirroring drew out in an endless extension. Looking back on this now, I recall being struck by standing within a space that existed for me, yet was not 'really there'. So used as I was to sitting and looking at such spaces in the cinema or on DVD, it seemed incredible to be able to move *inside* this construction. According to Claire Bishop, 'installation art creates a situation into which the viewer physically enters, and insists that you regard this as a singular entity' (Bishop 2005: 6).

Given the experience I describe above, the term 'immersion' might seem appropriate for thinking about an artwork into which one physically enters. Immersion is an already familiar term often used to describe the way gamers become embedded within a game-world, placed within a sensory audio-visual environment that captures their attention. This blanket term, however, obscures a more nuanced understanding of what a gamer's encounter entails. As I argued in Chapter 4, games are not so much about being immersed within a stable virtual environment, but about experiencing a series of *different* spatio-temporal structures, each of which contains attractors operating to both limit and expand the possibilities of agency for the gamer. Installations constructed using technological interfaces equally offer a viewer varied spatio-temporal structures, but these operate through a distinct spatio-temporal imperative.[1] In this chapter I pay particular attention to installations created using time-based media, as such media 'take hold' of space, and in doing so incorporate the viewer's body within the interface in diverse ways.

There are many kinds of installations, but given the central argument of this book time-based installations are of the greatest relevance, as they exploit the possibilities of technological interfaces more than installations without a strong temporal element in their organizations. Although I mainly consider recent digital works and earlier video pieces that include competing elements, I also make reference to other works as their precursors. As I stated of my brief examination of animation and digital games technologies, I do not aim for coverage of the historical chronologies of installation art, but instead look to examples demonstrating the impact of technologies on gallery spaces, and use them to work through the impact of these changes on their status as viewing interfaces.[2] The term 'installation' is relatively opaque, increasingly employed as an umbrella term as the artworks that come under its cover are extremely diverse, and may involve no moving parts, digital, video or for that matter celluloid. The *Thames and Hudson Dictionary of Art and Artists* entry for installations describes them as 'multi-media, multi-dimensional and multi-form works which are created temporarily for a particular space or site either outdoors or indoors, in a museum or gallery'. The multi-form nature of installations generates their competing elements, but this is not in itself enough to allow them to stand as examples of technological systems. For the purposes of my argument, the artwork needs also to include some kind of moving image or sound element, as these introduce the temporal qualities that are a key element of the overall experience that I address.

Generally speaking, installation art can be seen as an evolving process, no longer a static object, but as a work that unfolds in relation to both the viewer and its location, a perspective drawing attention to the ways in which a viewer engages with the work of art.[3] Although Julie Reiss suggests that 'the emphasis on space [in installation art] is ultimately geared towards creating the opportunity for an experience for a viewer' (Reiss 1999: 123), my particular interest is not about only space, but also the temporal experiences created by for a viewer by an installation through the intervention of a technology. As I have already described for digital effects cinema and games, installations are structured around competing elements, although their organizations are quite distinct from the former two examples. Where the competing elements of digital effects cinema are embedded in narrative organizations, and those of games within the architectural possibilities offered by different games platforms, both are displayed on a single screen. By contrast, the multi-form state of installations is constructed through competing elements often placed in physically distinct locations. In a more spatially dispersed organization, rather than being only accessible through a single screen such as a computer or television monitor or via projection, time-based elements can exist in a number of different ways – as an array of monitors or a series of projections embedded within the spatial organization of several elements.

I am not suggesting that these more physically dispersed organizations have occurred as a direct consequence of digital technologies, as projection of celluloid on multiple screens, such as William Rahan's *Surface Tension* (1975), pre-exists these works. Over the last 30 years, however, video, and subsequently digital, recordings and projections on multiple television or projection screens have become a more common practice, a movement paralleling the expansion of technologies into the world-view more generally. In the high-technology environments of many cultures, looking at space, whether it is a building draped in the hardware of plasma screens or a different place made accessible through the technological connections afforded by webcams or rapidly uploaded digital stills, technology is interceding in how we look at the world. In this context, the organizations of installations provide another means of looking at the relationship between viewers and interfaces. Their distinct-iveness lies in the ways the spatial experience of distributed attention is extended into a more physical dimension, and this may or may not involve being literally caught in place by the time-based attractor of a technological system.

The impact of time-based elements on a viewer's engagement with spatial organ-izations is visible in Michael Landy's *Scrapheap Services* (1995).[4] This installation has been exhibited as a room-sized exhibit at the Tate Modern, and is constructed around a number of different elements. These include a hanging video monitor playing an 'advert', five standing figures, dummies dressed in red jumpsuits, static representations of figures undertaking various activities associated with rubbish clearing, two large signs, several bins and sets of bin bags, and finally a large metallic rubbish mulcher painted in red. Strewn across the floor like autumnal leaves are paper figures, which the dummies collect and decant into the red vulture machine (see Figure 5.1). In the Tate Modern exhibition of this artwork, the number of people entering was limited, and their response to the hanging video monitor, the only time-based element of the installation, was revealing. Many people who entered the room stalled in their progress into the depth of the room because they were drawn to the audio-visual playback of the video, standing looking up at it for a few minutes before wandering across the room, headed towards the exit, perhaps taking some time to look more closely at the different figures inside the room.[5] Such a pattern of viewing can be described through the model I have been developing throughout this book.

To put this briefly, *Scrapheap Services'* competing elements form an architecture defined by its spatio-temporal organization. The space created by each of the com-peting elements as they are spread across the room is under pressure from the timespan configured by the time-based interface of the video. Although each com-peting element has the capacity to draw and distribute viewers' attention throughout the space of the room, causing them to move in particular directions within the three-dimensional space of the room, the time-based element tends to attract them more strongly. For instance, the small red rubbish bin towards the corner of the room has less visual pulling power than the large red vulture machine that stands at the far end of the room, and this in turn is trumped by the audio-visual video element that catches people's attention as soon as they enter the space of the installation. The

*Figure 5.1* The video monitor of *Scrapheap Services* is visible in the upper left of the image. The other elements of the installation are spread throughout the exhibition space. Michael Landy, *Scrapheap Services* (1995) © the artist. Courtesy of Thomas Dane, London.

capacity of an installation to distribute attention operates, then, beyond the dimensions of a screen, working instead according to the spatio-temporal co-ordinates of a more physically dispersed architecture.

If this organization is taken as a spatial snapshot, viewers might appear to be able freely to negotiate their way through the installation, drawn by the arrangement of the individual elements, with the virtual routes for moving between the different elements defined by their combinations and permutations. Since *Scrapheap Services* includes a temporal element which functions as an attractor, such a snapshot only offers an abstract mapping out of potential pathways through the installation, as within any system an attractor acts as an influence drawing many of the possible routes towards and around it. The attractor is not, however, an end-point in itself, as attractors only reconfigure the multiplicity of equally likely outcomes so that some routes become more likely than others. In an installation, each element is situated in a particular space, and in standing in its own spatio-temporal location precludes a route passing into that same spatio-temporal location. Nevertheless, it draws other routes towards it, and in doing so deforms the system so that out of all the virtual possibilities only some will become actualities. In *Scrapheap Services* the video monitor, with its mode of direct address to anyone walking into the installation, drew many viewers in its direction, with the large size of the vulture subsequently drawing viewers towards the far end of the space, from which they finally exited.

Each competing element of *Scrapheap Services* contributes to the structure of the installation, and viewers' agency lies in how they move through the installation. This includes both whether or not they visit all its different elements and also the interpretation they make of the piece, according to their dispositions and the content of the installation itself – a meditation on the 'waste of human capital caused by firms shedding surplus staff in pursuit of cost-cutting and greater productivity' (Rainbird 2004). Taken too superficially the idea of agency might imply that there is freedom to make one's way through the installation as one wishes, but, as I argued in an earlier chapter, just as a social agent operates within a multivalent grid of habitus and field, a viewer operates within the structure of an installation. As such, the video monitor places a constriction on the open play of the installation, a constriction that can be understood as a structure with which viewers negotiate in order to generate an understanding of the installation, acquiring degrees of agency as they do so. Equally, the video monitor reveals the impact of a technology on a system; more specifically, the impact of a time-based technology on its spatial dimension. Through the process of negotiating with the structure, viewers also, then, experience the impact of a time-based technology that is embodied in their encounter with perturbations of the spatio-temporal interface of the installation.

In the following, I explore this idea more fully, drawing out the ways different installations offer a series of experiences of technological systems, sometimes allowing viewers to simply watch, at other times enfolding them within the system itself, and finally literally incorporating the viewer as a part of the installation. This discussion will introduce two sets of concerns. First, I examine the organizational differences between installations and the other media I have approached in order to lay out the distinctive way a viewer is placed by installation. Second, I look at a range of different installations in order to explore in more detail the kinds of technological embodiments that they offer.

## Entering the interface

Throughout, I have used the ideas of competing elements and architecture to approach digital effects cinema, split-screen live-action cinema and animations, as well as digital games. Each stands as an interface through which viewers encounter the text as technological systems, as well as story- and game-worlds. The presence of competing elements has the effect of inscribing the interface, making the technological status of the image and sounds more explicit. At the same time they generate an architecture through which a viewer or gamer gains agency, with different organizations offering distinct kinds of engagements. As I have just described in relation to *Scrapheap Services*, time-based installations too offer interfaces through which we can gain insights about technological encounters. Just like cinema and digital games, time-based installations constructed around competing elements operate by distributing attention, requiring viewers or gamers to enact a choice-making process through which they can synthesize a meaning from the interplay of sounds and images, one upon which they can then build an interpretation with its own attendant agencies and identifications. Although my approach of using a model based on competing elements and architectures could tend towards erasing the diversity of media forms discussed in this book, these vary from each other in many ways, including their formal organizations, content and modes of exhibition. For my purposes, these forms also offer distinctive spatio-temporal organizations and, importantly, they can be characterized by the means through which a viewer intersects with these organizations.

To keep in place a sense of the distinctiveness of the different interfaces, I have used the relationship between character, space and action to tease out the relationships between the elements of their spatio-temporal organizations, distinguishing seamless and inscribed interfaces in digital effects cinema, split-screen live-action and animated cinemas, as well as the unifying position of the gamer in digital games. In installations we find yet another kind of organization. Though at first sight using the relationship between character, space and action to approach installations may seem a bit too much of a stretch, staying with this formulation is useful since it distinguishes between the interfaces and the consequent differences in the encounters a viewer may have with these interfaces. Beginning with character: many installations include a figure, whether as a still or moving image, a voice or a sculpture, but these figures rarely equate to characters in the same sense as we find in narrative cinema. As such, the role of an installation 'character', perhaps more appropriately called a figure, is not necessarily to exert any unifying principle over the space and action of the installation. Instead, the character/figure is only one element amongst several, and is not privileged as the site through which meaning emerges. Character/figure, space and action, then, can be thought of as separate entities, each of which makes contributions to an interface, but which operate differently according to the individual installation.

Given this, it is also necessary to revisit the terms 'space' and 'action', as without the presence of character they take on other roles as structuring elements within the organization of an installation. In my earlier discussions of the interplay of character, space and action, I have taken action to mean the actions of characters within the story-world. In the context of an installation, it seems appropriate to state that it is the space of the installation which acts, and, furthermore, that the space of the installation acts directly on the viewer, rather than via a story-world. Although such a perspective immediately locates the viewer in a distinctive way at the interface of an installation, it is in some ways also self-evident, as artworks are spatial organizations whose expressive 'work' is to provoke a response in the viewer. But the presence of a time-based technology in the installation reveals something that remains only implied in the statement that artworks are spatial organizations that act on someone, which is that an interface is temporal as well as spatial. If space is understood to act upon viewers, a view that in any case relies on a sense of temporality since an action is durational, then a time-based technology adds a more explicit temporality to the action of an installation on viewers as they encounter its interface. Since moving image technologies and soundscapes have a temporal axis, when included in an interface they have the potential to intercede by shifting the viewing experience away from an engagement with the space of the artwork towards an engagement with its spatio-temporal organization.

This idea broadly links back to my earlier introduction of the concept of time-space in relation to some digital effects cinema. Timespaces emerge as sections within a digital effects film when space need no longer be simply understood as being contained by a unified relationship between character, space and action. A timespace is a temporalized space having meaning beyond supporting the actions of characters, and competes with character-based actions for a viewer's attention. When present together these competing elements form the structure of a complex linear interface, but since they operate within a narrative organization their impact nevertheless remains in the service of the narrative. In *The Matrix*, for instance, the effects can act as vehicles narrating the story of the conflict between the humans and machines, as much as the characters within the story-world. By contrast, the spatio-temporal interface of an installation addresses the viewer, its competing elements operating directly as perceptual cues to be made sense of by the viewer, rather than already having the cohesion of an overarching narrative. To more fully articulate the interplay of character/figure, space and action I consider two particular installations: one built around several kinds of figures but no characters, Fred Wilson's time-based work *Me and It* (1995); and Bruce Nauman's installation *Going Around the Corner Piece* (1970), which includes a figure by virtue of incorporating the body of its viewer. Through these two pieces I lay out how competing elements are more fully dispersed within a gallery space, and in being so organized allow viewers to enter into the dispersed and complex architecture of time-based installations, becoming part of the process of the installation.

*Me and It* consists of three competing elements, two time-based video loops played through separate monitors and a covered static display of figurines; all three elements are arranged in a row to be frontally viewed.[6] Although the frontal display precludes a viewer literally entering the space constructed by the installation, the ability of the spatio-temporal organization to act on viewers requires not simply that they are present, but that they act as the unifying point through which the perceptual cues of the three competing elements meet and gain meaning. Looking at *Me and It* in more detail, the covered display is located at the centre and consists of miniatures depicting African-American stereotypes recognizable as domestic slaves from the plantation era. On the right-hand screen (as faced by the viewer) there is a looped video of a figure, Fred Wilson, contorting his features in an attempt to recreate the expressions of the figurines. On the left-hand screen a second video loop shows a set of figures being smashed with a hammer. Between them, the display and monitors create competing elements constructed from their visual elements and also the sounds of smashing. As viewers stand in front of this installation they are invited by the interplay of elements to distribute their attention between them so as to make sense of what they are watching.

In terms of spatial structures, there are three elements to look at, but since two have a temporal axis generated from their status as looped video footage, viewers are not able to exert full temporal control over how they watch the images. Instead, they have to negotiate a way through the static standing figures and the continually running loops of competing sounds and imagery. This quality marks a distinction between spatio-temporal competing elements and a series of static photographs or canvases seen in the same location. A triptych of canvases, for instance, is also constructed from three related images, but as static works the viewer can contemplate each singly or compare between the three, but always on their temporal terms.[7] Even Gerhard Richter's *48 Portraits* (1972, 1998), which creates an extremely large array of images to look at, still allows viewers to make their own decisions over what they do or do not look at.[8]

The competing elements of *Me and It*, the two monitors and the figurine display, form the architecture of the viewing interface, with the looped videos acting as attractors drawing attention away from each other and the static figurines. Although there are numerous virtual possibilities for making sense of the intersections of the three sets of images, in watching through any particular cycle only certain actualizations will occur. While watching Wilson's facial contortions, I found my eyes sliding to the figurines, seeking out the one with an equivalent expression and then moving further along to see which figurine was being smashed. In choosing to opt for this means of looking, it would have been easy to miss Wilson's fatigued and collapsing expression as he gives up his attempts to recreate an exaggerated grin. A description of *Me and It* requires, then, not only a statement of its narrative around representation and racial stereotyping, but also access to the experience of engaging with the attractors of the installation. This includes a sense of watching and hearing the interplay of mimicry and destruction in relation to the static figurines, and of catching the moments of transition from expression to expression, where the mask of performing for the video camera slips in register. *Me and It* is about the dynamism created by the competing elements as they distribute a viewer's attention, and how that brings a liveliness to the installation's interrogation of its historical objects.

Describing installations as architectures, separating out the components that contribute to their impact, reveals something not only about experiencing the installation, but also the impact of its technological aspects. The figures of *Me and It*, though recognizable as stereotypes, are not important as characters, but because of the ways in which their expressions and gestures contribute to the overall action of the installation. The deployment of an action in this sense is linked to the installation's spatial and temporal configurations and the ways in which these provoke a response in the viewer. Some of the spatio-temporal organization is content based: it is clear that the piece is interrogating derogative racial imagery that accumulated in a particular geographic location and historical era of African-American experience. Other aspects of the spatio-temporal organization can be understood in terms of how the installation takes up space within a location and takes on temporality through its time-based media. As this description begins to make clear, the spatial term within the interplay of character, space and action is complex, not simply because it is really a spatio-temporal term, but also because it consists of the space taken up by the installation within the gallery, the environment established by the contents of the installation and the way the viewer inhabits the space in relation to the installation.

Where competing elements created from timespaces, split-screen or avatar-versus-AI-space all coexist within the frame of a single screen, creating an inscribed interface, in installations the competing elements may be spread across several screens or a single screen surrounded by elements which do not require technology: standalone figures, paintings, sculptures or textiles or furniture. While some installations are organized as a frontal array of elements, in many the viewer is able to move through or around the piece as it 'challenges the aesthetics of frontality, that is, the paradigm of cinematic screen and monitor' (de Oliveira *et al.* 2003: 167). As a consequence of their location *within* a physically dispersed array of competing elements, the viewer's engagement with an installation represents a different mode of encounter, one bringing together the artist and viewer in a discursive moment. Ronald Onorato suggests that 'the aesthetic power of installation art does not reside in the singular, commodified object but in an ability to become, rather than merely represent, the continuum of real experience by responding to specific situations' (Onorato and Davis 1997: 13). Although this is often meant in terms of how a viewer interprets the social, political or aesthetic paradigms of artwork, it could also be a statement about how installations offer a continuum of the experience of technological interfaces. Central to this continuum of experience are the ways the time-based element of an installation give a viewer a means of entry into its interface.

Over the last two decades, as installations have entered into the relative mainstream of public galleries from their beginnings in the peripheries of more experimental spaces, it has become possible to walk into a gallery space and be not entirely sure about what the experience will entail or the kind of space you are going to enter. Walking around the Open Systems exhibition at the Tate Modern was one such occasion as it drew together the work of 31 international artists to examine how art was reconceived in the late 1960s and early 1970s.[9] The exhibition focused primarily on different kinds of installation work, only some of which involved sound and/or image technologies. In the final room I encountered *Going Around the Corner Piece*, which at first glance seemed to be constructed as an interrogation of space: a solid white cube placed in the centre of a white room and taking up a least three-quarters of its volume. Taking a closer look, I saw it was indeed a cube within a room, but with the addition of four video monitors placed on the floor, one at each corner, plus four surveillance cameras placed on the opposing diagonal of the wall. These technologies alter the spatial configuration of the installation, changing the way space acts. Since the cameras are the means through which figures enter into the organization of the installation, they do more than represent a surveyed figure; instead, they place viewers at an interface where they experience surveillance, both by themselves and by anyone else who happens to be present. This experience, however, is not quite what the viewer might expect.

At first glance, the cameras look as though they are pointing into the monitor screens that will show the recorded images, and by this logic you expect to see yourself, from the back, approaching the monitor. This expectation is thwarted as the feed is linked into the monitor around the corner, setting up the unexpected spatio-temporality of the piece. On turning the corner to face the monitor around the corner, you only briefly see yourself in motion as your receding back approaches and turns the corner; to be fully visible requires standing still at the corner's right-angle. Although *Going Around the Corner Piece* can be described as an interrogation of how 'narcissism and voyeurism are simultaneously nurtured and frustrated' (Criqui 1997), engaging with *Going Around the Corner Piece* also reveals the distinctive way a viewer encounters the interface and becomes enfolded within the technology of a system. To encounter the interface viewers engage with its competing elements by looking and seeing the cube in space, noticing the monitors and cameras, and so expect to find themselves visible within it. The competing elements are therefore completed by the appearance of the body of the viewer. Although the model of competing elements that I have presented requires that a viewer completes a synth-esis of meaning from the competing elements, and so is always embodied to some degree, the presence of a viewer is different in each of the interfaces.

For digital effects and split-screen cinema, I argued that the process of making a meaning from competing elements is embodied because it involves drawing together attention that has been distributed. To carry out this synthesis requires an action embed-ded within the spatio-temporality of the progression of the images, an action that entails an orientation to the competing elements. However, there is no trace of the body of the viewer within the text, as the actions of a synthesis are enacted as pre-dominantly mental ones.[10] With digital games a trace of bodily presence does exist, since the game does not play without a gamer's active engagement with a controller of some kind. Online games evoke a stronger sense of a gamer's presence, since multiplayer games often rely on interaction between the players online, as well as via their avatars in the game-world. The ability of gamers to create their own avatars and exchange materials online extends this presence. The actual body, however, is not aurally or visually evident, beyond the stand-in of the avatar icons and/or text.

Installations, by contrast, presume the presence of the viewer: 'installation pro-vides places for exchange in which the audience becomes an integral part of the work' (de Oliveira *et al.* 2003: 107). In some time-based installations, the body of the viewer is literally incorporated into its organization, and in *Going Around the Corner Piece*, to be visible, at least to oneself, involves either of two actions: walking away or standing still. In their different ways these two options pose a conundrum that works against the expectations set up by the installation.[11] Given the cameras and monitors we might well expect to more fully see ourselves, but can only glimpse our receding backs as we turn the corner; to see our own faces requires that we stand still on the threshold of stepping out of view. As the room is set up with directional arrows there is a sense of breaking the rules by standing still and, as the piece operates through the sign system of internal surveillance monitors, there is an expectation of motion along corridors. Whatever expectations we may have of the installation, how we experience it, take part in or resist its structures, making sense of *Going Around the Corner Piece* involves a series of embodied adaptive negotiations with the installation in which a viewer can acquiesce to the parameters of the camera and monitor or be caught in the bind of resisting the movement so central to the piece.

Installations, both time-based and spatial, offer a range of possibilities through which a viewer may interact with its interfaces. And just as narrative frameworks or game rules decrease the likelihood of some modes of interaction while at the same time increasing the likelihood of others, installations have thicker and thinner routes of engagement. For instance, the space of *Going Around the Corner Piece* is expanded by its camera technology, integrating the spatial deformation of a solid cube nesting within an unfilled space with the technologized reconfiguration of being able to see oneself receding from the camera. The relatively undifferentiated space of the cube nested within the room is therefore marked by the technology, which, in addition to reconfiguring its spatial organization, imposes a temporality that places a more rigorous limit on how the installation can be experienced. The attractor of the technology limits the temporal possibilities of the piece, which in turn elicits a limited set of instances for engaging with the piece. Viewers can walk around the installation, they can stand on the corner, stalling the process, or they can walk away, leave through the door or stand on the periphery of the system. Through these different modes they can engage in an interaction with the installation that is either interlaced or undone. There is little in the way of in-between.

In an equivalent way to online games, where a player intersects with the game and other gamers, the presence of other people adds a further dimension to the experience of an installation. Although this is something not well described in relation to film-viewing, the audience also makes a difference there. How many times has a film seemed funnier because you have caught the mood of the crowd, and how much scarier has it been because someone in the audience is triggering everyone else with their shrieks? Equally, how many times have you felt affronted because the crowd thinks something is funny and you do not? Similarly, other people in an installation make a difference, as they can get in the way, make intriguing or irritating remarks, or add to the installation as they allow themselves to be incorporated into or refuse its operations; whichever way, they add another dimension of possibilities. *Going Around the Corner Piece* comes alive with other people present, even if they only engage with the structures imposed by the technology. When I saw the piece two women already in the room decided to play catch-up, and in doing so exploited the interplay of visibility/invisibility established through the relationship between the camera and monitors.

Entering the interface of an installation represents another kind of encounter with competing elements and technological interfaces. Although similar to other texts in terms of having an architecture of competing elements which distribute a viewer's attention, there are a number of differences. Using the interplay of character, space and action to mark these differences, characters do not control the meaning of an installation, though figures do contribute to the space of an installation. Installation spaces are often physically dispersed, creating a different kind of interface for a viewer, as well as being the site of action. As I have suggested through *Me and It* and

*Going Around the Corner Piece*, there are two consequences to this dispersal. Installations, whether they include time-based media or not, engage viewers not to simply show them something, but to act, to make them part of the process through which the installation is completed. This is not simply meant in the sense of viewers activating the meanings of a text as they consume it, but separate elements of the installation converge on the body of the viewer, making them the locus at which some of the possible meanings are activated. In the following, I pursue this idea more fully by considering the impact of technologies on gallery space, and subsequently on the agency of a viewer who enters into those spaces.

## The taking of space: temporal incursions

The increasing presence of moving image and sound technologies has changed the spatio-temporal organizations of artworks within gallery spaces. The claim that '[c]inema provides the dominant cultural experience [of immersion] that Installation must explore' (de Oliveira *et al.* 2003: 23) suggests not only that cinema's interface is more prevalent, but also that it is also somehow all-encompassing. Central to such a claim is the term 'immersion', which I have already discussed in relation to games, but which is worth revisiting since it is a concept that has been used in a number of different ways. Immersion refers to the total occupation of the mind, and is associated with ideas of absorption, engrossment and enthralment. It is 'a type of experience in which the subjective awareness ... appears to merge with the artwork, so as to create a sensation of a new, more powerful, experience of totality' (de Oliveira *et al.* 2003: 49). Perhaps because the idea of spectacle in cinema studies had been so influential in the decades prior to the emergence of immersion as a critical term, the latter has become strongly associated with spatial organizations rather than temporal ones.

The use of the term to describe virtual environments encourages this connection further, as these aim to create virtual spaces in which users can believe themselves to be embedded within a space. Virtual spaces are constructed with an emphasis on display, so that their users can visually and aurally take in and explore the environments. For instance, the National Center for Supercomputing Applications (NCSA) in the USA has created CAVES (Cave (or Computer) Automatic Virtual Environments), in which scientists are able to look more closely at digitally modelled hurricanes or DNA sequences.[12] Art installations have been quick to exploit these new technologies; for instance, works based on a similar principle include Jeffrey Shaw's iterations on a digital city in *The Legible City* (1989–91) and *The Distributed Legible City* (1998). In *The Legible City* viewers sat on a stationary bicycle and 'moved' through streets projected in front of them. The buildings of the streets were not, however, of conventional icons, but of three-dimensional words that named the buildings. The 'cyclist' controlled his or her speed and direction, and made his or her own way within the virtual space. There were three versions of *The Legible City*: Manhattan, Amsterdam and Karlsruhe, with the Manhattan variant one of the very first interactive installations.

*The Distributed Legible City* included all the opportunities of the original version but introduced a multi-user capacity. In *The Distributed Legible City* two or more cyclists interacted via remote locations, with each simultaneously present in the virtual environment. These cyclists could accidentally or intentionally meet each other, and, as well as the architecture, saw abstract avatar representations of each other. Once close enough, the cyclists were able to communicate through the technologies of the interface. Instead of being the main focus of attention, the textual landscape coexisted with the avatars, becoming a location for communications. As a website for the project comments: 'In other words the artwork changes from being merely a visual experience, into becoming a visual ambiance for social exchange between visitors to that artwork'.[13] The closest mainstream cinematic equivalent is three-dimensional i-Max films, in which a viewer may feel more surrounded as the sounds and imagery of the scenes appear much closer, sitting out from the flat screen, a feature especially exploited in travelogue-type films of pyramids, shipwrecks, safaris, though also used in animated features such as *Alien Adventure 3-D*. *Superman Returns* (2006) is the first feature to also be released for 3-D exhibition at i-Max cinemas, with segments of 3-D imagery included in the otherwise 2-D experience.

Such descriptions privilege the immersive spatiality of these technologies, which consequently tends to overlook their temporalities. This is perhaps unsurprising since the works themselves emphasize the experience of space rather than the time spent inside their spaces. Other works, however, do draw attention to the temporalities of immersion, creating complex interfaces revealing the ability of technology to frame and reframe the world around us. A brief look at how these interfaces have developed gives some insight into how technologies reframe not only the spatiality of the world, but also its temporalities. In the following section I explore how the inclusion of time-based media in artworks creates interfaces through which viewers experience technologies in different ways. As I move through this section I look at the way viewers are increasingly incorporated into the interface. As such they are embodied not only through their agency in constructing a synthesis of meaning from competing elements, but also through the way their physical presence is addressed by the artwork.

Historically, galleries have placed a greater emphasis on space than time. Whatever the ideological intentions behind creating museum and gallery space, the effect was to create a space in which art could be contemplated. Commenting on this aspect of gallery space in the late nineteenth and early twentieth centuries, Brian O'Doherty states:

> Unshadowed, white, clean, artificial – the space is devoted to the technology of esthetics. Works of art are mounted, hung, scattered for study. Their ungrubby surfaces are untouched by time and its vicissitudes. Art exists in an eternity of display, and though there is lots of 'period' (late modern), there is no time.
>
> (O'Doherty 1999: 15)

Influential for introducing the concept of the 'white cube' of the gallery, O'Doherty also thinks through how the frame and edge of an artwork establish a relationship with a viewer within gallery spaces. Whereas late nineteenth-century art was hung as an assemblage of self-contained entities, over the twentieth century various movements interrogated the boundaries of art by exploring the edges of work, shapes of frames, as well as moving beyond the canvas to create environments and installations: 'space now is not just where things happen; things make space happen' (O'Doherty 1999: 39).

Going over the edge of the canvas has been explored in many different works, including *Salon de Madame B, à Dresden* and *Chocolate Room*. Designed in the mid-1920s, though only exhibited in 1970 in New York, in *Salon de Madame B, à Dresden* Piet Mondrian took his distinctive colour and grid systems off the flat canvas and placed them on the six surfaces of a room. Similarly, Ed Ruscha's *Chocolate Room* (1970) immerses its viewers within a room whose walls and ceiling are hung with chocolate-coated silk-screen panels, leaving no distance between the edge of the artwork and the room; indeed, the room is the artwork. *Chocolate Room* is an unusual piece because of its olfactory dimension. As is often true in exhibitions, it is possible to wander into a room and be unsure of where you are and what you are looking at. *Chocolate Room* can be one such space, as people stand looking bemusedly at the brown walls, not quite registering the wave of chocolate on the air they are inhaling. It is only when this occurs that they realize they are within an artwork, immersed in a chocolate space.[14]

The incorporation of technological elements into works of art alters the spatial constructions of artworks even further, although their impact on temporality depends on the extensiveness of the time-based production of sound and images. Technologies have the potential to incorporate a temporal dimension to the explorations of gallery spaces, and in doing so things can make time as well as space happen. In exhibitions in which artworks stand or hang in gallery spaces, viewers walk through, taking the work in, standing before it, looking, rejecting or enjoying it. All of these actions occur in a space where viewers have control over the temporality of their looking. While potential distractions might include a crowd, or other demands on one's time, static artworks are available to be looked at for as long as a viewer wants. Technology alters this aspect of a viewer's relationship with the piece when it takes space over by adding temporality. The visibility of this temporal incursion is, however, contingent on the balance between the spatial and temporal impact of the technology, or, put another way, how a technology can make time happen in space. For instance, looking at the earliest time-based works reveals how technologies may alter the kinds of imagery produced, but it does not follow that this is experienced as a temporal transformation. Even if a spatial organization is contingent on a technological mechanism, the temporal axis may remain apparently fixed.

Although installation art, a name given to works from the 1970s onwards, is most frequently associated with technological interventions, earlier twentieth-century artists also used machines in their work, including Marcel Duchamp and Man Ray's

*Rotary Glass Plates* (1920) and Laszlo Moholy-Nagy's *Light Space Modulator* (1930). Moholy-Nagy captured the astonishing light effects created by the apparatus *Light Space Modulator*, a sculpture composed of continuously rotating panels cut from glass, metal and wood, illuminated in such a way that they cast dramatic shadows against the wall, in the film *Lightplay: Black-White-Grey* (1930). Christiane Paul suggests that both these works are precursors of digital art because they are rule governed in the sense that they rely on their machine components to create their imagery:

> Duchamp's *Rotary Glass Plates* (*Precision Optics*), created in 1920 with Man Ray, consisted of an optical machine and invited users to turn on the apparatus and stand at a certain distance from it in order to see the effect unfold, while the influence of Moholy-Nagy's kinetic light sculptures and his idea of virtual volumes – 'the outline or trajectory presented by an object in motion' – can be traced in numerous digital installations.
>
> (Paul 2003: 13)

Duchamp's *Rotoreliefs* (1935) also rely on a machine (a turntable) to turn painted discs, which when viewed in motion gain depth perspective, taking on a three-dimensional shape.[15] Although these examples demonstrate the impact of introducing mechanisms to an artwork, they also reveal how this does not in itself establish a strong experience of temporality, since even though rule governed they nonetheless revel in a hypnotic spatial immersive quality. The set rotations of *Rotoreliefs* are mesmerizing, and the shifting patterns of light and dark in *Lightplay*, along with the glimpses of the intricacies of the mechanical objects themselves, are fascinating, and draw a viewer to stand by in order look and see.[16] Despite the obviousness of the rule-governed or mechanistic elements of these two installations, it is the hypnotic quality that has the greatest impact, as the temporal axis of the piece does not place limits on a viewer's spatial engagement. The temporal quality of both works, though defining of their spatiality, remains submerged behind the viewer's experience of the spatial. The organization of the elements is balanced in such as way as to obscure the technological capture of temporality, while the pioneering possibilities for spatial display are the primary emphasis of the piece.

The impact of technology on the temporal experience of viewing becomes more marked when the sensation of time begins to exist beyond the boundaries established by the viewer. This sensation of time taken into hand by another order of control is very clear in the experience of looking at Marcel Broodthaers' *Bateau-Tableau* (1973).[17] A slide-projection installation consisting of 80 slides, *Bateau-Tableau* is based on a familiar image, a nineteenth-century oil painting of a sailboat at sea that includes a rowing boat with three figures in the lower left foreground. Broodthaers has taken photographs at varying distances from the painting, giving the impression of someone's attention shifting between a full view of the canvas and one moving over the detail of a specific area of the canvas. These include two of the men in the rowing boat, the colour detail of one of the men's jackets and extreme close-ups of the brushstrokes, so close that the content of the painting gives way to

147

the materiality of paint and visible evidence of an artist's hand. One interpretation is as follows:

> The slide projection, *Bateau-Tableau* (1973), breaks down the iconography of the pictorial and symbolic and reflects Broodthaers' interest to displace realistic representations. By projecting a slide of a traditional maritime painting of a ship, Broodthaers accentuates the basic elements of the art object to make visible and decode its materiality.[18]

This interpretation, however, does not remark on the central place of technology in controlling the viewer's gaze. Not only does Broodthaers' choice of areas on the painting's spatiality direct a viewer's gaze, but the timing mechanism of the slide projector denies viewers control over the time of their contemplation, either making them wait too long for the next image or not giving them enough time to look at the one displayed. *Bateau-Tableau*, then, controls a viewer's spatio-temporal relationship to a work of art, and this control establishes the primary point of engagement, rather than the painting, which is arguably secondary in this particular installation. The 'work' of the installation is to take over the process by which viewers direct their attention across an image, as their agency is reduced to the decision to stay or move on.

Another work which controls a viewer's spatio-temporal relationship to an artwork is Sam Taylor-Wood's *Still Life* (2001), in which a temporal dimension is added to a work that overtly recalls and relies on the tradition of still-life paintings.[19] *Still Life* is a short DVD-based film projected via a framed plasma screen. At first glance, if you happen upon the beginning of the loop, *Still Life* gives the illusion of being a typical painting of its kind. A succulent selection of apples, pears, plums, grapes and peaches is arranged in a flat wicker bowl on a wooden table, carefully lit to pick up the fruit's rich colour tones. The only oddity is the twentieth-century biro placed in the foreground near the bowl on the table (see Figure 5.2). Over 3 minutes and 44 seconds, the fruit decays, beginning to soften and finally rot into brown mulch, puffing out fungus that expands and contracts over surfaces as it encroaches beyond the limits of the bowl to cover areas of the table. The images are carefully resolved into a smooth transition, and only the collapsing peach and the peculiar motion of the flies towards the end of the loop draw attention to the time-lapse technique. *Bateau-Tableau* and *Still Life* present the two opposite extremes of temporal experience. *Bateau-Tableau*, in taking agency away from the viewer, makes its technological intervention both evident and disruptive, while *Still Life*'s seamless progression displaces its obvious technological intervention into the background, and in doing so gives its viewers access to temporal immersion. The interest of *Still Life* lies not in its spatial composition but in its temporal decomposition. *Bateau-Tableau* and *Still Life*, then, draw attention to their technological construction, placing some degree of emphasis on how they alter the processes through which a viewer engages with or approaches an artwork.

Interfaces inscribed by competing elements have the capacity to take this temporal shift further. The dispersed competing elements offer a more complex architecture

*Figure 5.2 Still Life* is a formal composition recalling still-life paintings. Over its duration of 3 minutes and 44 seconds, the fruit decays, puffing out mould before collapsing in on itself. Sam Taylor-Wood, *Still Life* (2001) 35mm Film/DVD; © the artist. Courtesy of Jay Jopling/White Cube, London.

and agency through which a viewer might encounter the installation, but they also complicate the ways in which temporality can take hold of the spaces of an image. Nam Jun Paik is a central figure in the development of time-based video installations using television monitors in which 'the individual image becomes part of a total composition – all these are possibilities for video artists, ways of incorporating time as another dimension in the field of sculpture' (Herzogenrath 1988: 16). Paik's *Video Fish* (1975) includes a linear array of television monitors. In front of each were placed equivalently sized fish tanks containing live goldfish and plants.[20] The goldfish swam in front of various kinds of video footage, including the dancer Merce Cunningham, airplanes and swimming fish, weaving together the natural and the synthetic. The organization of the installation distributes a viewer's attention both across its face and into its depth, since the different sets of imagery draw a viewer's eyes and are additionally refracted through fish swimming across the visual field. The interplay of these multiple time-based images establishes a temporality by virtue of a viewer's experience of the continually changing competing elements.

Unlike in *Bateau-Tableau*, the technology, though ultimately controlling in *Video Fish*, creates competing elements, establishing an architecture in which the space and time of the installation are organized so that viewers are able to exert agency over how they view the different elements. As David Joselit suggests, Paik creates 'a dynamic field of patterns that is alternatively overwhelming and mesmerising' (Joselit 2000: 2). The mesmerizing quality of *Video Fish*, similar to the rotating patterns of *Lightplay*, is counteracted by the continuity of dispersed and fragmentary action. This is an interface that draws you in, offers spatial immersion while in the same moment refusing the kind of temporal immersion evident in *Still Life*. With *Video Fish* it is not possible to simply contemplate time and experience it as a seamless duration. Instead, the durational interface is multiple, and it is possible to attend to only some elements out of many, a process which again exposes the partiality of experience. A consequence of the presence of competing elements is to emphasize that experience emerges out of a multiplicity of lived-times, with the individual a figure who is embodied according to choices contingent on the availability of a limited set of elements from within a larger construction. Such partiality is a quality of any time-based interface inscribed by competing elements, though its pressure or discomfort on an individual varies. In digital effects the narrative trajectory provides the 'payback' covering over any losses, as do the narrative structures of split-screen cinemas. Digital games, too, distract from the gaps in their architecture through their goal-oriented and insistent AI agents. Installations, lacking a narrative or game organizations, leave it to the viewer to mind the gap.

How viewers mind the gap, how they allow themselves to become entwined with an installation, embodies their experience of the technological interface. With *Video Fish* exposure of the partiality of experience revealed by the competing temporal and spatial elements is far from unpleasant, perhaps because swimming fish, even when embedded within a complex array of elements, are relaxing to watch. By contrast, Bruce Nauman's multi-monitor installations employ a confrontational mode of engagement. In Nauman's larger scale 4×3 stacked array of screens, *Violent Incident* (1986), the increasingly violent gestural and aural actions of a mixed-sex couple are reiterated in different ways, confronting the viewer with violence escalating from a mean joke to murder within 18 seconds.[21]

The scenario is a simple dinner party where one of the figures plays a joke, pulling a chair out from under the other and causing them to fall; the initial response of goosing rapidly moves from shouting to slapping and stabbing, and culminates in murder. Using hired actors, Nauman orchestrated the action in different ways. Variations include the reversal of male/female roles so that both a man and a woman instigate the violence; a sequence of a rehearsal where the director's instructions are audible; and, slow motion segments of the chair-pulling action. These different iterations of the same actions abut one another on the array of screens, so that the linearity of one sequence dissipates as it connects into the linearity of another. As this occurs, even the most banal of the early gestures becomes more fraught with aggressive meaning, as the later violence, which coexists with it on the array, infuses everything on the multiple-screen interface. The confrontational nature of the rapidly escalating and repetitive violence makes *Violent Incident* an uncomfortable interface. Its complex architecture gives plenty of scope for a viewer to exert agency in making sense of the different images, allowing a spatio-temporal engagement with the interface; but, inflected by the tensions provoked by the sounds and imagery of the piece, the engagement is a fractious one.

One of the defining features of installations is the way they place the viewer as a figure who completes the piece, the pivot around which the actions of the spatio-temporal elements forge a dynamic interplay. Installations whose spatial organizations allow the viewer to move 'within' their spaces embed viewers in a more physically assertive way, literally surrounding them, allowing the body of the viewer to be more visibly present within the operations of the installation. The potential to surround the viewer in the shift away from frontality can be seen by looking at two of Bruce Nauman's smaller installations, *Good Boy, Bad Boy* (1985) and *Clown Torture* (1987). *Good Boy, Bad Boy* relies on frontal display, and its use of two actors (Tucker Smallwood and Joan Lancaster) looking directly into camera initially creates a more intimate engagement with the interface. This mode of engagement begins to break down through the duration of the aural dimension of the installation, as viewers almost feel as though they are being torn between the two competing elements.

The soundspace of *Good Boy, Bad Boy* is created by the two talking heads speaking the same words, 100 phrases with the same basic structure: 'I was a good boy. You were a good boy. We were good boys. That was good.' Each set of statements cycles through this conjugation and the variations include: I was a good girl; I am a virtuous man; I am an evil man; I'm alive; I play; I like to shit; I pay. The incantation ends on 'I don't want to die. You don't want to die. We don't want to die. This is fear of death.' Initially the two are in synch, but as they loop through repetitions of the phrases, shifting from a performance with flattened emotional cadence to one of extreme anger, the individual speech patterns of the two actors become dissonant – two voices saying the same phrases are heard several beats apart. Making sense of the whole involves viewers in distributing their attention across the visual and aural interfaces, and having to make the effort to choose between what to hear and what to see by shifting between the determining structures of the screens and voices. In standing in front of this installation, the impact of its space, created by the figures on the monitor, is to act by pulling the viewer across different axes of the competing voices and competing images, a process that involves 'filling space and taking up time'.[22] The sense of being surrounded is stronger in *Good Boy, Bad Boy* because its direct address of talking heads fills up space. When this becomes confrontational, through both its lack of synchrony and increasing aggression, the effort of remaining in front of the shouting faces is pronounced, a process that evokes a stronger feeling of physical orientation within the installation.

Lack of synchrony is also a device of Nauman's *Clown Torture* (1987). Two monitors, each displaying a clown figure, face each other across the diagonal of a room, their voices filling the space with a repetitious: 'It was a dark and stormy night. Three men were sitting around a campfire. One of the men said, "Tell us a story Jack." And Jack said, "It was a dark and stormy night. Three men were sitting around a campfire. One of the men said, 'Tell us a story Jack'. And Jack said, 'It was a dark and stormy night. . . .'"' The clown's frustration is expressed in his different vocal deliveries of this same loop. Integrated into these monologues are peals of laughter, which grate against the words of the speaking clown. In the version of *Clown Torture* I saw, the two monitors were placed in a diagonal of a small square room that effectively formed a corridor, ensuring the viewers had to pass between the competing images.[23] Unlike the frontal display of *Me and It*, *Video Fish*, *Violent Incident* and *Good Boy, Bad Boy*, *Clown Torture* requires viewers to more fully change their physical orientation if they are going to engage with the piece, as to look between both screens you had to almost fully turn your body. The installation in this sense surrounds the viewer, extending the process of embodiment into a physically active one as well as a mental or gestural one. In this way, perception becomes visible. Since viewers do not simply orient their audio-visual apparatus, but have to physically turn, a movement that manifests and reveals the partiality of perception, as in *Clown Torture* the viewer has to turn away and miss something in order to see something else. Where competing elements inscribe the screen, revealing the partiality of perception, installations that surround the viewer inscribe that partiality on the body of the viewer through their capacity to literally turn bodies in space and time.

Such a process of physical embodiment is exploited in installations that extend beyond the relatively tight organizations of sound and image of screen arrays. The multiple components of image and sound projections and static objects used in Tony Oursler's installations, or the multiple large-screen installations of Bill Viola such as *The Five Angels For the Millennium* (2001) and *Going Forth By Day* (2002), made possible by digital projection, aim to turn more than the heads of the viewers, seeking to reorient their whole bodies in space. Encountering Tony Oursler's *Introjection* exhibition, for instance, relied on the viewer moving through an installation constructed from the competing elements of furniture, standalone video monitors or projections, and being verbally hailed by uncanny human-like scrunched figures.[24] Often lying crushed or obscured under the otherwise domestic furniture of chairs and sofas, these figures' accusations, apparently directed towards the passing viewer, provoke an engaged viewer to turn and look, and so be reincorporated into the installation. Moving within the parameters of the installation, viewers are able to turn within the aural and visual architecture of the installation, looking at what they have already passed by, seeing and hearing it again once it has been reconfigured by the newest element in their encounter.

In these artworks, time-based technologies take hold not only of the space of the competing elements, but of the viewer. Antonia Hirsch's *String Theory* (2003), though a smaller installation, works in a similar way.[25] The installation is first encountered as a series of rhythmic sounds reminiscent of a heartbeat. As exhibited at the Vancouver Art Gallery, *String Theory* was placed on the edge of a hallway, to be crossed through in order to access the main rooms of the gallery. Rather than being drawn to the sounds, viewers are likely to find themselves within the installation, suddenly aware of the growing intensity of the beat. Once the sound registers viewers may begin to reconsider their space, looking around until they notice a small 10×11 cm screen placed at the base of the wall. On this screen a woman is skipping with a luminescent rope that is highlighted against a black background, but which then disappears behind her body with the repetition of each skip. To see this part of the installation, the viewer has to pause and bend. The sounds of these two installations are attractors that perturb not only the synthesis of meanings, but also a physical progression through the space.

Where Oursler's *Introjection* includes a number of static elements, which can be revisited by viewers following their incorporation into the installation, Bill Viola's multi-screen installations incorporate a viewer but, since they are completely time-based, refuse the option of revisiting the space as time has already moved on. The darkened rooms in which both *The Five Angels For the Millennium* and *Going Forth By Day* are exhibited establish a space that is configured by the proximities not only of visual elements, but also of aural ones.[26] The ability of aural elements to distribute attention is already evident in *Introjection* and *String Theory*. Bruce Nauman's *Raw Materials* (2004), however, takes the process further. *Raw Materials* was a sound-only exhibition at the Turbine Hall at the Tate Modern, generated from 22 spoken and sung competing textual elements taken from Nauman's already existing work, including *Good Boy, Bad Boy*. As Emma Dexter suggests, in this architecturally complex soundscape 'Nauman was particularly interested in controlling the behaviour of the visitor or spectator' (Dexter 2004: 20).

Sound is also important in *The Five Angels For the Millennium*, as a viewer can be standing in front of one screen and be distracted by the explosion of sound and image on one of the other four. A similar effect is in play in *Going Forth By Day*, though in this installation the competing elements have a different content. Because every screen of *The Five Angels* contains a figure in water it is tempting to try filling in the gaps with some kind of linking narrative. On each, a figure is submerged in water, or re-emerges from it, at times diving into the water's surface, or hovering over it, in a continuous loop of slow motion sequences. The colour, a saturated blood-red that shifts to grey-blue, evokes a sense of being both cleansing and sinister.[27] *Going Forth By Day* includes no such suggestion of continuity. *Fire Birth* acts as the first screen since it frames the doorway through which viewers walk, only to retrospectively realize they have walked through fire, while the other four screens, *The Path*, *The Deluge*, *The Voyage* and *First Light* are approached within the space of the room (see Figure 5.3). Taken together the piece opens into a meditation on the cycle of life, on individuality, society, death and rebirth. Despite their different content, both installations are often described in terms of Viola's interest in spirituality and cycles of being: 'in the rehearsed narratives of Viola's work there is a concentrated effort made to be witness to miraculous events, small and large, inexplicable and reasonable, that can be part of our lives' (Svich 2004: 73).

Perhaps because a quality of contemplation informs much of Viola's work, especially *The Passions*, the idea carries over into commentaries on *The Five Angels For the Millennium* and *Going Forth By Day*. Yet, while there is much to contemplate in the slow moving imagery of each screen, the influence of the surrounding ones is never far away, competing elements whose audio-visual textures intercede in a viewer's engagements with the installation, attractors that distribute attention across the room as a whole. In *Going Forth By Day*, the roaring water of *The Deluge*, for instance,

*Figure 5.3 Going Forth By Day*, a five-part projected image cycle of video/sound, fills a large exhibition space. The on-rush of sound in *The Deluge*, shown at the far end of the room, draws attention away from the other elements of the installation. Installation view of Bill Viola, *Going Forth By Day* (2002) © the artist. Photo: Mathias Schormann. Courtesy of Bill Viola Studio.

intercedes in the viewer's contemplation of the relative quiet of a long line of people strolling through the wood in *The Path*, or the death of an elderly man in *The Voyage*, or the exhaustion of rescue workers in the aftermath of an accident in *First Light*. Even as questions of spirituality rightly inform many commentaries on Viola's work, it is also appropriate to invoke the presence of technology. Both *The Five Angels For the Millennium* and *Going Forth By Day* contemplate cycles of birth, living and death, but because they are created from time-based competing elements, allow the viewer to only do so within a constantly changing environment. There are at least two ways of negotiating with the competing elements of the interface, both of which reveal an embodied experience of technology. Viewers can allow themselves to be distracted by the competing elements, turned by the attractors of escalating sound or movement of imagery, or they can refuse to be distracted, allowing the competing elements to pass them by as they confine themselves to contemplating a single image. Either of these options is equally possible and within the volition of the viewer, and therefore they act as a site of agency to which viewers also bring their dispositions and interpretations. Additionally, they reveal the dynamics of experiencing a time-based technological interface. Viewers are able to contemplate the image or hop between competing elements, but in either case they are experiencing a lived-time marked by having to let other temporal elements pass by them. A viewer's embodiment is never absolute, but contingent on their orientation to the interface.[28]

Time-based media, then, take hold of space in installations, creating spatio-temporal architectures within which viewers encounter technological interfaces. The action of these spatio-temporal organizations is to incorporate the viewer into the process of the artwork. As I have described in the foregoing paragraphs, this incorporation varies from an embodiment based only on frontally distributed attention to one in which viewers are surrounded by competing elements and so made more aware of the partiality of their perception. Even as it makes viewers aware of the partiality of their perception, however, the interface also offers agency in allowing viewers choices in how they orient themselves in relation to the competing elements of the artwork. The ability of installations to surround a viewer makes explicit the ways in which installations work on bodies, causing them to take on orientation in space and time.

Some installations take the process of bodily incorporation further, and, rather than inscribing competing elements on the body by orienting it in space, include the body as a competing element in the installation itself. For instance, Olafur Eliasson's *Your Double Lighthouse Projection* consists of two circular roofless 'rooms' placed within a larger gallery space (see Figure 5.4).[29] In the larger room a computer-controlled system shifts the colour spectrum, while the second room is bathed in white light. As the larger room is sequentially illuminated with blues, greens, yellows, reds and so forth, the light changes what a viewer sees. My own experience was of first looking at the changing colours of the walls and then noticing how the different light appeared to alter the skin tones of the other people present, as the technologically mediated colour space acted directly on the viewer. One of the green tones was especially effective in giving a rather un-lifelike 'veiny' quality to the skin. These two observations were followed by my oscillating between looking at the skin of my friends' faces and that of my hands, to try and see what effect the shifting spectrum of light was having on my skin. The immersive potential of being bathed in different coloured light is broken by the competing elements of seeing the effect of the light on oneself and others, where the competing elements include, in addition to the installation, the body of the viewer and that of everyone within the space. The bodies of viewers are literally part of the interface, bathed in the same light as the installation, effectively making them an aspect of the screen.

The body is active in other ways within *Your Double Lighthouse Projection*, as the playfulness of being in the colour changing room is only part of the installation. The second part involves entering the smaller room, bathed in white light, where the retinal memory of colour experienced in the first room affects the colour seen in the second room. At this point it becomes clear that the competing elements of *Your Double Lighthouse Projection* not only give access to the artwork by displaying the changing array of colours, but also form a technological interface which intercedes in how we see. The changing light of the larger room is computer controlled so that technology controls the colours seen, and this colour in turn literally influences how

155

*Figure 5.4* Installation view of *Your Double Lighthouse Projection* (2004) in the Tate Modern, London. © Olafur Eliasson. Photo: Marcus Leigh & Andrew Dunkley 2004.

the second room is seen. The technology of light display in one space generates a reaction in a viewer, which, through exploiting the temporality of retinal memory, is carried into the second space within the body of the viewer, and so in turn has an impact on the viewer's perception of the second space. The installation generates a fascinating example of embodied viewing. Not only is the viewer immersed in the light space, but the viewer's body is essential to the effect of the installation.

Installations frequently consist of competing elements, not all of which may be moving images or sound, and these cue and distribute attention, creating architectures within which viewers gain agency as they make an interpretation of the whole. Because the organization of an interface does not rely on the centrality of a character to organize the meaning of space, the viewer becomes active within the installation. Although viewers are always active, in the sense of being interpretive agents, something also true of viewers of films and players of games, installations activate the viewer in a different sense. Since viewers are the site at which the meaning of space is organized, they are central to the process of the installation. The embodiment offered by the elements of the interface allows viewers to shift their attention between the conceptual meaning of the artwork and the technology of images or sounds. Given this, installations are human–technology interfaces whose aspects point as much towards the technology as they do towards the aesthetics of the artwork. Standing in front of or within an installation, viewers encounter an extended network, and in attempting to make sense of what they are seeing and hearing they bring their dispositions and their cultural knowledge to bear on their direct experience of the installation. The embodied agency of this process lies in the combination of drawing on one's own history and of being in the moment of the installation, which includes the presence of other people in the space, friends or strangers, as well as the actual installation itself. The synthesis of meaning an individual makes occurs within the specificities of that context, and as such it is embodied and engaged with the world, even as it is tied into the interface.

Olafur Eliasson's *The Weather Project*, part of the Unilever Series exhibited in the Turbine Hall at the Tate Modern, reveals the contradictory nature of the dynamics of a body being incorporated into a technological interface.[30] Although *The Weather Project* is a technological interface without a time-based element, it has an unusual relationship with time and space. Constructed from a semicircular opaque disc behind which was an array of hundreds of narrow-band mono-frequency lamps giving out yellow light, the installation was hung high in the Turbine Hall. The semicircle was topped by a series of mirrors suspended along the entire length of the ceiling, giving the overall impression of a full sphere whose wash of colour carried along the length of the Turbine Hall, a technologically mediated version of a most extraordinary sunset (see Figure 5.5). Although the array of lights and the wiring, along with the smoke machines that were part of the installation, were visible from directly beneath the semi-spheric disc, these potential competing elements were not an obvious point of interest for the participants in the installation. Instead, despite adjectives such as 'acrid' and 'creepy' being used to describe the smoke-filled installation, many people took great pleasure in accepting the illusion of *The Weather Project*, basking in its yellow glow and playing visual games with their reflections on the ceiling above.[31]

As I have described for other installations, the competing elements form the architecture of the installation, the spatial organization of the sun-disc and mirroring exerting a direct impact on its viewer. In playing games with their reflections the viewers incorporated their bodies into the installation, and in so doing they revealed the dialectic of captivity and captivation so central to *The Weather Project*, and argu-ably to technology more generally. A shorthand tag for *The Weather Project* was the Sun; the installation's invocation of a sunset makes this seem an obvious choice, but it also makes clear how the installation acts on the viewer by holding still an object whose transitions through space are elemental. It holds an image of the sun captive by taking it out of time, but in the same gesture creates another temporal dimen-sion based on captivation. One of the ways viewers found to negotiate their way through the installation was to give themselves over to it, apparently taking the space of the Turbine Hall for themselves, even as they were caught within a dynamic of captivity and captivation. They were captivated by the space of the installation, which is based on holding a temporal moment still, and the viewer in turn is held captive as they give their time freely, passing it by watching stillness.

*Figure 5.5* Olafur Eliasson, *The Weather Project*, 2003. Turbine Hall, the Tate Modern, London (The Unilever Series). © Olafur Eliasson. Photo: Jens Ziehe.

*The Weather Project* reveals the contradictory status of engaging with technological interfaces. They engender both captivation and captivity, and it is only through seeking agency in their architectures that we can negotiate our way through.

# 6

# FINDING OURSELVES AT THE
# INTERFACE

[A] positive transformative aesthetic environment requires
finding, rather than losing oneself, and remaining connected
to the present time and space in order to ground what you are
experiencing in the dynamic ecology of that context.

(Jackson 2001: 351).

Viewers encounter the technological status of moving images at an interface. A
cartoon viewed on an iPod and a multi-screen gallery installation can be understood
as occupying different positions on the same continuum of experience. A consequence is that we should pay close attention to the interface so that we can
understand how and where we find ourselves in relation to contemporary moving
images. It is easy, at least if you live in a part of the world where technological
accessories are increasingly the norm, to imagine the following digital encounter. As
you are sitting within a wi-fi zone of a café, clicking across webpages on your laptop
and listening to an MP3 player, your mobile rings just as an email pings in. In such a
moment of convergence there is a sense of being pulled in several directions by the
'calls' of the disparate competing elements of your technological interfaces. In this
scenario there is a potential for distraction and dispersal, and ultimately inaction.
However, by becoming accustomed to this space we learn to find ourselves as we
enact agency, as long as we remain open to the possibilities of agency in our
encounters. It is necessary that we also maintain an open stance to the agencies of
our encounters with the interfaces of moving image technologies.

I have argued that moving images increasingly show the traces of technologies. In
the era of digital technologies these exist in the context of a broader set of changes
in practice, which are themselves evident either through an accelerated proliferation
and diversification of pre-existing devices or through the introduction of new kinds
of organizations. Although mostly I have discussed the visible impact of technologies, I want to briefly comment on the emergence of these visible traces as indices
of a digitally mediated series of developments within filmmaking and art practices.[1]
I have discussed at several points films relying on the use of a digital intermediate
(DI). The first to use extensive digitally mediated colour manipulation was *Pleasantville*,

released in 1998. Only two years later, a full DI was used for colour grading *O Brother, Where Art Thou?*, and since then the digital intermediate has become more commonly used, a transformation of filmmaking practice made possible by the increasing capacity of computers to handle the massive amounts of information created in transferring analogue footage into digital information. As we know, the extent to which these changes are visible depends on the film. *O Brother, Where Art Thou?* and *The Aviator* use DIs to generate seamless interfaces, whereas *Pleasantville* and *Sin City* have more inscribed ones. The future of inscription via a DI is yet to emerge, but where the rise of the DI points to the proliferation of digital technologies within the filmmaking industry, Rotoshop technologies reveal their capacity to also enable diversifications.

Rotoshop belongs in a chronology leading back to rotoscoping, an animation technology first developed in the 1910s. Rotoscoping involved tracing the movement of live-action figures and then using the tracings as a template for the movements of animated figures. Over the intervening years this practice has diversified as new technologies have become available. In the digital era, for instance, motion capture has again exploited live action as templates for modelling the movements of digitally constructed figures, either embedded in live-action films or in full animations. Rotoshop is taking this process in another direction. Rotoscoping and motion capture, though visible through the distinctive quality of movement they introduce, are usually embedded within a seamless interface, keeping the technological interventions involved relatively hidden. By contrast, as was shown in relation to *Snack and Drink* and *Waking Life*, Rotoshop introduces a visible digital inscription to the interface, which disturbs the conventional spatio-temporal dynamics of the imagery. The UK release of two further examples of Rotoshop films coincides with my writing this conclusion: *A Scanner Darkly* (2006) and *Renaissance* (2006). In the former film, the visible blend of live action and digital animation conveys the blurred reality of the central character, Arctor/Fred. A similar argument of proliferation and diversification can be made with regard to installations.

Since the video camera become available in the 1970s, video footage has been displayed using various arrays of television monitors. Digital technologies have had several influences on the constructions of time-based installations. First, DV recording devices alter the aesthetic parameters and manipulability of the imagery. Second, digital projectors have transformed the ways projection can be used in gallery spaces. Their mechanisms are silent – imagine the cacophony if *The Five Angels For the Millennium* were to be projected using five film projectors – and their small size also allows for more versatility in the placing of the projected image on shapes, an aspect that Tony Oursler has exploited in recent work in which he has projected eyes, lips and noses, as well as his own face, onto small free-standing shapes.[2]

As even this brief outline suggests, proliferating digital technologies not only mark the changing contours of a media landscape, they also reconfigure what such a landscape offers to its viewers and consumers. In this context of transformation, the question of loss has often arisen, but whether the losses of contemporary cinema can be attributed to the rise of digital technologies is a far from straightforward question. Digital effects are too simplistic a target when seeking reasons for the apparent vacuity of contemporary mainstream filmmaking, as the aesthetic and ideological indolence of *any* work of art is more likely to be a consequence of its place in a network of influences, which includes economic, industrial and technical contexts, as much as creative mediocrity.

My contention is that the information base of a landscape created from digital technologies is different to that of analogue systems. Digital information is indeed dispersed by comparison to analogue information, flowing through networks, reducible to zeros and ones as bits combine to generate fragments that will eventually make up an image or sound. As viewers, however, we have no access to this form of information, gaining comprehension of it only through interfaces such as films and television, digital games and gallery installations. These different digital interfaces inscribe the presence of technologies in very distinct ways, allowing us the opportunity to experience and think about how these technologies enable a range of spatio-temporal embodiments. Some of these experiences may be generative and productive encounters, others may not be, disassembling and reducing us to mere watchers of a system. Giving an account of digital inscriptions reveals the diversity of our experiences of technologies, embodied encounters that exist within and between the determinism of the interface and the choices made in viewing. I have argued through a synthesis of insights taken from cinema studies and social sciences that we can find ourselves in relation to digital technologies in two different ways: through an understanding of the emergence of digital inscriptions and the impact of these inscriptions on how we view.

All moving imagery exposes a viewer to a technological interface, but when technological practices are inscribed on the interface of screen(s) or installations through the presence of competing elements they allow a viewer to more easily find the work of that interface. Whereas a seamless interface gives direct access to the content of the image, its temporal quality refuses an axis of contemplation through which its construction might otherwise start to become clear, making it harder to find oneself in relation to a transformational digital aesthetic. The temporality of our experience of technological interfaces is central to the ways in which we gain agency.

Walking into an exhibit of Jeff Wall's work, for example, I was immediately struck by both the size of the works and also their luminosity, a quality enhanced by displaying the works as large transparencies on light boxes: *A Sudden Gust of Wind (after Hokusai)* is exhibited as 2.3×3.7 m (approx.) transparency.[3] One of the most arresting things about this work is the extraordinary impression of movement captured within its still frame. Not simply evident in the turning and reactive bodies of the four figures in the foreground, this is also visible in the bend of the trees, which reiterates the motion of the flowing paper trail sweeping from left to upper right across the image. It is as though every individual movement caught in the still image supports and expands every other movement also caught in the image. The longer I stood in front of *A Sudden Gust of Wind*, the more the paradox of this statement

161

began to pose questions about the image's status, allowing its artifice to start leaking through. Although seemingly a snapshot of a moment in time, its too perfect interplay of reiterating movements, apparently captured in the single click of a shutter, became implausible. In reading the exhibition notes the paradox is solved, as *A Sudden Gust of Wind* is a composite of more than 100 images taken over a period of a year and digitally manipulated to create the seamless interface of the final image. Analogue technologies have always been able to harness space and time, but digital technologies are taking this process further. The example of *A Sudden Gust of Wind* demonstrates their capacity to create a unified arrangement of figures in space, while erasing differences in time, resolving numerous images from different spatio-temporal moments into a single one. Nevertheless, because the digital technologies work through an exaggeration of co-ordinated movement, it is possible for the interested viewer to find them and begin to tease apart the processes behind the construction of the image.

Many digital technologies and techniques are being used to manipulate and create the spaces of moving images, but these have a very different kind of temporal organization to *A Sudden Gust of Wind*, and so they offer distinct kinds of interfaces for viewers to experience. Their status as moving images denies the viewer time to contemplate the artificial constructions of the imagery. Although awareness of image construction may come with repeated viewings using a DVD or from circulating digital discourses, seamless interfaces aim to distract from the work of their construction, drawing viewers into their story-worlds instead. Competing elements, by contrast, though not necessarily drawing attention to their status as constructed imagery, inscribe an interface with more complex spatio-temporal organizations that gesture not only towards the technological changes otherwise hidden behind a seamless interface, but towards the nature of technological encounters. Competing elements are the place where we begin to directly encounter an interface, and the work of this book has been to elucidate what it is that we find there. In looking across a number of media, including animation, digital effects cinema, digital games and time-based gallery installations, the emergence of inscribed interfaces has provided insights into the ways technologies are experienced as spatio-temporal organizations which embody the viewer.

This book has presented textual organizations in a distinctive way by arguing that they are architectures composed of competing elements, and that making sense of a text involves generating a pathway through those elements under the influence of a text's attractor(s). It is from this perspective that questions of agency and embodied viewing emerge. Understanding a screen interface in this way takes for granted its spatio-temporal organization, and it follows that any encounter will always occur through an orientation within the structures of an architecture. Viewers are embodied in the sense that they orient themselves within a spatio-temporal organization. When speaking of different kinds of cinema and digital games, because this orientation occurs in an 'unreal' location such an orientation might be described as disembodied or dispersed, and this could well be true if the encounter is only taken from the perspective of the human figure engaged within this process. That is, in being engaged with something that takes someone away from human–human interaction, their place within the world is diminished since their attention is elsewhere. However, if such encounters are understood as engagements with technological interfaces, then they are always about the interaction between a human and a technology. To simply state that such an interaction is disembodied is to miss the details of the interaction and what it allows us to say about how humans experience the spatio-temporal dynamics of technological interfaces.

I began my narrative with animation to explore the ways in which technologies that intercede in how we view the world can be made visible or invisible. The presence of competing elements makes such technological interventions more visible, and as it does so also introduces more than one spatio-temporal organization onto the interface of the screen. From the different organizations of competing elements and architectures discussed in relation to digital effects and split-screen cinema, as well as digital games, when technology's ability to intercede is apparent, another facet of experience becomes evident. Technological interfaces make explicit the partiality of experience by marking out the striations in spatio-temporal organizations. If perception is understood as an orientation within the world, then it involves engaging with one particular spatio-temporal organization at the expense of others, or being confronted with the possibility of understanding the world through more than one spatio-temporal organization. When tied into a view that human experience is contingent rather than all-encompassing, perception and experience are understood as situated both within the moment of perception and also within world-views mediated by and mediating interplays of political, social, cultural and economic discourse. One's awareness of the world is always partial, but in offering a point of view that is apparently unmediated, any seamless technological interface sets aside such a partiality of experience. Even though we may be informed and politicized viewers who can knowingly consume such imagery, whether at the cinema, on television or through the internet, the spatio-temporal perspective offered by them displaces the partiality of experience. Competing elements, by distributing attention across different spatio-temporal organizations on the same interface, reintroduce partiality.

This can be understood in terms of experience more generally, but I use it here to more specifically speak to encounters with technological interfaces. Technologies alter our spatio-temporal familiarity with the world, and an interface constructed around competing elements presents an equivalent perspective in which we find evidence of technologies' transformative impact. Such encounters do not cause us to be disembodied; rather, we are placed within different spatio-temporal orientations and organizations. One of the consequences of being placed within these organizations is the revelation of both the possibilities and limits of agency in our encounters with technological interfaces. The numbers of technological interfaces that frame how we see the world are rapidly expanding their influence, and there are questions to be asked about who controls and creates those interfaces and for what reasons. The reality of our exposure to a media landscape colonized by numerous interfaces leading to an environment constructed around competing elements is that a viewer

163

will never be able attend to everything. The outcome does not have to be as negative as this would seem to suggest. Instead, we can find agency in our relational negotiations within the spatio-temporal architecture of a system. A facet of digital technologies, and of technologies more generally, is not that they separate us from the world, but rather that they create within it distinct kinds of engagements. Given the continuing pressure towards technological innovation, moving image interfaces not only take us to representations of other worlds, but are also themselves articulations of the impact of ever-changing networks of interactions between humans and technologies.

# NOTES

## INTRODUCTION

1 The collection was available as a free download from i-Tunes in April 2006. *Aan Rika* was animated by Juan de Graaf, and the poem was written by Piet Paaltjens, who lived 1835–94. Paaltjens is the pen name of François Haverschimdt, a Dutch minister and novelist.

2 As I argue in Chapter 3, split-screen devices are not in themselves a consequence of digital technologies, as they have been used in filmmaking since at least the 1920s. However, digital and electronic media have enabled an acceleration in the use of these kinds of devices.

3 See, for instance, ideas on the proliferation of information in society throughout the later twentieth century and early twenty-first century in Terranova (2004).

4 For a discussion of independent digital filmmaking, see Willis (2005).

5 *Ping Pong* was seen as part of the Open Systems exhibition at the Tate Modern in 2005.

## 1 RE-ANIMATING THE INTERFACE

1 For a series of essays detailing discussions of the concept of the 'illusion of life' in animated works, see Cholodenko (1990).

2 *Snack and Drink* was animated by Bob Sabiston. Sabiston developed the Rotoshop software package, which as also used in the feature-length animations *Waking Life* and *A Skanner Darkly*.

3 A number of histories of American animation have already been written. These mainly cover the cinematic era between 1910 and 1960s. See, for instance, Crafton (1984), Klein (1993), Solomon (1994) and Barrier (1999).

4 For a selection of essays addressing the reception and practices of early cinema, see Elsaesser and Barker (1990).

5 Winsor McCay drew the Little Nemo strips *Little Nemo in Slumberland*, for the *New York Herald* between 1905 and 1911, and *In the Land of Wonderful Dreams*, for the *New York American* between 1911 and 1913.

6 Interestingly, the presence of animation technologies does not completely disappear, but is displaced into other kinds of discourse that surround the animations themselves. For instance, in his discussion of animations between 1895 and 1928, Donald Crafton (1984) mentions some of the advertising materials that draw attention to the technologies of animation.

7 In *The Contest* (1923), Koko leaps between the space of a live-action projection room and an animated circus show; in *Koko the Convict* (1926), banished to 'prison' by their animator, both Koko and Fitz jump between their live-action home space, their prison and also an animated cityscape.

8 The *Silly Symphonies* were not the first animations to use such detailed drawing styles, but remain early examples of this style within an industrialized studio organization. Winsor McCay's *The Sinking of the Lusitania* (1917), for instance, includes some extremely detailed work.

9 Mark Langer (1992) has argued that the multi-plane camera was in fact expensive and complicated, and so only used in brief segments on the more prestigious Disney productions, and had fallen out of use by the mid-1940s.

10 Paul Wells (1998) describes this tendency as hyper-realism.

11 Norman Klein argues that late silent era animation remained embedded in the two traditions of graphic comic strip style and vaudeville gag, but these gave way to the increasing influence of live-action cinema in terms of spatial organization and dramatic structure mediated through the work of the Disney Studio (Klein 1993).

12 At the Fleischer Studio depth perspective was generated by using miniature three-dimensional models. The Color Classic shorts *Peeping Penguins* (1937) and *Hunky and Spunky* (1938) made use of these models during landscape sequences. The dimensional model was usually used without characters, focusing on a camera movement across space, a device used to arresting effect in the opening credits of the otherwise unsuccessful *Hoppity Goes to Town* (a.k.a. *Mr Bug Goes to Town*) (1941). The sequence begins with an outer space nebula and travels down to earth into the three-dimensional cityscape of New York.

13 The distinctive spatial constructions of the UPA animators were visible in the two cartoons contributed by the studio to the Snafu series: *A Few Quick Facts: Inflation* (1945, Osmond Evans) and *A Few Quick Facts: Fear* (1945, Zack Schwartz). In *A Few Quick Facts: Fear* Snafu appears as a knight on a shining horse riding into a darkened space. From this darkened space various elements of the animation appear – the eyes of a fearsome beast, internal organs, a hypodermic needle. The minimal use of spatial detail both breaks away from the conventional narrative structures evident in the other Snafu cartoons and also establishes a space where anything might materialize.

14 The short *Luxo Jr in Light and Heavy* (1991) involves Luxo pushing around a marble sphere and a plastic football. Although the actuality of physical laws of gravity and weight is clearly an aim of the animators, they also put in place a series of lighting set-ups appropriate to the surface of plastic and marble. Importantly, the set-ups look like those of a studio, making it appear to be an exercise in lighting conventions rather than realistic ones.

15 Jay David Bolter and Richard Grusin point to something similar in their discussion of *Toy Story*, although they see this particular film as a remediation evoking immediacy. That is, the transposition of the conventions of cel-animation into digital animation provides nothing other than a reworking of old conventions in a way that erases the presence of a new technological system. It is an example of 'a transparent interface ... that erases itself, so the user is no longer aware of confronting a medium, but instead stands in an immediate relationship to the contents of that medium' (Bolter and Grusin 1999: 23–4).

16 For a more detailed discussion of this interplay of influences in *The Matrix*, see Hunt (2004).

17 I mean camera movement here in the sense that digital animators, although they do not work with a physical camera, are able to chose between 'camera' positions within their modelled environments, focusing on different parts of its digital construction, zooming in and out of a space, cutting within the dimensions of a complex construction, as well as the more fluid camera motion that signals an unreal space – that is, a space which could not be filmed in reality because of the physical limitations of taking a camera into such as location. Similarly, while cel-animation could include camera movements, with zooms, pans and tilts, digital technologies allow faster and more extensive shot compositions. The difference I am pointing to here is not of kind but of scale.

18 Katharine Sarafian, a producer at Pixar, provides some insight into the workings of Pixar in her article on digital aesthetics. See Sarafian (2003).

19 The animators discuss this aspect of their work in an interview on the Behind-the-Scenes 'Making Of' *The Incredibles* segment of Disc 2 of the Collector's Edition of *The Incredibles*.

20 A useful comparison can be made with the falling live-action shots seen in *Medicine Man* (1992) when the characters are climbing through the trees in the Amazon rain forest. By contrast to the untethered digital shots, these were achieved using cameras attached to bungee ropes, and retain a sense of weightedness associated with being attached to something.

21 The self-reflexivity of *Duck Amuck* has been written about in other contexts. See Thompson (1975) and Polan (1985).

22 Tex Avery is frequently cited as a central figure in these changes, and indeed he spent time at both studios in the late 1930s and 1940s, when his animation influenced a turn away from cute pastoral figures to fast-paced and adult-oriented gag structures (Wells 1998).

23 For a more detailed account of the animation techniques used in *Flatworld*, see Pilling (2001).

24 Paul Wells (2002) uses this phrase in an interview with Caroline Leaf.

25 Paul Ward (2004) has discussed the use of Rotoshop in *Waking Life*, and also addresses the consequence of Rotoshop for work practices within animation communities.

## 2 DIGITAL EFFECTS AND EXPANDED NARRATIVE SPACE

1 Christopher Nolan was speaking about the making of *Batman Begins* to Jeff Otto (2005).

2 Although the first computer animations of the 1960s were analogue, for instance those animations making up *Catalog 1961*, by the 1970s John Whitney had begun to work with digital computers following his time as an artist in residence at IBM (Moritz 1997).

3 Prior to their work with computer animation, both John and James Whitney were renowned for their ability to set abstract shapes in motion to music in works such as *Film Exercises 1–4*, made between 1943 and 1944.

4 Michelle Pierson, for instance, discusses the consumption of special effects discourse within the broader history and context of film-going culture (Pierson 2002).

5 To help the uninitiated, websites give lists of films and instructions for how to access easter eggs. See http://www.dvdreview.com/eastereggs/.

6 Since the web-based viewers of *My Little Eye* are persecutory figures within the narrative, this is a curious device belonging in the tradition of horror films by aligning viewers with the perspective of the murderer or monster.

7 Vivian Sobchack (2004) has discussed the impact of video technology on viewing habits, and Laura Mulvey's (2006) recent work also looks at the impact of DVD players on how viewers view.

8 At its beginning, cinema was only one visual show amongst many, competing with other kinds of spectacular displays, such as numerous live shows, including theatre, vaudeville, circus, as well as dioramas and panoramas. For further descriptions of the kinds of shows that early cinema competed with, see Friedberg (1993) and Rubin (1993).

9 I have not addressed how a viewer may engage with the spectacular elements of texts. There are a number of different ways of approaching this question, one of which is through pleasure: Yvonne Tasker (1993) considers the pleasure of spectacular bodies in action films, and Michelle Pierson (2002) the enjoyment of effects as effects. These views are countered by Winston Wheeler Dixon (1998) and Andrew Darley (2000), who both express reservations about the transparency or self-referentiality of effects.

10 Rick Altman has discussed the problem of the 'dominant' in the classic model of Hollywood cinema, where an emphasis on models privileging relationships based on causality has tended to marginalize other elements of films. Altman comments that 'the notion of classical narrative necessarily involved concentration on a narrow range of targeted features, with a consequent levelling of all but certain key differences among texts' (Altman 1992: 14–15).

11 Many of the recent commentaries dealing with the question of spectacle versus narrative have two key points in play. These are formal questions about narrative trajectory and the contributions of various plot elements, which are combined with a more experiential view of the impact of spectacle on a viewer. Andrew Darley's view of spectacle is an example that combines both positions:

> If, ultimately, the spectacular aspect has always been viewed as subordinate to and in a sense subject to the control of a repressive narrative logic, this is precisely because

spectacle is, in many respects, the antithesis of narrative. Spectacle effectively halts motivated movement. In its purer state it exists for itself, consisting of images whose main drive is to dazzle and stimulate the eye (and by extension the other senses).

(Darley 2000: 104)

12 For contrasting views on the relationship between narrative and spectacle, see, for instance, Geoff King (2001), who argues that the spectacular elements are separate from narrative but form an aspect of the overall experience of the film through their quality of 'impact'. This differs from Warren Buckland's (1998) view, in which he argues that spectacular sequences contain narrative information and so can never be held apart from narrative.

13 For further discussions of the impact of digital technologies on the economic and creative practices of Hollywood, see Prince (1996, 2004).

14 A number of studies include detailed discussions of early effects, tracing their emergence and subsequent development through the studio system. See Brosnan (1977), Schecter and Everitt (1980), Finch (1984) and Pinteau (2004).

15 The team working on the 1933 *King Kong*, which included Willis O'Brien (as supervisor) and Marcel Delgado, made extensive use of rear projection, especially innovative miniature projection, and travelling mattes in conjunction with stop–motion modelling, often in miniature sets, to bring the figure of Kong, the dinosaurs and the human figures close together within the same shot (Finch 1984).

16 In relation to their work on the *Jurassic Park* films, the digital modellers discuss their approach as an attempt to achieve an ever-greater closeness to the actual world. They role-played creature scenes in order to understand the dynamics of particular kinds of actions, and studied movements of living heavy animals in order to copy the subtle 'jiggle' of their skin and muscle ripple. The subsequent developments of heavy creature modelling are evident in a comparison between the brachiosaur display scenes of *Jurassic Park* (1993) and *Jurassic Park III* (2001), with the creature's flesh of the later film more enfolded and the sway of the body with movement more pronounced. The '*Making of Jurassic Park III*' is on the DVD release of *Jurassic Park III* and includes brief discussions of the thinking behind the muscle and skin software developments between the later film and the first *Jurassic Park*.

17 In the same way that Industrial Light and Magic authorized a book about its history, Digital Domain has also been party to an official history of its work. See Bizony (2001).

18 For a discussion of morphing techniques pre-dating digital technologies, see Wolf (2000).

19 Vivian Sobchack, while observing that the morph calls 'to the part of us that escapes our perceived sense of "selves" and partakes in the flux and ceaseless becoming of Being – that is, our bodies at the cellular level ceaselessly forming and reforming and not "ourselves" at all', notes that the transformation occurs in time *and* space (Sobchack 2000: 136).

20 In the 1960 version of *The Time Machine*, directed by George Pal, a similar effect can be seen. For its era, the early *The Time Machine* is unusual in including sequences where space changes in time within a single framing. These elements are a direct, if rare, precursor to later digital animation of space in live-action films, one also used in the 2002 version of *The Time Machine*. In both of the films the presence of dynamic spatial elements is most evident during George/ Alexander's journey through time. One instance of this shows the changing growth of vegetation – the opening of flowers and also a ripening apple. For the 1960 version, the ripening apple was achieved through animation of a matte painting so lifelike that its brief appearance on screen almost goes unnoticed as animation. These animated sequences appear only very briefly in the 1960 film, but the digital equivalents of the 2002 version are on screen for longer.

21 Tom Kenny (1998) discusses the construction of the soundscape for *Titanic* as a combination of many sound sources, some wild and some studio based.

22 This is a different concept to 'elastic reality', a term Lev Manovich uses to mean digitally constructed images that could not have been filmed conventionally, but which assume a 'realistic'

image of the event. He uses the example of the feather that opens and closes *Forrest Gump* to illustrate his point (Manovich 2001).

23 This kind of effect is not to be confused with the ability of filmmakers to animate figures, something which they have done since the 1900s through a range of techniques including stop–motion modelling, rotoscoping and animation, computer animation and animatronics. All these techniques have been used to give movement to mythological creatures (*The 7th Voyage of Sinbad* (1958) and *Jason and the Argonauts* (1963)), dinosaurs (*The Lost World* (1925), *Jurassic Park*), numerous monsters (*King Kong* (1933 and 2005) and *Godzilla* (1998)) and ghosts (*Ghostbusters* (1984) and *Casper* (1995)) in live-action films. *Toy Story* (1995) saw the arrival of the first fully computer-generated animation film. Despite their differences, in each the effects are used to animate a figure that subsequently acts in the equivalent way to live-action characters.

24 The collection of essays *Timespace: Geographies of Temporality* also uses the term specifically to mean a relationship between time and space within human geography (May and Thrift 2001).

25 For discussions of time and space in narrative organizations, see Brannigan (1992) and Bal (1997).

26 For a full discussion of the various uses of effects in *The Perfect Storm*, see Duncan (2000).

27 *Hotel Rwanda* was originally filmed on Super35mm and then transferred to an anamorphic ratio stock. This caused the introduction of too much grain, a problem fixed by using a digital intermediate (Goldman 2005).

28 Immediacy is used in relation to effects cinema by Jay David Bolter and Richard Grusin (1999), while scripted space is a term introduced by Norman Klein (2005).

29 Michael Allen and Kevin Martin both discuss the use of effects in *Gladiator*. Martin, for instance, talks about the influence of *Triumph of the Will* on the pomp of the Rome scenes. Within *Gladiator* the effects shot that begins in the clouds and descends into Rome, and which segues into a sequence of shots showing the assembled army, is reminiscent of Hitler's arrival at Nuremberg in the earlier film. See Martin (2000) and Allen (2002).

30 Details of the making of *Gladiator* can be found in Scott and Parkers (2000).

31 Deborah Tudor (2002) discusses the issue of masculinity in *Gladiator*.

32 The character-based deployment of effects is discussed in detail in an interview with the cinematographer Wally Pfister, in which he argues that the aim was to create a real-world rather than fanstastical look for *Batman Begins* (Pizzello 2005).

33 The spidey-cam was introduced in one of the final shots of *Spider-Man*, but was used more extensively in *Spider-Man 2*. It is a computer controlled camera rigged to cables so that it can be swung between buildings or along streets. The controller is able to rotate the camera so as to twist during the recording of a swing, thus achieving the motion of swinging and twisting through the air.

34 Paul Grainge considers the impact of colour on memory and nostalgia in the intertextual play of colour and past in *Pleasantville* (Grainge 2003).

35 The *Sin City* comic book series, written by Frank Miller, and comprising six volumes, was originally published in 1992. Miller is also the author of the 'Dark Knight Returns' Batman series, which is an influence for *Batman Begins*.

36 In the colour filming of these scenes the plasters were fluorescing, and the soft edge of this glow is visible on the black and white images of the final version of *Sin City*.

37 In interviews, Robert Rodriguez has discussed how such strongly edged lighting was created around Marv's figure as he stood with his back to the wall. Impossible to achieve through conventional lighting and filmmaking techniques, Mickey Rouke was backlit standing against knee-high green-screen, and the wall was then added behind him (Pavlus 2005).

38 The cinematographer Janusz Kaminski discusses the use of colour bleaching in *Minority Report* as a means through which to characterize the mood and control of power within the film's different spaces (Holben 2002).

## 3 ENCOUNTERING THE INTERFACE

1 Jonathan Crary comments:

> Western modernity since the nineteenth century has demanded that individuals define and shape themselves in terms of a capacity for 'paying attention,' that is, for a disengagement from a broader field of attraction, whether visual or auditory, for the sake of isolating or focussing on a reduced number of stimuli.
>
> (Crary 2001: 1)

2 For example, Vivian Sobchack remarks: 'electronic presence randomly disperses its being *across* a network, its kinetic gestures describing and lighting on the surface of the screen rather than inscribing it with bodily dimension (a function of centered and intentional projection)' (Sobchack 2004: 159).

3 For an overview of ideas about attention, see Pashler (1998).

4 Mike Figgis discusses his use of DV cameras in an interview with Greg Lindsay (2003).

5 Laura Mulvey (2006) also discusses the ability of video and DVD to alter our relationship to the temporality of images.

6 Paul Dourish states than an affordance is 'a property of the environment that affords action to appropriately equipped organisms' (Dourish 2001: 113).

7 For a discussion of the relationship between habitus and field, see Bourdieu (1990).

8 The idea of dispositions equates with thinking about textual interpretation in film studies. For an overview of these debates, see Kinder (2002b).

9 The Devonshire Hunting Tapestries are a collection of four 15th-century tapestries and were viewed at the Victoria and Albert Museum, London, in March 2006.

10 *Roaring Forties: Seven Boards in Seven Days* (1997) was viewed at the Tate Modern, London, in July 2006.

11 Though *Pleasantville* used extensive post-production colour correction, *O Brother, Where Art Thou?* was the first film to be fully converted to a digital format, the digital intermediate.

12 I do not mean that the linearity of the plot is singular, as many plots feature threads that develop across the duration of a film; instead, I mean that the emphasis within the image is singular.

13 The filmmakers speak of the need to ensure that the colour elements of an otherwise predominantly black and white image look like they are within the same frame, rather than literally standing out as a separate element. See Fisher (1998).

14 Although the kinds of texts I am working with here are not conceived of in terms of mathematics, the idea of attractors within a spatio-temporal system is useful.

15 Paul Driessen is a Dutch animator who began his career working on *The Yellow Submarine*. The two pieces I work with here, *The End of the World in Four Seasons* and *The Boy Who Saw the Iceberg*, are based around multiple screens. *The End of the World in Four Seasons* uses eight panels, while *The Boy Who Saw the Iceberg* uses two panels.

16 There is an analogy between the attractor and field:

> [E]ach field prescribes its particular values and possesses its own regulative principles . . . . Two properties are central to this succinct definition. First, a field is a patterned system of objective forces (much in the manner of a magnetic field), a *relational configuration endowed with a specific gravity* which it imposes on all the objects and agents which enter in it. In the manner of a prism, it refracts external forces according to its internal structure.
>
> (Wacquant 1992: 17)

17 For discussions of representations of science and technology in the horror and science fiction genres, see Frayling (2005), Telotte (2001a), A. Tudor (1989) and Wood (2002).

18 For a more full discussion of the editing strategies used in *Hulk*, see Hollyn (2003).

## 4 DIGITAL GAMES: FATAL ATTRACTORS

1 Though the terms 'computer games' and 'video games' have had a longer usage, more recently the term 'digital games' has been introduced by scholars in the field.

2 Les Haddon makes this connection between domestic computer technologies and the rise in domestic digital gaming in an early commentary on digital games (Haddon 1993).

3 I am using 'play' in a very general sense here to mean that a player or gamer is required to intercede in some way in order to allow a game to progress. The nature of the play depends on the game itself, and in digital games can include puzzle-solving, strategy and control of the avatar in ways determined by the genre of the game, such as a sport simulation or first-person shooter.

4 See, for instance, the brief overview of early digital games history by Kirriemuir (2006).

5 For two historical views of digital game development which pay attention to the emergence of three-dimensional games, see Poole (2000) and Wolf (2001).

6 This is somewhat different to Henry Jenkins' use of the term narrative architect. In an interesting intervention in the narratology debate in games, Jenkins seeks to 'argue for an understanding of game designers less as storytellers and more as narrative architects' (Jenkins 2006: 674).

7 An AI agent is any character or object with which a player can interact. The AI agent is under the control of the game AI, rather than the player, although the player will aim to neutralize its presence within the game-world if the AI agent is an enemy. If the AI agent is a friend or neutral, then the player either learns from it or ignores it.

8 A combine is a military drone within the *Half-Life* games. They will always launch an attack on the Freeman-Avatar, and represent the means through which the AI constrains the spaces available to the gamer.

9 The anthology of essays collected in *Understanding Digital Games* provides a broad range of chapters addressing all the major debates within games studies. See Rutter and Bryce (2006).

10 James Newman usefully outlines this frequently contentious debate in his chapter on 'Narrative and Play'. See Newman (2004).

11 I use 'play space' here to mean the spaces of the game in which a gamer intersects with the AI agents, the obstacles and puzzles. The information spaces, or info-spaces, are those spaces containing information that may be consulted during play, but are not necessarily essential to it.

12 The Playstation 2 system can also be taken online via broadband or dial-up connections, something that would significantly alter the architecture of the interface.

13 The communities of online gamers have been extensively studied. See, for instance, T.L. Taylor's (2006) study on the interactions of gamers in online communities.

14 Jesper Juul (2005) uses the term 'above discussion' in his work on game rules, and this is appropriate here since these kinds of moves are an aspect of the rules of a digital game.

15 Both Sherry Turkle (1997) and Lev Manovich (2001) make this claim for new media.

16 An alternative spatial configuration is 'top down', more familiar from older 2-D games but also still in use in the *Pokémon* series on Gameboy. In this view, the gamer is able to see the whole of the play space as a continuous interface.

17 Within cinema studies, the different perspectives allow different degrees of distance from the actions carried out by the protagonist. Whether this operates for gamers is not yet clear, but it is mentioned by Geoff King and Tanya Kryzwinska in their essay on the relationship between film studies and games, in which they also outline other aspects of film studies analysis that are relevant to thinking about games (King and Kryzwinska 2006).

18 The game AI is the artificial intelligence section of a game's programming which allows non-player characters to react as though they have intelligence regarding the interventions of the gamer. The greater the sophistication of the AI, the greater the illusion of an intelligent response from the game.

19 For instance, in the ongoing discussion I refer to works by Steven Poole, Janet Murray, Marsha Kinder and Lev Manovich, all of whom cite *Myst* as a key game in the 1990s.

20 The last of the series, *Myst V: The End of Ages*, was released in 2005.

21 *Red Faction* (2000) introduced a 'geo-mod' facility whereby structural damage could only accumulate up to the point at which the architecture of a place became unstable. At that point the integrity of the play space came under threat, and presumably also the avatar. A similar view of physical integrity ensures that avatars can injure themselves if they misfire their grenades, and so forth.

22 Ken Birdwell was involved in the team that developed *Half-Life*. His contribution to the collection on game design provides an interesting insight into the ups and downs of the process of game design. See Birdwell (2006).

23 Many gamers publish their reviews and observations about games online. Some simply consider the action of the games, but others, such as Robert Hunicke, also give an account of their experience of the game's spatial environment (Hunicke 2006).

24 *Tomb Raider: Legend* also contains a binocular button with 'RAD', a device that gives clues as to the nature of the otherwise invisible obstacle ahead. It allows the gamer to discover whether it will be a mechanism or an unstable or hazardous area.

25 For Andrew Darley surface play does not include an entry into the image involving '... the poetic level ... a more profound dimension of semiotic resonance and semantic depth' (Darley 2000: 164).

26 Seth Giddings and Helen Kennedy (2006) have suggested that a gamer's experience is more usefully considered 'cyborgian' rather than interactive. Although the move toward cyborg experience may well be appropriate, it seems premature in the current era of games. At the moment, in playing a game the player becomes embedded within multiple play spaces, and can alter the state of the game. However, the state machine is pre-programmed to adjust in this way, and as such the game itself remains unaltered. The machinic interface remains unaltered in its encounter with a gamer, and it is for this reason that I resist the idea of cyborgian.

## 5 GALLERY SPACE/TEMPORAL ZONING

1 Although I do make occasional reference to works only encountered in other people's writing, the majority of pieces discussed are ones that I have directly experienced in visits to various galleries. The materials considered are therefore limited, but given the importance of having been 'in' the spatio-temporal architecture of an installation, this limit is an inevitable one.

2 For more complete commentaries on time-based artworks and installations, see Reiss (1999), Rush (1999), de Oliveira *et al.* (2003) and Bishop (2005).

3 For a brief overview of process art, see Fernández (2006).

4 *Scrapheap Services* was viewed in June 2005 when exhibited as part of the Still Life/Object/Real Life permanent collection at the Tate Modern, London.

5 The video is 11 minutes 21 seconds long, but, as is true of many installations, few people watched the whole loop through.

6 *Me and It* was seen as part of the Fred Wilson: Objects and Installations 1979–2000 exhibition at the University of California Berkeley Art Museum, March 2003.

7 A further comparison can be made with Bill Viola's *Nantes Triptych* (1992), in which three moving images are arrayed in a frontal organization, showing a series of images whose temporal organization is under the control of a technological interface. The three screens depict a birth on the left, a death on the right, and in the middle a body floating in water, often described as the metaphysical journey between the states of becoming alive and of dying. As is well known, the images of the dying woman are of Viola's mother as she lay in a coma at the end of her life.

8 *48 Portraits* is a series of paintings based on the headshots of 'illustrious men' found in an old encyclopaedia. Richter carried out this work in order to interrogate the illusion of neutrality conveyed by the presentation of words and imagery in encyclopaedia. As displayed at the

Open Systems exhibition in the Tate Modern in 2005, the 48 portraits were arranged together towards one side of a single wall space.

9 Open Systems: Rethinking Art c.1970 was curated by Donna De Salvo and ran at the Tate Modern from 1 June to 18 September 2005.

10 It might be appropriate to argue that a number of physical actions, such as squirming, laughing, shifting with boredom, make a contribution to a viewer's synthesis, but none of these leaves traces in the text.

11 Going Around the Corner Piece belongs in context with Nauman's other 'corridor installations' created in the late 1960s and early 1970s, in which he experimented with controlled spaces and camera placements to explore the relationship of the body to the act of perception. For a full overview of Nauman's work, see Morgan (2002).

12 The website http://cave.ncsa.uiuc.edu/ provides more background information on the various CAVES which have been developed in the USA.

13 The following website includes a video of people interacting with The Distributed Legible City: http://www.icinema.unsw.edu.au/projects/prj_dislegcity.html.

14 Chocolate Room was installed as part of the Ed Ruscha at MOCA exhibition in Los Angeles in October 2004. Given that Ruscha's work often uses Hollywood iconography, the overwhelming olfactory impact of this encounter might be described as an example of 'smello-vision'.

15 An example of these Rotoreliefs was exhibited as part of Dreaming With Open Eyes at the Art Gallery of Ontario in Toronto. The website http://www.elasticmind.com/arch/roto/ allows users to interact with a digital version of a rotorelief.

16 I am referring here to the film Lightplay, and not the original sculpture, which is screened as part of the Still-Life/Object/Real-Life exhibition on display at Tate Modern.

17 Marcel Broodthaers' Bateau-Tableau was viewed as part of the Open System exhibition at Tate Modern in August 2005.

18 Quoted in http://www.manifesta.es/eng/artistas/artistas/broodthaers.htm/, accessed 12 August 2005.

19 Still Life was viewed at Tate Modern when it was exhibited as part of its permanent display entitled Still-Life/Object/Real-Life.

20 This version of Video Fish was seen at the Centre Pompidou, Paris, in 2003.

21 Violent Incident was viewed in the Nauman Room at Tate Modern in 2003.

22 Nauman used this term to describe his thinking behind Good Boy, Bad Boy (Dercon 2003: 306).

23 There are different versions of Clown Torture, some including four screens. This two-monitor version of the installation, Clown Torture: Dark and Stormy Night With Laughter, was viewed in London at the Whitechapel Gallery exhibition Faces in the Crowd: Picturing Modern Life from Manet to Today, in 2004–05.

24 Introjection: Tony Oursler Mid-Career Survey 1976–1999, Museum of Contemporary Art, Los Angeles, 2000.

25 Viewed at Vancouver Art Gallery, March 2006.

26 Both The Five Angels for the Millennium and Going Forth By Day were exhibited at the Guggenheim-Bilbao in November 2004. The Five Angels for the Millennium was also viewed at the Tate Modern in 2003.

27 Each screen has its own audio track that mixes freely within the space, and each is individually titled: Departing Angel, Birth Angel, Fire Angel, Ascending Angel, Creation Angel.

28 This argument represents a different position on the place of technology in Bill Viola's work from that of Mark Hansen. Hansen suggests that Viola's installations bear witness to life because their use of decelerated digital imagery leads to an encounter with affectivity. My argument, by contrast, looks to the ways technological interfaces intercede in and reveal our processes of perception. The key distinction in our approaches lies in Hansen seeing Bill Viola's imagery as a technology that reveals aspects of being human, whereas I see Viola's installations as saying something about the intersections of humans with technological systems. See Hansen (2004a, 2004b).

29 Viewed at the Tate Modern in May 2004.
30 For a collection of essays specifically addressing *The Weather Project*, see May (2003).
31 *The Weather Project* was in the Turbine Hall between October 2003 and March 2004, and each time I visited people were gathered in groups within the installation.

## 6 FINDING OURSELVES AT THE INTERFACE

1 Digital technologies are also altering access to filmmaking technologies and the distribution of films. Cheaper technologies, digital recording devices and computer-based editing packages make lower budget filmmaking more feasible. Digital technologies also alter the opportunities for distribution, especially as the capacity for downloading feature films is coming online. For further discussion of the impact of digital technologies on filmmaking and distribution, see Telotte (2001a) and Trinh (2005).
2 The Lisson Gallery, London (2003), showed Tony Oursler's projections of distorted faces onto various spheroid shapes, each of which had its own soundscape. Short clips of two pieces from this exhibition can be accessed through the past exhibition links at www.tonyoursler.com. Oursler also exploited digital projection technology in *The Influence Machine*, a more expansive display of projected faces and sound shown after dark in Soho Square in London in early November 2000. The faces were of key figures in media history, including John Logie Baird and the Fox Sisters.
3 A number of Jeff Wall's photographs were viewed as part of the exhibition Jeff Wall Photographs 1978–2004 held at the Tate Modern in 2005. *A Sudden Gust of Wind (after Hokusai)* is an early example of Wall's digital work, and is modelled on a nineteenth-century woodcut by the Japanese artist Hokusai.

# BIBLIOGRAPHY

Aarseth, E. (1999) 'Aporia and Epiphany in *Doom* and *The Speaking Clock*: Temporality in Ergodic Art', in M.-L. Ryan (ed.) *Cyberspace Textuality*, Bloomington: University of Indiana Press.

Allen, M. (2002) 'The Impact of Digital Technologies on Film Aesthetics', in D. Harries (ed.) *The New Media Book*, London: BFI Publishing.

Altman, R. (1992) 'Dickens, Griffith, and Film Theory Today', in J. Gaines (ed.) *Classical Hollywood Narrative: The Paradigm Wars*, Durham: Duke University Press.

Arnheim, R. (1958) *Film as Art*, London: Faber.

Atkins, B. (2003) *More Than a Game: The Computer Game as Fictional Form*, Manchester: Manchester University Press.

Bal, M. (1997) *Narratology: Introduction to the Theory of Narrative*, 2nd edn, Toronto: University of Toronto Press.

Barrier, M. (1999) *Hollywood Cartoons: American Animation in its Golden Age*, Oxford: Oxford University Press.

Bendazzi, G. (1994) *Cartoons: One Hundred Years of Cinema Animation*, London: John Libbey.

Birdwell, K. (2006) 'The Cabal: Valve's Design Process for Creating Half-Life', in K. Salen and E. Zimmerman (eds) *The Game Design Reader: A Rules of Play Anthology*, Cambridge, MA: The MIT Press.

Bishop, C. (2005) *Installation Art: A Critical History*, London: Tate Publishing.

Bizony, P. (2001) *Digital Domain: The Leading Edge of Visual Effects*, London: Aurum.

Blandford, S., Grant, B.K. and Hillier, J. (2001) *The Film Studies Dictionary*, London: Arnold.

Bolter, D.J. and Gromala, D. (2003) *Windows and Mirrors: Interaction Design, Digital Art, and the Myth of Transparency*, Cambridge, MA: The MIT Press.

Bolter, D.J. and Grusin, R. (1999) *Remediation: Understanding New Media*, Cambridge, MA: The MIT Press.

Bordwell, D. and Thompson, K. (2000) *Film Art: An Introduction*, 6th edn, New York: McGraw-Hill.

Bourdieu, P. (1977) *Outline of a Theory of Practice*, Cambridge: Cambridge University Press.

—— (1990) *In Other Words: Essays Towards a Reflexive Sociology*, Cambridge: Polity Press.

—— (1992) *An Invitation to Reflexive Sociology*, Cambridge: Polity Press.

Brannigan, E. (1992) *Narrative Comprehension and Film*, London: Routledge.

Brosnan, J. (1977) *Movie Magic: The Story of Special Effects in the Cinema*, London: Abacus.

Buckland, W. (1998) 'A Close Encounter with Raiders of the Lost Ark: Notes on Narrative Aspects of the New Hollywood Blockbuster', in M. Smith and S. Neale (eds) *Contemporary Hollywood Cinema*, London: Routledge.

—— (1999) 'Between Science Fact and Science Fiction', *Screen* 40: 177–92.

Cholodenko, A. (ed.) (1990) *The Illusion of Life: Essays on Animation*, Sydney: Power Books.

Crafton, D. (1984) *Before Mickey: Animated Film 1898–1928*, Cambridge, MA: The MIT Press.

Crary, J. (2001) *Suspensions of Perception: Attention, Spectacle, and Modern Culture*, Cambridge, MA: The MIT Press.

Criqui, J.-P. (1997) 'Bruce Nauman – Kunstmuseum Wolfsburg', *Artforum* 36. Available online at http://www.gobelle.com/p/articles/mi_m0268/is_n3_v36/ai_20381893 (accessed 4 August 2005).

Darley, A. (2000) *Visual Digital Culture: Surface Play and Spectacle in New Media Genres*, London: Routledge.

de Landa, M. (2002) *Virtual Science and Intensive Philosophies*, New York: Continuum.

de Oliveira, N., Oxley, N. and Petry, M. (2003) *Installation Art in the New Millennium: The Empire of the Senses*, London: Thames and Hudson.

Deleuze, G. (1992) *Cinema 1: The Movement-Image*, London: The Athlone Press.

Dercon, C. (2003) 'Keep Taking it Apart: A Conversation with Bruce Nauman', in J. Kraynak (ed.) *Please Pay Attention Please: Bruce Nauman's Work*, Cambridge, MA: The MIT Press.

Dexter, E. (2004) 'Raw Materials', in *Bruce Nauman: Raw Materials*, London: Tate Publishing.

Doane, M.-A. (2002) *The Emergence of Cinematic Time: Modernity, Contingency, the Archive*, Cambridge, MA: Harvard University Press.

Dourish, P. (2001) *Where the Action Is: The Foundations of Embodied Interaction*, Cambridge, MA: The MIT Press.

Duncan, J. (2000) 'Perfecting the Storm', *Cinefex* 82: 94–113.

Elsaesser, T. and Barker, A. (eds) (1990) *Early Cinema: Space, Frame, Narrative*, London: BFI Publishing.

Fernández, M. (2006) '"Life-Like"', in A. Jones (ed.) *A Companion to Contemporary Art Since 1945*, Oxford: Blackwell Publishing.

Finch, C. (1984) *Special Effects: Creating Movie Magic*, New York: Abbeville Press.

Fisher, B. (1998) 'Black-and-White in Colour', *American Cinematographer* 79: 235–38.

Frayling, C. (2005) *Mad, Bad and Dangerous: The Scientist and the Cinema*, London: Reaktion Books.

Friedberg, A. (1993) *Window Shopping: Cinema and the Postmodern*, Berkeley: University of California Press.

Furniss, M. (1998) *Art in Motion: Animation Aesthetics*, London: John Libbey.

Giddings, S. and Kennedy, H.W. (2006) 'Digital Games as New Media', in J. Rutter and J. Bryce (eds) *Understanding Digital Games*, London, Sage Publications.

Goldman, M. (2005) 'Digital Intermediate 2005'. Available online at http://preview.millimeter.com/digital_intermediate/dig_interm_2005 (accessed 14 April 2006).

Grainge, P. (ed.) (2003) *Memory and Popular Film*, Manchester: Manchester University Press.

Haddon, L. (1993) 'Interactive Games', in P. Hayward and T. Wollen (eds) *Future Visions: New Technologies on the Screen*, London, BFI.

Hansen, M. (2004a) *New Philosophy for New Media*, Cambridge: MA: The MIT Press.

—— (2004b) 'The Time of Affect, or Bearing Witness to Life', *Critical Inquiry* 30: 584–626.

Hayles, N.K. (1999) *How We Became Posthuman: Virtual Bodies in Cybernetics, Literature, and Informatics*, Chicago: University of Chicago Press.

Heath, S. (1981) *Questions of Cinema*, Bloomington: Indiana University Press.

Herzogenrath, W. (1988) 'The Anti-Technological Technology of Nam Jun Paik's Robots', in *Nam Jun Paik: Video Works 1963–88*, London: Hayward Gallery.

Holben, J. (2002) 'Criminal Intent', *American Cinematographer* 83: 34–45.

Hollyn, N. (2003) 'The View from the Cutting Room Ceiling: Tim Squyres on Hulk'. Available online at http://www.editorsguild.com/newsletter/JulAug03/hulk.html (accessed 4 June 2005).

Huizinga, J. (1971) *Homo Ludens: A Study of the Play Element in Culture*, London: Beacon Press.

—— (2006) 'Nature and Significance of Play as a Cultural Phenomenon', in K. Salen and E. Zimmerman (eds) *The Game Design Reader: A Rules of Play Anthology*, Cambridge, MA: The MIT Press.

Hunicke, R. (2006) Online posting. Available online at http://www.intelligent-artifice.com/2006/06/halflife_2_revi.html (accessed 14 June 2006).

Hunt, L. (2004) 'The Hong Kong/Hollywood Connection: Stardom and Spectacle in Transnational Action Cinema', in Y. Tasker (ed.) *Action and Adventure Cinema*, London: Routledge.

Hutchins, E. (1995) *Cognition in the Wild*, Cambridge, MA: The MIT Press.

Jackson, T.A. (2001) 'Towards a New Media Aesthetic', in D. Trend (ed.) *Reading Digital Culture*, Oxford: Blackwell.

Jenkins, H. (2006) 'Game Design as Narrative Architecture', in K. Salen and E. Zimmerman (eds) *The Game Design Reader: A Rules of Play Anthology*, Cambridge, MA: The MIT Press.

Joselit, D. (2000) 'Planet Paik: Nam Jun Paik's Works', *Art in America* 23: 21–26.

Juul, J. (2005) *Half-Real: Video Games Between Real Rules and Fictional Worlds*, Cambridge, MA: The MIT Press.

Keane, S. (2001) *Disaster Movies: The Cinema of Catastrophe*, London: Wallflower.

Kenny, T. (1998) '*Titanic*: Sound Design to James Cameron's Epic Ocean Saga'. Available online at http://www.geocities.com/Hollywood/Academy/4394/titanic.htm (accessed 13 July 2005).

Kerr, A. (2006) *The Business and Culture of Computer Games: Gamework/Gameplay*, London: Sage.

Kinder, M. (1991) *Playing with Power in Movies, Television and Video Games: From Muppet Babies to Teenage Mutant Ninja Turtles*, Berkeley: University of California Press.

—— (2002a) 'Hot Spots, Avatars and Narrative Fields Forever: Bunuel's Legacy of New Digital Media and Interactive Database Narrative', *Film Quarterly* 55: 2–15.

—— (2002b) 'Narrative Equivocations Between Movies and Games', in D. Harries (ed.) *The New Media Book*, London: BFI Publishing.

King, G. (2001) *Spectacular Narratives: Hollywood in the Age of the Blockbuster*, London: I.B. Tauris.

King, G. and Kryzwinska, T. (2006) *Tomb Raiders and Space Invaders: Videogame Form and Contexts*, London: I.B. Tauris.

Kirriemuir, J. (2006) 'A History of Digital Games', in J. Rutter and J. Bryce (eds) *Understanding Digital Games*, London: Sage Publications.

Klein, N. (1993) *Seven Minutes: A Cultural History of the American Cartoon*, London: Verso.

—— (2005) *The Vatican to Vegas: A History of Special Effects*, New York: The New Press.

Lahti, M. (2003) 'As We Become Machines: Corporealized Pleasures in Video Games', in M.J.P. Wolf and B. Perron (eds) *The Video Game Theory Reader*, London: Routledge.

Langer, M. (1992) 'The Disney–Fleischer Dilemma: Product Differentiation and Technological Innovation', *Screen* 33: 343–60.

Laurel, B. (1993) *Computers as Theatre*, London: Addison Wesley.

Lindsay, G. (2003) 'Musing on Modern Film with Mike Figgis, Director of Hotel'. Available online at http://www.blacktable.com/lindsay030806.htm (accessed 16 August 2005).

Lubin, D.M. (1999) *Titanic*, London: BFI.

McCarthy, J. and Wright, P. (2004) *Technology as Experience*, Cambridge, MA: The MIT Press.

McCullogh, M. (2004) *Digital Ground: Architecture, Pervasive Computing and Environmental Knowing*, Cambridge, MA: The MIT Press.

McNay, L. (2000) *Gender and Agency: Reconfiguring the Subject in Feminist and Social Theory*, Cambridge: Polity Press.

Maltby, R. with Craven, I. (1995) *Hollywood Cinema: An Introduction*, Oxford: Blackwell Publishers.

Manovich, L. (2001) *The Language of New Media*, Cambridge, MA: The MIT Press.

Martin, K. (2000) '*Gladiator*: A Cut Above', *Cinefex* 82: 13–31.

May, J. and Thrift, N. (eds) (2001) *Timespace: Geographies of Temporality*, London: Routledge.

May, S. (ed.) (2003) *Olafur Eliasson: The Weather Project*, London: Tate Books.

Mellencamp, P. (1995) 'The Old and the New: Nam Jun Paik', *Art Journal*: 41–45.

Merleau-Ponty, M. (2002) *The Phenomenology of Perception*, Routledge Classic Series, London: Routledge.

Morgan, R.C. (2002) *Bruce Nauman*, London and Baltimore: Johns Hopkins University Press.

Moritz, W. (1997) 'Digital Harmony: The Life of John Whitney, Computer Animation Pioneer', *Animation World Magazine*. Available online at http://www.awn.com/mag/issue2.5/2.5pages/2.5moritzwhitney.html (accessed 13 July 2005).

Moszkowicz, J. (2002) 'To Infinity and Beyond: Assessing the Technological Imperative in Computer Animation', *Screen* 43: 293–314.

Mulvey, L. (2006) *Death 24x a Second: Stillness and the Moving Image*, London: Reaktion Books.

Murray, J. (1997) *Hamlet on the Holodeck: The Future of Narrative in Cyberspace*, New York: The Free Press.

Newman, J. (2004) *Video Games*, London: Routledge.

O'Doherty, B. (1999) *Inside the White Cube: The Ideology of the Gallery Space*, Berkeley: University of California Press.

Onorato, R. and Davis, H. (1997) *Blurring the Boundaries: Installation Art 1969–1996*, New York: Data Art.

Otto, J. (2005) 'Interview: Christopher Nolan: We Chat with the *Batman* Filmmaker'. Available online at http://filmforce.ign.com/articles/622/622719p1.html (accessed 31 July 2005).

Pashler, H.E. (1998) *The Psychology of Attention*, Cambridge, MA: The MIT Press.

Paul, C. (2003) *Digital Art*, London: Thames and Hudson.

Pavlus, J. (2005) 'Black and White and Red All Over: Robert Rodriguez and Crew Create a Digital Noir Setting for *Sin City*'. Available online at http://www.cameraguild.com/index.html?magazine/stoo0405.htm~top.main_hp (accessed 29 July 2005).

Pierson, M. (2002) *Special Effects: Still in Search of Wonder*, New York: Columbia University Press.

Pilling, J. (2001) *2-D Animation*, London: RotoVision.

Pinteau, P. (2004) *Special Effects: An Oral History*, New York: Harry Abrahms.

Pizzello, S. (2005) 'Wally Pfister, ASC Helps Director Christopher Nolan Envision the Dark Knight's "Origin Story" in *Batman Begins*', *American Cinematographer* 86: 108–15.

Polan, D. (1985) 'A Brechtian Cinema? Towards a Politics of Self-Reflexive Film', in B. Nichols (ed.) *Movies and Methods*, vol. II, Berkeley: University of California Press.

Poole, S. (2000) *Trigger Happy: The Inner Life of Video Games*, London: Fourth Estate.

Prince, S. (1996) 'True Lies: Perceptual Realism, Digital Images, and Film Theory', *Film Quarterly* 49: 27–38.

—— (2004) 'The Emergence of Filmic Artefacts: Cinema and Cinematography in the Digital Era', *Film Quarterly* 57: 24–33.

Rainbird, S. (2004) 'Are We as a Society Going to Carry on Treating People This Way?' Michael Landy's *Scrapheap Services*'. Available online at http://www.tate.org.uk/research/tateresearch/tatepapers/04spring/rainbird_paper.htm (accessed 27 July 2006).

Reiss, J.H. (1999) *From Margin to Center: The Spaces of Installation Art*, Cambridge, MA: The MIT Press.

Rollings, A. and Morris, D. (2000) *Game Architecture and Design*, Scotsdale: Coriolis.

Rouse, R. (2005) *Game Design: Theory and Practice*, 2nd edn, Plano: Wordware Publishing Company.

Rubin, M. (1993) *Showstoppers: Busby Berkeley and the Tradition of Spectacle*, New York: Columbia University Press.

Rush, M. (1999) *New Media in Late 20th-Century Art*, London: Thames and Hudson.

Rutter, J. and Bryce, J. (eds) (2006) *Understanding Digital Games*, London: Sage Publications.

Ryan, M.-L. (2001a) 'Beyond Myth and Metaphor: The Case of Narrative in Digital Media', *Games Studies* 1. Available online at http://www.gamestudies.org/0101/ryan (accessed 23 October 2004).

—— (2001b) *Narrative and Virtual Reality: Immersion and Interactivity in Literature and Electronic Media*, Baltimore: Johns Hopkins University Press.

Sarafian, K. (2003) 'Flashing Digital Animations: Pixar's Digital Aesthetic', in A. Everett and J.T. Caldwell (eds) *New Media: Theories and Practices of Digitextuality*, AFI Film Reader, New York: Routledge.

Schecter, H. and Everitt, D. (1980) *Film Tricks: Special Effects in the Movies*, New York: Harlan Quist.

Schenkel, T. (1988) 'Storytelling as Remembering: Picturing the Past in Caroline Leaf's *The Street*', in J. Canemaker (ed.) *Storytelling in Animation: The Art of the Animated Image*, Los Angeles: American Film Institute.

Scott, R. and Parkers, W. (2000) *Gladiator: The Making of the Ridley Scott Epic*, London: Macmillan.

Sobchack, V. (1992) *The Address of the Eye: A Phenomenology of Film Experience*, Princeton: Princeton University Press.

—— (ed.) (2000) *Meta-Morphing: Visual Tranformation and the Culture of Quick Change*, Minneapolis: University of Minnesota Press.

—— (2004) *Carnal Thoughts: Embodiment and Moving Image Culture*, Berkeley: California University Press.

Solomon, C. (1994) *The History of Animation: Enchanted Drawings*, New York: Outlet.

Svich, C. (2004) 'A Process of Perception: A Conversation with Bill Viola', *Contemporary Theatre Review* 14: 72–81.

Tasker, Y. (1993) *Spectacular Bodies: Gender, Genre and the Action Cinema*, London: Routledge.

Taylor, L. (2003) 'When Seams Fall Apart: Video Game Space and the Player', *Games Studies* 3. Available online at http://www.gamestudies.org/0302/taylor (accessed 12 June 2004).

Taylor, T.L. (2006) *Play Between Worlds: Exploring On-Line Game Culture*, Cambridge, MA: The MIT Press.

Telotte, J.P. (2001a) *Science Fiction Film*, Cambridge: Cambridge University Press.

—— (2001b) 'The *Blair Witch Project*: Film and the Internet', *Film Quarterly* 54: 32–39.

Terranova, T. (2004) *Network Culture: Politics for the Information Age*, London: Pluto Press.

Thompson, R. (1975) 'Duck Amuck', *Film Comment* 11: 39–43.

Trinh, M.-H.T. (2005) *Digital Film Event*, London: Routledge.

Tuan, Y.-F. (2001) *Space and Place*, Minneapolis: University of Minnesota Press.

Tudor, A. (1989) *Monsters and Mad Scientists: Cultural History of the Horror Movie*, Oxford: Blackwells.

Tudor, D. (2002) 'Nation, Family and Violence in *Gladiator*', *Jump Cut* 45. Available online at http://www.ejumpcut.org/archive/jc45.2002/tudor/index.html (accessed 16 January 2005).

Turkle, S. (1997) *Life on the Screen*, New York: Touchstone Books.

Vaz, M.C. (1996) *Industrial Light and Magic: Into the Digital Realm*, London: Virgin Books.

Wacquant, L.J.D. (1992) 'The Structure and Logic of Bourdieu's Sociology', in P. Bourdieu, *An Invitation to Reflexive Sociology*, Cambridge: Polity.

Ward, P. (2004) 'Rotoshop in Context: Computer Rotoscoping and Animation Aesthetics', *Animation Journal* 12: 32–52.

Wells, P. (1998) *Understanding Animation*, London: Routledge.

—— (2002) *Animation: Genre and Authorship*, London: Wallflower Press.

Wheeler Dixon, W. (1998) *The Transparency of Spectacle: Mediations on the Moving Image*, Albany: State University of New York Press.

—— (2001) 'Twenty-Five Reasons Why it's All Over', in J. Lewis (ed.) *The End of Cinema as We Know It: American Film in the Nineties*, New York: New York University Press.

Willis, H. (2005) *New Digital Cinema: Reinventing the Moving Image*, London: Wallflower Press.

Wilson, P.N. (1996) *The Closed World: Computers and the Politics of Discourse in Cold War America*, Cambridge, MA: The MIT Press.

Wolf, M.J.P. (2000) 'A Brief History of Morphing', in V. Sobchack (ed.) *Meta-Morphing: Visual Tranformation and the Culture of Quick Change*, Minneapolis: University of Minnesota Press.

—— (ed.) (2001) *The Medium of the Video Game*, Austin: University of Texas Press.

Wolf, M.J.P. and Perron, B. (eds) (2003) *The Video Game Theory Reader*, London: Routledge.

Wood, A. (2002) *Technoscience in Contemporary American Film: Beyond Science Fiction*, Manchester, Manchester University Press.

## FILMS

*2001: A Space Odyssey* (1968, Stanley Kubrick; UK/US)

*24* (TV) (2001–; US)

*7th Voyage of Sinbad, The* (1958, Nathan Juran; US)

*Aan Rika* (2005, Juan de Graaf: Netherlands)

*Abyss, The* (1989, James Cameron; US)

*Alexander* (2004, Oliver Stone; US)

*Anchors Away* (1945, George Sidney; US)

*Antz* (1998, Eric Darnell and Tim Johnson; US)

*Aviator, The* (2004, Martin Scorsese; US)

*Batman Begins* (2005, Christopher Nolan; US)

*Bedknobs and Broomsticks* (1971, Robert Stevenson; US)

*Boy Who Saw the Iceberg, The* (2000, Paul Driessen; Canada)

*Bringing Up Baby* (1938, Howard Hawks; US)

*Bug's Life, A* (1998, John Lasseter; US)

*Casper* (1995, Brad Silberling; US)

*Charlie and the Chocolate Factory* (2005, Tim Burton; US)

*Contest, The* (1923, Fleischer Bros; US)

*Dad's Dead* (2003, Chris Shepherd; UK)

*Daffy Duck in Hollywood* (1938, Warner Bros.; US)

*Dark City* (1998, Alex Proyas; US)

*Day After Tomorrow, The* (2004, Roland Emmerich; US)

*Dough for the Do-Do* (1949, Warner Bros; US)

*Dr Jekyll and Mr Hyde* (1932, Rouben Mamoulian; US)

*Duck Amuck* (1953, Warner Bros; US)

*Dumbo* (1941, Ben Sharpsteen; US)

*Enchanted Drawing, The* (1900, James Stuart Blackton; US)

*End of the World in Four Seasons, The* (1995, Paul Driessen; Canada)

*Entre Deux Soeurs* (1990, Caroline Leaf; Canada)

*Fantasia* (1940, Disney; US)

*Feeling My Way* (1997, Jonathan Hodgson; UK)

*Felix Takes a Hand* (1922, Pat Sullivan Studio; US)

*Few Quick Facts: Fear, A* (1945, Zack Schwartz; US)

*Few Quick Facts: Inflation, A* (1945, Osmond Evans; US)

*Finding Nemo* (2003, Andrew Stanton; US)

*Fight Club* (1999, David Fincher; US)

*Final Fantasy: The Spirits Within* (2001, Hironobu Sakaguchi; US/Japan)

*Final Flight of the Osiris, The* (2003, Andy Jones; US)

*Flatworld* (1997, Daniel Greaves; UK)

*Futureworld* (1976, Richard T. Heffron; US)

*Gerald McBoing Boing* (1951, United Productions of America; US)

*Ghostbusters* (1984, Ivan Reitman; US)

*Gladiator* (2000, Ridley Scott; US)

*Godzilla* (1998, Roland Emmerich; US)

*Great Train Robbery, The* (1903, Edwin S. Porter; US)

*Hellboy* (2004, Guillermo del Toro; US)

*Hollow Man* (2000, Paul Verhoeven; US)

*Hoppity Goes to Town* (a.k.a. Mr Bug Goes to Town) (1941, Fleischer Studio; US)

*Hotel* (2001, Mike Figgis; UK/US)

*Hotel Rwanda* (2004, Terry George; US)

*How a Mosquito Operates* (1912, Winsor McCay; US)

*Hulk* (2003, Ang Lee; US)

*Hunky and Spunky* (1938, Fleischer Studio; US)

*Incredibles, The* (2004, Brad Bird; US)

*Jason and the Argonauts* (1963, Don Chaffey; US)

*Jurassic Park* (1993, Steven Spielberg; US)

*Jurassic Park III* (2001, Joe Johnston; US)

*Just Dogs* (1932, Disney Studio; US)

*King Kong* (1933, Merian C. Cooper; US)

*King Kong* (2005, Peter Jackson; US)

*Knick Knack* (1989, John Lasseter; US)

*Koko the Convict* (1926, Fleischer Studio; US)

*Last Starfighter, The* (1984, Nick Castle; US)

*Little Nemo* (1911, Winsor McCay; US)

*Looney Tunes: Back in Action* (2003, Joe Dante; US)

*Lost World, The* (1925, Harry O Hoyt; US)

*Lost World: Jurassic Park, The* (1997, Steven Spielberg; US)

*Luxo Jnr* (1987, John Lasseter; US)

*Luxo Jnr in Light and Heavy* (1991, John Lasseter; US)

*Man with a Movie Camera* (1929, Dgiza Vertov; Russia)

*Manipulation* (1991, Daniel Greaves; UK)

*Matrix, The* (1999, Andy Wachowski and Larry Wachowski; US)

*Matrix No. III* (1972, John Whitney; US)

*Medicine Man* (1992, John McTiernan; US)

*Memento* (2000, Christopher Nolan; US)

*Minority Report* (2002, Steven Spielberg; US)

*Monsters, Inc.* (2001, Pete Doctor; US)

*Mummy, The* (1999, Steven Sommers; US)

*Mummy Returns, The* (2001, Steven Sommers; US)

*Music Land* (1935, Disney Studio; US)

*My Little Eye* (2002, Marc Evans; US)

*Napoleon* (1927, Abel Gance; France)

*O Brother, Where Art Thou?* (2000, Ethan and Joel Coen; US)

*Old Mill, The* (1937, Disney Studio; US)

*Pearl Harbor* (2001, Michael Bay; US)

*Peeping Penguins* (1937, Fleischer Studio; US)

*Perfect Storm, The* (2000, Wolfgang Petersen; US)

*Pirates of the Caribbean: The Curse of the Black Pearl* (2003, Gore Verbinski; US)

*Pleasantville* (1998, Gary Ross; US)

*Remains to Be Seen* (1986, Jane Aaron; US)

*Renaissance* (2006, Christian Volckman; France)

*Saving Private Ryan* (1998, Steven Spielberg; US)

*Scanner Darkly, A* (2006, Richard Linklater; US)

*Second Class Mail* (1984, Alison Snowden; UK)

*Secret Adventures of Tom Thumb, The* (1993, the Bolex Brothers; UK)

*Shrek* (2001, Andrew Adamson and Vicky Jenson; US)

*Sin City* (2005, Robert Rodriguez; US)

*Sinking of the Lusitania, The* (1917, Winsor McCay; US)

*Skeleton Dance, The* (1929, Disney Studio; US)

*Sky Captain and the World of Tomorrow* (2004, Kerry Conran; US)

*Snack and Drink* (2000, Bob Sabiston; US)

*Snow White and the Seven Dwarfs* (1937, Disney Studio; US)

*Song of the South* (1946, Harve Foster and Wilfred Jackson; US)

*Spider-Man* (2002, Sam Raimi; US)

*Spider-Man 2* (2004, Sam Raimi; US)

*Street, The* (1976, Caroline Leaf; Canada)

*Superman Returns* (2006, Bryan Singer; US)

*Swordfish* (2001, Dominic Sena; US)

*Tell-Tale Heart, The* (1953, United Productions of America; US)

*Time Machine, The* (1960, George Pal; US)

*Time Machine, The* (2001, Simon Wells; US)

*Timecode* (2000, Mike Figgis; US/UK)

*Titanic* (1998, James Cameron; US)

*Tom Thumb* (1958, George Pal; US)

*Topper* (1937, Norman McLeod; US)

*Toy Story* (1995, John Lasseter; US)

*Trial and Retribution* (TV) (1997–2006, UK)

*Triumph of the Will* (1935, Leni Riefenstahl; Germany)

*Tron* (1982, Steven Lisberger; US)

*Troy* (2004, Wolfgang Petersen; US)

*Twister* (1996, Jan de Bont; US)

*Waking Life* (2002, Richard Linklater; US)

*War of the Worlds* (2005, Steven Spielberg; US)

*Water Babies* (1933, Disney Studio; US)

*Westworld* (1973, Michael Crichton; US)

*Who Framed Roger Rabbit?* (1988, Robert Zemickis; US)


## GAMES

*Arcanum* (2001, Sierra and Troika Games: PC)

*Enter the Matrix* (2003, Shiny Entertainment and Atari: Playstation 2)

*EverQuest* (1999, Sony Online Entertainment: online game)

*Grand Theft Auto III* (2001, Rockstar: Playstation 2)

*Half-Life* (1997, Valve: PC)

*Half-Life 2* (2004, Valve: PC)

*Halo* (2003, Microsoft: XBox)

*Max Payne* (2001, Take 2 Interactive: PC)

*Max Payne 2* (2003, Take 2 Interactive: PC)

*Midnight Club 3* (2005, Rockstar: PSP)

*Myst III: Exile* (2002, Focus Multimedia Ltd: PC)

*Primal* (2003, Sony: Playstation 2)

*Red Faction* (2001, THQ: Playstation 2)

*Spiderman* (2002, Activision: Playstation 2)

*Tomb Raider: Last Revelation* (1999, Eidos Interactive: PC)

*Tomb Raider: Legend* (2006, Eidos Interactive: Playstation 2)

# INDEX